China's Revolutions in the Modern World

China's Revolutions in the Modern World:

A Brief Interpretive History

Rebecca E. Karl

VERSO
London • New York

First published by Verso 2020
© Rebecca E. Karl 2020

1 3 5 7 9 10 8 6 4 2

Verso
UK: 6 Meard Street, London W1F 0EG
US: 20 Jay Street, Suite 1010, Brooklyn, NY 11201
versobooks.com

Verso is the imprint of New Left Books

ISBN-13: 978-1-78873-559-9
ISBN-13: 978-1-78873-560-5 (UK EBK)
ISBN-13: 978-1-78873-561-2 (US EBK)

British Library Cataloguing in Publication Data
A catalogue record for this book is available from the British Library

Library of Congress Cataloging-in-Publication Data
Names: Karl, Rebecca E., author.
Title: China's revolutions in the modern world : a brief interpretive
    history / Rebecca E Karl.
Description: London ; New York : Verso, 2020. | Includes bibliographical
    references and index. | Summary: "China's emergence as a
    twenty-first-century global economic, cultural, and political power is
    often presented as a story of what Chinese leader Xi Jinping calls the
    nation's "great rejuvenation," a story narrated as the return of China
    to its "rightful" place at the center of the world. In China's
    Revolutions in the Modern World, historian Rebecca E. Karl argues that
    China's contemporary emergence is best seen not as a "return," but
    rather as the product of revolutionary and counter-revolutionary
    activity and imaginings. From the Taipings in the mid-nineteenth century
    through nationalist, anti-imperialist, cultural, and socialist
    revolutions to today's capitalist-inflected Communist State, modern
    China has been made in intellectual dissonance and class struggle, in
    mass democratic movements and global war, in socialism and
    anti-socialism, in repression and conflict by multiple generations of
    Chinese people mobilized to seize history and make the future in their
    own name. Through China's successive revolutions, the contours of our
    contemporary world have taken shape. This brief interpretive history
    shows how"-- Provided by publisher.
Identifiers: LCCN 2019038428 (print) | LCCN 2019038429 (ebook) | ISBN
    9781788735599 (paperback) | ISBN 9781788735612 (ebook ; US) | ISBN
    9781788735605 (ebook ; UK)
Subjects: LCSH: Revolutions--China--History. | China--Politics and
    government.
Classification: LCC DS740.2 .K37 2020 (print) | LCC DS740.2 (ebook) | DDC
    951.05--dc23
LC record available at https://lccn.loc.gov/2019038428
LC ebook record available at https://lccn.loc.gov/2019038429

Typeset in Minion Pro by Hewer Text UK Ltd, Edinburgh
Printed and bound by CPI Group (UK) Ltd, Croydon, CR0 4YY

For my teachers:
Arif Dirlik, Marilyn B. Young,
Harry Harootunian

Contents

Introduction

We are Marxists, and Marxism teaches that in our approach to a problem we should start from objective facts, not from abstract definitions.

—Mao Zedong (1942)[1]

Ideologies must become dramas if they are not to remain mere ink printed on paper.

—Antonio Gramsci (1917)[2]

In 1926, Mao Zedong began a short consideration of class analysis in China with a query: "Who are our enemies? Who are our friends? This is a question of primary importance for the revolution."[3] An early attempt to understand China's social structure in Marxist perspective articulated in the absolutely antagonistic terms of "friends" and "enemies," class analysis allowed Mao to present China's past and contemporary situations as necessary revolutionary stages of struggle in the securing of China's future. This type of rethinking of past, current, and future time is characteristic of all modern historical analysis. Among others, it raises the question: With what facts— which past and which present and in the name of which future—does one write a book on China's revolutions in *today's* profoundly unrevolutionary times? The current volume explores that question by asking what the meaning of revolution is as a problem of and in the modern history of China, as well as of and in the world. In approaching

---

1   Mao Zedong, "Talks at the Yan'an Forum on Art and Literature" (1942), available at *Marxists Internet Archive*, marxists.org.

2   Antonio Gramsci, "Red October" (October 13, 1917), *Prison Notebooks*, vol 1, New York: Columbia University Press, 2011.

3   Mao Zedong, "Analysis of Classes in Chinese Society" (1926), in Stuart Schram, ed., *Mao's Road to Power*, vol. 2, New York: Routledge, 1992.

answers to that question, the facts from which we begin matter a great deal.

Here, then, we can find the first of this book's major approaches to the question: while modern revolutions in China have of course always been Chinese, they always have been global as well, not only because world contexts and texts helped shape the conditions of successive revolutionary struggles in China, but because those successive struggles helped constitute the contexts and texts of the modern world. From the outset, what this intertwining indicates is that revolutions are a modern global phenomenon, even as they are also a fact of and in modern Chinese history. The book's second major approach flows from this: "modern" is not merely a chronology or description. Rather, it refers to an experience of time—a temporality—and a form of historical becoming—a historicity. When, for example, peasant women after 1949 re-narrated their individual pasts as histories of oppression rather than as ones of gendered fate, they demonstrated, in however a state-managed fashion, that they were ready for and capable of making a future that fate may not have foretold. The conditions of the past became not a restraint on the time of the present, but rather an opening to a new experiential future.

From the mid nineteenth century onward, this transformed modern temporality and historicity corresponded, directly or indirectly, to the violently imposed connectedness of an emerging world order under an evolving global capitalist regime. This book's insistence on viewing the China-global nexus through the centrality of violence and capitalism places the discussion within a particular worldview: one that reckons with the inherent structural violence of the capitalist world in which China is embedded (and that is embedded in China), and one that takes seriously that there is no pure internality or externality to modern historical inquiry. In other words, any attempt to think about the recent past in the present *forces* a simultaneously global and local historical perspective. In this light, for example, the Taiping Revolution of the mid nineteenth century cannot be understood without grappling with how structures of capitalist accumulation, possession, and dispossession had intruded into China in ways that did not permit even intensely local spheres of social life to escape their transformative logics. Exploring the Taipings thus entails a consideration of how various uneven preexisting and enduring systems of social, cultural, political, and economic life in China were *necessarily* transformed—structurally and conceptually—in their forced confrontation with capitalist logics that exceeded their local domains. The book takes up how, as each successive revolution was mobilized and took hold in China, different parts of past organizations of Chinese life were rethought and remade in the process of conceptualizing and creating new presents, as well as new possibilities for the future.

In the last two centuries, the mutual embedding of China in the world and the world in China has been informed and shaped through a number of crises whose historical narrative contours are ever in flux. The problem of narration—Which facts do we use to tell our story? How is the story organized? In whose voice is it told?—constitutes the third and overarching approach of this book. China's revolutions—or, we might say, revolutions in what we know today as "China"—have, since the mid nineteenth century, raised questions about what "modern China" was to be as a geography or spatial entity, a polity or state, a nationality or cluster of ethnicities, a congeries of cultural entities, a class politics, a gendered sociality, and more. These questions repeatedly forced seemingly settled narratives into crisis. In the Republican Revolution of 1911, for example, the dynastic system and its Confucian ideological underpinnings were rejected as antiquated and unable to answer to the challenges of the capitalist world and its many possible futures. Having come through a century of revolutionary practice, a reworked and attenuated version of Confucian ideology has now been re-embraced by Xi Jinping in the name of the Communist Party as a way to enforce unitary cultural-nationalist pride and social obedience in a severely divided economic and ethnic environment. In presenting this history, it would be a mistake to narrate China as enacting an endless circular return to some primordial origin, or as fulfilling a linear march to a predestined goal. Rather, narrating China's modern history—as with all such histories in different ways and for different reasons—allows us to explore how concrete actors at particular points actively and repeatedly engaged texts from many places and times, thus compelling ideological and material encounters with traces of China's past that opened up new imaginings for China's present and future. What makes these questions modern, then, is the structurally *necessary*—and not merely contingent—nature of these engagements. "China" becomes "China" in the world through modern revolutions only in the globally entwined material and ideological conditions created for the re-narration of the past in light of new demands on the present and new hopes for the future.

In the course of the revolutions that have remade China in the world, the geographical extent of the fluid borders of the imperial dynastic order were hardened into national state boundaries. The resultant nation is neither timeless, nor natural, nor culturally homogeneous, nor mono-ethnic; its territorial claims are far from universally accepted. Indeed, for more than a century, the contestation over China as a polity and a territory has been a vital problem in and of socio-political struggle, in and of revolutionary process. One major aspect of modern struggles has revolved around the question of who is Chinese and how to be a modern Chinese—a subject of recurring fraught politics, social disputes, and cultural debates. Elements of these conflicts have been bound up, especially in the twentieth century, with the emergent politics of "China" as a state form: Should the state be founded upon an urban-based bourgeois hegemony, a thinly disguised (or entirely undisguised) Confucian patriarchy, a semifeudal agrarian state capitalist bureaucracy, a sociopolitical dictatorship of the proletarian-peasant alliance, a party-state oligarchy, or something else entirely? These were and remain deeply intertwined subjects of fierce struggle at the intellectual, political, cultural, and social levels. They were first systemically broached in the nineteenth century with the challenges posed to the dynastic system and its corresponding version of "Chinese-ness" by successive revolutionary movements, which were intent not on replacing one dynasty with another, but on transforming the entire system along with its underlying social and cultural logics.

A major arena of revolutionary concern and endeavor—particularly after the full-scale intrusion of capitalist production and manufacture into China's coastal regions in the wake of the Opium Wars of the 1840s and '50s, and then more insistently after the Sino-Japanese War of 1894–1895—has been the struggle over what constitutes a modern sociopolitical economy. This struggle shaped the entirety of the twentieth century and is still ongoing. The nineteenth-century antecedents to its full systemic articulation fundamentally unsettled the dynastic and global capitalist worlds, so that by the late nineteenth century the problem of economic organization and goals moved to the forefront of revolutionary and counterrevolutionary theorization, in China as elsewhere. Socialism and capitalism have been the two major poles along which this question has been posed and vigorously contested. In the early twenty-first century, these questions, having gone through a century of structural transformation and philosophical dispute, continue to animate the Chinese and global scene.

This book traces how questions of Chinese-ness, modernization, sociopolitical organization, culture, economic thinking, class, gender, ethnicity, and globality became mutually defining aspects of revolutions in China. The structure of the volume is as follows: each of the main chapters presents a revolutionary moment of the past one and a half centuries in chronological and thematic terms, exploring how certain questions emerged and in which forms they came to be repeatedly posed. Between the main chapters are "interludes" that narratively and analytically move from one revolutionary moment to the next, or that fill in episodes that require more concentrated consideration. The book contends that the questions raised in and by the many revolutions of modern China never emerged all at one time, other than once in China's history: that is, during the revolution led by the Chinese Communist Party (CCP) under the leadership of Mao Zedong. In proposing a vision and method for fundamental domestic social-cultural transformation and a simultaneous ideological-structural challenge to the global capitalist system, the 1949 revolution was intended to settle these questions once and for all—if not with firm answers of form and content, then at least with settled approaches to how they should be asked as well as sociopolitically and culturally addressed. The post-1949 emphasis on politics as a mass mobilizational form, on the political primacy of the peasant-proletarian leadership of the party and society, on the relation between national liberation and socialist principles in China and globally, on Third Worldism as an alternative to normative US-led capitalist geopolitics: these and more were posed as genuine attempts to thoroughly uproot the Chinese and global present in favor of an utterly different future. The proposed permanence of these approaches lasted only a few decades. However, 1949 subtends this book as a fulcrum and a historical argument, albeit not as a teleology.

1919, 1949, 1959, 1969, 1979, 1989, 2009, 2019: the "nine years" have a particular claim on the twentieth and twenty-first centuries in China. Many anniversaries can be celebrated or forgotten in the name of the "nines." This book originally was conceived as a way to think the "nines" as history in the centennial year of the May Fourth Movement (1919). While nine is a consequential number in Chinese cosmology and numerology—associated with the imperial throne and with longevity ("nine" and "long," 九 / 久 [jiu], are homonyms)[4]— it has no particular modern significance, other than the coincidences provided in and by the past century of history. Yet, inspirationally, at the end of 1968 the Beatles released a track called "Revolution 9," included in their celebrated *White Album*. The piece is a sound collage that loops in on itself, repeating with variations and never resolving. The track can be seen as a history of the group's music that constitutes a reckoning with the past, a long dwelling in the present, and a hoped-for leap into the future. The narrative I offer here was written with "Revolution 9" as soundtrack and muse.

I start with the Taipings in the mid nineteenth century, the first of the modern revolutions in China, and I end with today's Xi Jinping regime, a powerful counterrevolutionary tendency that nevertheless must be counted as revolutionary. In between, I narrate revolutionary

---

4   Angela Zito reminded me of the imperial connection during a casual dinnertime conversation.

moments during which temporality—the experience of time—and historicity—historical becoming—were thoroughly scrambled; that is, when the rereading of the past in the present required and also facilitated a reconceptualization of the future. This is, to be sure, a retrospective and selective narrative, as is every presentation of any past. My narrative, therefore, is not offered as an attempt to unify a putative "China" existing outside of time. Rather, it is intended to show how revolution—that quintessentially modern form of fundamental social transformation—repeatedly created and recreated "China" and "the world," with its fissures and unevenness, its unresolved politics and social turbulences, its economic organizations and claims to exceptionalism, its cultural and historical pretensions, as well as its suppressions and oppressions. It treats revolutions as discrete spatial events, as well as latent historical challenges in and through both global and domestic time. The narrative rejects any ahistorical premise of China's inevitable overcoming or ethno-cultural rise to destined global power and nationalist hegemony. The book hence challenges the contemporary state's cultural narrative of "restoring China to its ancient prominence and glory," as Xi Jinping put it in 2012, by denaturalizing the nationalist aspirations for what is called the "great rejuvenation of the Chinese nation" (*weidade zhongguo fuxing* / 伟大的中国复兴). It does so by centrally positioning the repeated challenges that modern revolutions posed to any naturalized and settled notion of what "China" was, is, or could be.

CHAPTER 1

The Taipings

> It may seem a very strange, and a very paradoxical assertion that the next uprising of the people of Europe, and their next movement for republican freedom and economy of Government, may depend more probably on what is now passing in the Celestial Empire . . . than on any other political cause that now exists.
>
> —Karl Marx (1853)[1]

> The War of the Taiping Heavenly Kingdom was a peasant revolutionary war waged against the feudal rule and national oppression of the Qing Dynasty in the middle of the 19th century.
>
> —Mao Zedong (1949)[2]

In 1850–1851, a group of dispossessed peasants and disappointed scholars banded together in the marginal wild regions of Guangxi Province, in the South of Qing China, under the banner of an idiosyncratic ideology in opposition to local authorities bent on disciplining them. With a leader, Hong Xiuquan, who claimed to be the younger brother of Jesus Christ—thus the Christian God's younger son—this unlikely group propelled themselves and their movement, now named the Taipings, from their mountainous redoubt to become one of the major internal threats to the stability of the Qing dynasty in the mid nineteenth century. In the course of fifteen or so years, those who came to identify with the Taipings (whether strongly or loosely) swept north in ever larger and more violent military campaigns, finally to occupy much of the most fertile regions of the South while centering their rule in the old Ming dynastic capital city, Nanjing. Initially, Qing

---

1   Karl Marx, "Revolution in China and in Europe," *New York Daily Tribune*, June 14, 1853.

2   Mao Zedong, "The Bankruptcy of the Idealist Conception of History," September 16, 1949, in *Selected Works of Mao Tse-tung*, volume 4, marxists.org.

dynastic forces were quite ineffective in quashing what they called a "heterodox rebellion"—that is, one led by a non-Confucian and thus nonorthodox vision of the world. Eventually, however, the Qing was able to organize an effective military strategy to vanquish completely and thoroughly these pretenders to an alternative state and ideological form. By 1865, the Taipings were being systematically wiped out and their movement crushed; with an estimated 50 to 70 million dead at the hands of both sides, the Qing was able to re-establish some form of dynastic and domestic order over a destroyed and depopulated Southern landscape.

The Taiping Revolution (or Rebellion or Uprising or Insurrection) was a cataclysmic disordering of the Qing dynastic imperial world from within.[3] It also profoundly unsettled the European world in its apparent demonstration of Chinese revolutionary fervor so soon after the abject defeat of the Qing in the First Opium War (1842), on the one hand, and the 1848 pan-European wave of revolutions, on the other. While any posited direct relationship between Europe's 1848 and the Taipings must be seen as the result of a profound misrecognition or wishful thinking—Marx's view notwithstanding—the chronological proximity of the upheavals to one another left a deep impression on anyone who bothered to pay attention. Yet, those who came to call themselves proponents of the *taiping* (great peace) and who attempted to establish what they called the "Taiping Heavenly Kingdom" (1853–1864) were thoroughly products of mid-nineteenth-century southern Chinese conditions.

The initial mass of peasant participants had been displaced from their livelihoods in the decade after the First Opium War, when the

---

3 Recent scholarship treats the Taipings as a civil war rather than a rebellion or revolution. It could very well be called a "civil war," but the designation seems intended to avoid the politics of naming "revolution" as a problem in Chinese history. See Stephen Platt, *Autumn in the Heavenly Kingdom* (2012) and particularly Tobie Meyer-Fong, *What Remains: Coming to Terms with Civil War in Nineteenth-Century China* (2013). For the newest versions of Taiping scholarship, see the special issue of *Frontiers of History in China* 13:2, 2018.

geographical center of trade and commerce shifted from Canton (Guangzhou) up the coast toward Shanghai. Meanwhile, the Taiping leaders were mostly failed scholars, having repeatedly tried without success to pass the ever-narrowing funnel of civil service exams required of any educated man who wished to formally serve in the dynastic bureaucracy. Among the leaders and the led alike, many were susceptible—because of personal disappointments, individual intellectual propensities, or crass opportunism—to a number of different readings and interpretations of a variety of sacred texts excavated from China and abroad. These texts were syncretically mixed in a cauldron of social, political, economic, and cultural dislocation that soon lent newly created ideological precepts a social coherence and practical plausibility that found, at least at first, enthusiastic adherents. If, by the end of the revolution, the ideology had been rendered hollow; if, by the end of the revolution, its leaders had been corrupted and discredited; if, by the end of the revolution, its followers were disillusioned and felt trapped; if, by the end of the revolution, the forces of Qing dynastic order and stability proclaimed the righteousness of a sweeping, indiscriminate, and vengeful massacre of every last putative sympathizer . . . None of this denouement is particularly surprising, even if it was enormously deadly and tragic.

What *is* surprising, shocking even, is how attractive the Taipings were in the beginning stages of their movement's development—an attraction that helped propel them from the confines of their intensely local birthplace into an empire-wide movement of social upheaval and ideological contestation. The combination of social and ideological claims allows us to consider the Taipings a modern revolutionary movement. Their process exhibits an important modal characteristic of all modern revolutionary movements in China: it drew upon a wide range of global and domestic textual, practical, and ritual resources to plant itself in Chinese society, thence to offer approaches to social change at an unprecedented depth and breadth. In their very conceptualizations of the world, moreover, the Taipings proposed a rereading of China's past, present, and possible future in the light of a new form of historicity and temporality. Animated in large part by pre-modern or unmodern peasants and marginalized populations, the Taipings were nevertheless a very modern phenomenon.

Yet, unlike Mao Zedong and generations of Communist Party historians, we should not consider the Taipings the origin of the Chinese Communist Revolution that came to fruition a century later. Despite superficial resemblances—the huge peasant constituency of both revolutions, for example—there is no indication among Taiping texts or practices that there was even an embryonic understanding of class analysis and class struggle, or of socialist productive relations, both of critical importance to the Communist revolutionary movement a century later. Among the Taipings, there was an intense concern with land, its value-producing capacities, and its equitable redistribution; this is not surprising, given that China was at the time a predominantly socially and economically uneven agrarian society. Additionally, among the Taipings there was a concern with proper leadership and military tactics for what would come to be called, a century later, "guerilla" or "asymmetrical" warfare; again, this is to be expected among those who believed dynastic leadership had failed them and who were contending with vastly better armed forces in the service of often-corrupt local and provincial bureaucrats. There was, as well, concern with hierarchies, and with gendered modes of social production and reproduction—the former a feature of many bottom-up movements in China's past, and the latter perhaps more surprising than otherwise, as it had been foreshadowed in few prior domestic or global social movements. Maybe most intriguingly, there was great concern with what we might want to call, anachronistically, "propaganda" and "cultural information wars." Indeed, the placards placed in cities under siege by Taiping rebels along the way from their nascent villages to what was to become their final destination of Nanjing display a canny sensibility about the relationship between possibly aggrieved historical experiences of the present and broader textual strategies aimed at mobilizing people into disruptive social activity. The combination of these concerns—the technics as well as the epistemic foundations—is an argument for the modernity of the Taipings as a movement, whose transformative grasp of temporality and historicity was potentially locally and globally world shattering. It is no less, and no more, than this general transformative temporality and historicity that renders the Taipings a recognizable genealogical antecedent to Mao's Communist Revolution. Any claimed teleological relationship is entirely invented.

The origin story told of the Taipings focuses on the charismatic figure of their leader, Hong Xiuquan, who, in the course of sitting for the provincial bureaucratic exams in Canton in the mid 1830s, picked up a Christian tract introducing God and Jesus, their sacrifices, and their proposed mode of world salvation. At the time, Christian missionaries were circulating illegally in China; however, a short few years later they won the privilege of operating freely, through a legal clause included in the Nanjing Treaty that ended the First Opium War (1842). In Qing China, missionary religious freedom—as with "free trade" more generally—thus grew out of the barrel of imperialist guns. The particular tract Hong picked up happened to be from the hands of a Chinese convert working with the American Congregationalist Edwin Stevens from the Seamen's Friend Society. The tract was entitled "Good Words for Exhorting the Age." Hong was not immediately struck with religious fervor. Yet after several more exam disappointments over the course of a decade or so, Hong apparently turned to the Christian texts, which helped explain his now-incoherent experience of his world: though highly educated, he was unable to pass the exams that would lend him social and cultural legitimacy; unemployed, he was unable to sustain himself or bring credit to his family. Through his reading of these accidentally obtained texts, Hong embraced the story of Jesus's sacrifice. He began further study with the American Southern Baptist Isaacher Roberts, who encouraged him to defy local authorities and oppose traditional ancestor worship, among other prevalent social rituals.

By the mid 1840s, Hong was driven out of his hometown for his unorthodox behaviors—smashing ancestor tablets among them. He left the cities, linked up with some desperados in the mountains of Guangxi, and began to formulate a new type of ideological and conceptual understanding of the world, now informed by a sense of monotheistic justice and righteousness against apostate, evil dynastic authorities and polytheistic beliefs. Leading the "Society of God Worshippers," Hong declared himself Jesus's younger brother, the designated spokesperson for the one true God, sent to China to save the Chinese and the world from heathenism, the devil's depredations, and God's vengeful wrath. As countless scholars have shown, the belief system informing Hong's initial movement, a bit incoherent from the get-go, quickly got further muddled by the necessity to include more people in its leadership structures as a tool of social mobilization and cohesion. Monotheism, while retained as an ultimate principle, was stretched thin as different people came to claim the ability to channel and speak of and to God or Jesus, and as different leaders came to hold and wield power through their claimed channeling capacities. In the very beginning, however, Hong Xiuquan was the exclusive conduit of meaning from God/Jesus to his flock of believers.

Through the late 1840s, the movement grew in its backwater locality—Guangxi—where it soon became threatening to local officials, who swooped down upon it to suppress the now-burgeoning number of adherents, most of whom were out-of-work migrants and social marginals: coal miners, itinerant charcoal producers, and former drug runners for the now-displaced Canton-based opium-for-tea dealers who had monopolized trade with the British until the Nanjing Treaty put an end to such monopolies. The proclaiming of the movement as a form of "heterodoxy"—a necessary move by local officials to qualify their ineffective military defenses for coordinated Qing imperial assistance—put Hong on the map as a formal opponent of Qing neo-Confucian orthodoxy; this brought the weight of dynastic ideological censure and military violence upon him and his followers. From the beginning of 1851, when Hong named his band of followers the Taiping Heavenly Kingdom (*Taiping tianguo* / 太平天国)—where *tian* (heaven) referred specifically to the Christian God, rather than to the "son of heaven" of Confucian dynastic ritual—the movement gained in strength and credibility as it defeated the first dynastic military foray into the area. Finally ousted from their base in late 1851, the denizens, now swollen in number, began a long trek out of the mountains, heading north along an uncertain path that ultimately led to Nanjing. With news of their military prowess preceding them, the economic and social disorder of southern China, which had fallen into disarray because of long-standing trends now accelerating under the impact of the Nanjing Treaty provisions, helped produce many followers for the Taiping, including a renowned and much-feared all-female military corps composed of fighting Hakka women. The military campaigns through 1852 and 1853 proceeded north along the Yangzi River. With victories, the movement spread.

Meanwhile, ideological texts explaining and lending ideological coherence to the movement were promulgated, promoted, and often posted on placards hung on the walls of the cities under assault. Such texts as the "Taiping Ballad to Save the World" (*Taiping jiushi ge* / 太平救世歌) were meant to introduce the Taiping worldview while also competing with imperial dynastic classics for the attention and fealty of regular folks as well as of the educated classes. While most of educated society shunned the Taipings, and while Christian missionaries were supportive only until the blasphemous nature of the belief system became clear, those whose fortunes had been frustrated or destroyed by the Qing decline and imperialist assaults were particularly attracted to this new way of seeing the world and the future. At the same time, those in opposition attempted to escape before being swept up in the efforts of what were derisively called the "Yue bandits" to conquer ever-larger territories.[4] The back-and-forth fighting between the Taipings and the military forces of provincial and dynastic authorities produced spectacular violence and succeeded, ultimately, in depopulating and laying waste to large swaths of the Qing empire's most populous and economically productive regions.

---

4   There is a recently translated first-person account (written many years after the fact): Zhang Daye, *The World of a Tiny Insect: A Memoir of the Taiping Rebellion and its Aftermath*, tr. with introduction by Xiaofei Tian, Seattle, WA: University of Washington Press, 2013.

Taiping leaders—Hong Xiuquan, joined by a few other highly educated men, who would remain close allies until 1856, when internecine battles broke apart any remaining unity—elaborated an exceptionally detailed set of living and production precepts that were to provide guidance and educational materials to the rapidly developing settlements and fighting corps of Taiping rebels and their dependent families. Though never fully implemented, these precepts nevertheless indicate how thoroughly the temporal and the historical were being rethought through new conceptualizations of the ordering of everyday social life and the tasks of the present. In the most abstract terms, general introductory Taiping narratives tell of how God and Jesus came to earth to deliver sacred texts, and/or how Hong Xiuquan went to Heaven to directly discuss with God and Jesus the salvation of China and humankind; later, communication between Hong Xiuquan and God was narrated as having taken place via various outer-body voices. These direct and indirect visitations, and Hong's own claim to being Jesus's younger brother, conferred legitimacy upon Hong and gave the movement he led a source of textual and conceptual authority that lay well outside the dynastic order, even as it remained plausible to his followers. The salvation of the Han (Chinese) people from the evildoing of the Manchu Qing Empire—pictured in placards as snake demons—which worked its Satanism through Confucianism, was one major aim of the movement. Thus Confucius, at least in part, was rendered as the Devil in disguise, creating havoc on earth as part of the epic battle between God and Satan for the souls of humankind. And yet, Confucius was also partially redeemable, through the operations of *ren* (仁, benevolence), a key Confucian concept that took on enhanced meaning in the Taiping universe in its relation to Christian compassion. This temporal vision elaborated a global present as an urgent, historically extended and crucial moment of battle between a Heavenly universalism and a people doomed to damnation.

Underscoring this abstract vision, Taiping textbooks, so-called "three-character classics," were used in elementary schools and other institutions to inculcate the correct political and social attitudes and practices into children and adults. These books drew upon the common form of missionary-disseminated Bible study materials and classical Chinese primers to re-narrate all of history around the Creation, where the coming of Christ also then augurs the arrival of his younger brother, Hong Xiuquan, as savior. Hong's coming is thus an integral part of the Heavenly story, and the Heavenly story is an integral part of China's history. In this way, the "universalism" of Christianity, hitherto monopolized through the particular story of white Europeans, became inclusive of China, not coincidentally or incidentally, but as a matter of the very narrative of Christian creation and salvation. At the same time, China's dynastic history was narrated through the idiom of the fall of China to Satan (Manchu Qing Confucianism) and the potential in the here and now to fight to be saved. This deracialized, departicularized, and globally universal historical narrative—based as it was on a Christian theme—de-exceptionalized white missionaries and lent to the Taipings (comprised mostly of Han and Hakka Chinese) full agency in world history and their own salvation. Thus was China's contemporary temporality—as well as its past of the Three Dynasties and other more mythical times—written into world time as a matter not only of historical conceptualization but also of future experiential becoming.[5] This was an eschatology through which China's fate was narrated as inseparably intertwined with Europe's.

Another important text was the Taiping Diary, published with copper plate technology in 1862; the diary served as the official account of the movement and its ideals after the death of Yang Xiuqing, one of the Taipings' major figures. There were also plays, ballads, and popular forms used to promote Taiping ideology among the less literate and the less persuaded. The printed volumes by the Taipings were clearly aimed at proposing a *textual*—and thus ideological and practical—alternative to imperial dynastic authority; indeed, the number of volumes printed posed huge problems for the dynastic efforts to suppress the movement, during its high tide and in

---

5 Yao Dadui, "The Power of Persuasion in Propaganda," *Frontiers of History in China* 13:2, 2018, 193–210.

its aftermath. As scholar Huan Jin recently noted: "Their texts were so ubiquitous that Zhang Dejian 張德堅 (fl. 1850s), a Qing official, commented . . . 'The books are so numerous that they make an ox carrying a load of them sweat, and fill rooms to the rafters. Everyone is used to seeing them.'"[6]

Perhaps most well known of the Taiping texts and practices were the land laws. Resting upon the conviction that private property, and particularly clan domination of land use rights, needed to be abolished, the Taiping proposed an equitable distribution of land as a mode of creating conditions for social justice. Remarkably, in their vision, land was to be distributed to men and women alike, although the heterosexual household remained the naturalized unit in which men and women were to be socially located and through which society was to be reproduced, while the village—comprised of groupings of twenty-five families—was designated the natural unit of social life for rural society more generally. In the 1853 "Land System of the Heavenly Kingdom" it is noted that

> the division of land must be according to the number of individuals, whether male or female; calculating upon the number of individuals in a household, if they be numerous, then the amount of land will be larger, and if few, smaller . . . There being fields, let all cultivate them; there being food, let all eat; there being clothes, let all be dressed; there being money, let all use it, so that nowhere does inequality exist, and no man is not well fed and clothed.[7]

It was the aggregation of villages and the family households within them that would constitute the productive capacities of the Heavenly Kingdom; taxation would be levied on family production, and it would be equitable and far lower than the Manchu Qing rates then in effect. Rent to landlords was abolished. Gendered divisions of labor

---

6 Huan Jin, "Authenticating the Renewed Heavenly Vision: The Taiping Heavenly Chronicle (Taiping tianri)," *Frontiers of History in China* 13:2, 2018, 173–92.

7 Franz Michael, *The Taiping Rebellion: History and Documents*, Seattle, WA: University of Washington Press, 1971, 313–15.

were specified—women were to tend mulberry trees (for silk production) and spin and weave, and men were to till fields and engage in animal husbandry; meanwhile, social life was to be devoted to production and reproduction, to worshiping God, and to providing military staffing when required. Wealth accumulation, academic honor, and personal ambition were not encouraged. With education offered to all, the exam system for selecting bureaucrats was closely modeled upon the dynastic exams, in which Hong and others had so spectacularly failed. It must be noted that, in the event, not much of this was actually implemented, because of difficulties in holding territories and the constant violence visited upon nominally Taiping-held areas by Qing military forces and resisters among the occupied populations.

For a number of reasons and in a variety of ways, the Taiping Revolution failed. It fell apart of its own internecine struggles over power and doctrinal interpretation; it fell to corruption and disease; it fell to the sieges and massacres endured at the hands of dynastic military hostilities and accumulating strategic strength; and it fell to the withdrawal of any and all Euro-American missionary support. Despite the fact that the Taiping movement was, particularly in its latter stages, coterminous with such dispersed and largely unrelated uprisings as those of the Red Turbans, the Nian, and the Hui—whose respective crushings stretched dynastic military resources to the limit—its internal weaknesses also rendered the Taipings far less formidable in these later years than they had been while gathering force in the beginning. Despite this, the Taipings' vision of history as a global universal and of world time as providential and co-temporal competed for a while with the Qing dynastic defense of neo-Confucian social and political domination. Ultimately, though, its military forces were unable to defend the capital at Nanjing, and the increasing incoherence of the ideological sanction for Hong's turn to despotic leadership meant that adherents fled when they could and remained passive when they couldn't. As the noose tightened, the ideals of the Taipings receded ever further into a utopian abstraction that bore no relation to anyone's life or to any mode of governance and rule.

The final destructive massacre and empire-wide hunting down of leaders, followers, and all plausible adherents and legitimating texts bespeaks the elemental fear that had been struck in the heart of the Qing dynastic order. In this light, both Marx and Mao were wrong and right: the disruption of the Chinese empire by the Taipings was indeed cataclysmic. The revolution was peasant led; it was historically consequential because it forced a rethinking of temporal and historical premises of the Qing Chinese sociopolitical order and of global history. However, it did not lead to the forms of internationalist solidarity upon which Marx hinged his ideas of global revolution in the 1850s, nor did it usher in Mao's anti-feudal, anti-capitalist revolutionary movement. By the same token, Marx and Mao were right to designate the Taipings as a progressive phenomenon: in their reconceptualization of Chinese and global history as part of the same universal (Christian and millenarian though it was), and in their restructuring of temporality around a futurity secured by and through political and social transformative activity in the present, the Taipings proved themselves utterly modern.

China's modern revolutions thus start from then.

Interlude: Post-Taiping "Restoration"

> I read Western newspapers and they report on . . . the disorder in the
> Chinese polity . . . This has been going on for the past few decades.
> Since September or October of last year [1896], they have even more
> openly and brazenly publicized how wild and uncivilized the
> Chinese are, how ignorant and dishonest, how empty Chinese
> Confucianism is. The meaning is clear: they will move to eliminate
> China at once.
>
> —Liang Qichao, "On the Future Strength of China" (1897)[1]

In the post-Taiping reordering of the empire, many sociopolitical and
economic aspects of life were supposedly "restored," when in fact they
were being invented as part of an effort to stabilize the Qing and to
ward off further internal social threats to the dynasty. The Euro-
American powers assisted the Qing in their efforts, in part to ensure
that a central government—not too weak but not too strong—could
be forced, at gunpoint if necessary, to sign treaties disadvantageous to
itself but of great advantage to the capitalist, missionary, and other
expansions desired by the "free trade" leaders of the mid-nineteenth-
century global North. Known as "self-strengthening" (ziqiang/ 自 强),
this top-down program of restoration/invention entailed the renova-
tion of old institutions and the building of new ones. These included
the reorganization of the Qing military banner system into a more
modernized fighting force (eventually including a navy) equipped
with the latest weaponry, which closely tied the Qing military to
Euro-American weapons industries and advisors; the elaboration of a

---

1   Liang Qichao, "Lun Zhongguo zhi jiangqiang" (On the future strength of China),
Shiwu bao 31, June 1897. Liang demonstrates an advanced understanding of how imperial-
ism works to ideologically create its object of violence. See Rebecca E. Karl, *Staging the
World: Chinese Nationalism at the Turn of the Twentieth Century*, Durham, NC: Duke
University Press, 2002.

foreign diplomatic corps through the Zongli Yamen (Office for General Affairs), which took on the responsibility for negotiating trade and colonial/territorial matters that arose or were forced upon the Qing by various foreign powers; the Maritime Customs Service, under the direction first of the British Colonial Office and subsequently of Americans, charged with setting and collecting internal riverine transport taxes (*lijin* or *likin*/厘金) on behalf of the Qing court as well as on their own behalves;[2] the establishment of "arsenals" that were as tied to foreign military industry as they were to training new talent in new knowledges (foreign languages, translation, and "Western" science and technology), useful primarily not for Confucian bureaucratic purposes but for modern-world managerial tasks; and so on. These institutional reforms were accompanied by socioeconomic innovations: the repopulation of the Yangzi River valley with new peasant households, whose female labor was deployed to rebuild the regional specialization in sericulture (silk production), a trade ever more closely tied to urban centers and hence to global commodity markets;[3] efforts at industrialization along the coastal littoral near Shanghai, funded through public-private arrangements that socialized risk while privatizing profits; railroad building, financed primarily through territorial and other concessions granted to foreign powers; and so on. Qing fiscal discipline, never very strict, already had been dealt a huge blow by the growing scarcity of silver since the beginning of the nineteenth century, and then by the difficulty of gathering revenue during the Taiping Revolution; now, it went wildly out of control. Predatory debt regimes, enforced by colonial merchant banks backed by imperialist powers and underpinned by the British/American-dominated Customs Service,[4] were not far behind.

---

2 This was a system put in place during the Taiping Revolution, as a way to pay armies to fight the Taipings; it survived and was reorganized several times, always under foreign supervision, until well into the 1930s.

3 Lynda S. Bell, "From Comprador to County Magnate," in Joseph Esherick and Mary Rankin, eds., *China's Local Elites and Patterns of Dominance*, Berkeley, CA: University of California Press, 1990, 125.

4 Debin Ma, "Money and Monetary System in China in the 19th–20th Century: An Overview," *LSE Working Papers*, January 2012, 10.

The post-Taiping economic and political "restoration" helped transform Qing social relations by placing more socioeconomic power in the hands of landowners, usurers (who mediated trade, in part by indebting producers and advancing capital on speculative crops such as silk and tea), and urban commercial and merchant elites, as well as by welding more closely together those local and provincial elites with global capitalist concerns—the latter imposed upon and increasingly incorporated into China through visible and invisible imperialist expansion into the everyday workings of social life. The concomitant growth of urban treaty ports—Shanghai, Canton (Guangzhou), Xiamen (Amoy), Tianjin, and others—and such inland entrepôt cities as Wuhan/Hankou (at the intersection of several riverine commercial routes) brought various types of local elites—merchants, literati, and so forth—into "an unprecedented social mixing,"[5] as well as bringing this new mix into residential, political, social, and cultural proximity to colonial settlers from many countries, all of whom (aside from the Japanese) were now commonly lumped into the catchall category of "Westerner," who came from somewhere now homogeneously called "the West."

By the 1880s and 1890s, these transformations had seeped, unevenly, into everyday life, helping visibly or invisibly to restructure and recalibrate the rhythms and expectations of many. Agrarian producers were now often tied to the fluctuations of the global markets in which their commodity economy was increasingly embedded. Meanwhile, for elites accustomed to securing social status through state service, larger civil service exam quotas for those social sectors that had defended the dynasty against the Taipings led, in an immediate sense, to larger numbers of sons admitted to bureaucratic appointments. Primarily aimed at pacifying the Yangzi delta region, this helped further enhance the dominance of that area in relation to other regions of the empire. Small

---

5   Christopher Reed, *Guttenberg in China: Chinese Print Capitalism, 1876–1937,* Vancouver: UBC Press, 2004, 165.

but increasing numbers of educated sons also were sent to new-style schools, or even sent abroad to study new forms of knowledge. Some girls were now being schooled as well, although not systematically, while a movement against footbinding—that congeries of practices that had been visited upon many Chinese girls since at least the fourteenth century and that had become a firm part of the marriage market—grew in the interstices of urban society, albeit only gaining major ground and persuasive power after the 1911 Republican Revolution.[6]

Meanwhile, various intellectual endeavors attempted to make "Western" and "Chinese" knowledge systems compatible, or at least comparable, either by separating them out so that each would pertain to a different albeit equivalent domain (as with the late-nineteenth-century saying "Western function serves Chinese essence" [*zhongti xiyong* / 中体西用]), or by mixing and matching fragments of each system as needed and desired—thus arriving at a syncretism identifiable by neither system. In the latter vein, for example, a far-reaching reinterpretation of Confucius was undertaken by the renegade scholar Kang Youwei, who, by the early 1890s, had configured Confucius as essentially a reformer rather than a conservator of sociopolitical structure. By using Confucius to sanction not preservation but reform, Kang's syncretism, impeccably rooted in Confucian textual studies now updated with new perspectives derived from a reformist imperative, gained enthusiastic adherents among rebellious younger scholars even as it drew calumny from staid conservatives. Their relentless efforts to quash Kang and his followers persisted through the 1890s, even as new forms of thought outstripped Kang's audacity and came to inform a whole radical movement that led directly to anti-dynastic activity. These efforts—the quashing and the development of more radical thought and action—led to the relocation of some scholars to the

---

6 On the end of footbinding as a social and embodied practice, see Dorothy Ko, *Cinderella's Sisters: A Revisionist History of Footbinding*, Berkeley, CA: University of California Press, 2005.

relatively safer shores of Japan or Hong Kong, at a remove from Qing dynastic forces keen to jail or silence them.

The fall of the Qing and the Republican Revolution startlingly emerged from a combination of these social, intellectual, systemic, and military forces.

CHAPTER 2

The Collapse of the Qing and the Republican Revolution

> Has it occurred to you that men are our archenemy? . . . This situation is by no means confined to the ancient world and is just as prevalent in the modern world . . . nor is it a uniquely Chinese situation . . . There is no doubt that the Manchu court [of the Qing dynasty] should be overthrown, but I would like to point out that a Han sovereign or regime could be a disaster worse than the ones wrought by foreign rule.
>
> —He-Yin Zhen, "On the Revenge of Women" (1907)[1]

> Raise the Han, Raise the Han
> Destroy the Manchu, Destroy the Manchu,
> Destroy the thieving Manchu.
>
> —Military anthem, October 1911[2]

On February 1, 1912, the final abdication of the Qing was formalized at the Forbidden City in Beijing in a sad little tête-à-tête between the Empress Dowager Cixi and Yüan Shikai, the Qing's former number one general, who had turned to uncertain revolutionary sympathies. (Already a traitor to the Qing, Yüan was soon enough to become a traitor to the republic, but that was history yet to be written.) A new government had already been proclaimed a month prior, on January 1, in Nanjing, where revolutionary leaders had gathered and had already begun to rule in the dynasty's stead. The symbolism of the

---

1 Lydia Liu, R. E. Karl, and D. Ko, trs. and eds., *The Birth of Chinese Feminism: Essential Texts in Transnational Theory*, New York: Columbia University Press, 105, 106.

2 Cited in Henrietta Harrison, *Inventing the Nation: China*, London: Arnold Publishers, 2001, 133. This song was published in a pro-republican newspaper, *Minlibao*, in October 1911.

Gregorian calendrical timing of the proclamation was intentional: the dynastic time of the emperors was at an end, while the rural peasant time of lunar calendars was to be curtailed. A new China, a new nation among nations in solar time, was to prevail. Yet, historical time was also to begin anew: January 1912 was counted as year one of the republic. While no one stood on a rostrum in front of millions of cheering supporters—as was to happen in 1949 when Mao Zedong declared the establishment of the People's Republic of China from Beijing's Gate of Heavenly Peace (*Tian'an men* / 天安门)—the transfer of state power from the Manchu Qing to republican revolutionaries was no less momentous an occasion for being less immediately public.[3] While significant political, cultural, and economic continuities obviously remained, history was nevertheless set on a new path.

Starting from the October 10, 1911 uprising of military contingents in the city of Wuhan, the sequence of military and political events leading to the deposing of the dynasty proceeded relatively quickly, even if the revolution had been some five decades in the making. As various troops defected, thus leaving the Qing relatively undefended, Sun Yatsen, who at the time was in Denver, Colorado, raising funds for the revolutionary effort, heard of the events through media reports. He rushed back to China (first to New York, via the transcontinental railway built by imported Chinese labor, then by steamship to London, overland to France, and from there, by sea to Shanghai), where he was proclaimed the first president of the Republic of China (ROC). A Cantonese-born, American-educated (in the newly US-occupied Pacific territory of Hawaii) Western medicine doctor turned revolutionary agitator who resided in British colonial Hong Kong, Sun embodied a symbolic figure of modern Chineseness that appealed to ordinary as well as educated Chinese, both at the time and subsequently. While formally the provisional president for only a few months (ousted by the ever-traitorous Yüan Shikai), Sun

---

3   Public ceremonies attached to the new ROC kicked in very soon. See Henrietta Harrison, *The Making of the Republican Citizen: Political Ceremonies and Symbols in China, 1911–1929*, Oxford, UK: Oxford University Press, 2000.

remained in constant opposition to the constituted ROC government until his death in 1925. However, he was and remains heralded as "the father of the nation" (*guofu*/国父).

The Republican Revolution (also called the 1911 Revolution, or the Xinhai [辛亥] Revolution) succeeded in ousting the Qing through an almost-accidental accrual of ideological strength backed by military support. This coalition failed to translate into any enduring political unity. Despite the messiness of the denouement, the fall of the Qing marked an evental shift in China's modern history. This shift was informed by and pushed forward through a revolutionary rethinking of the basis of Chinese sociopolitical and economic organization; it was, in addition, underpinned by and promoted through nascent social revolutionary upheavals in gender, ethnic, national, regional, and global relations. All of these forces combined in various ways to bring to the fore and propose (unfulfilled) solutions to the *systemic* problems of modernity as a process of *necessarily* locally and globally intertwined temporal and historical experience.

The 1911 Revolution has been called, by Communist historiographical convention, a "bourgeois" revolution. In the idiom of Marxian party dogma—where socialist revolutions must be preceded by bourgeois ones—the overthrow of the Qing dynasty serves the historicist purpose. It would be a mistake to adhere rigidly to such claims, however. Fitting the leaders, the ideology, or the politics of the revolution into a categorical straitjacket not only misconstrues the subordinated relationship between China and the capitalist world but places China into a teleological trajectory formed by histories made elsewhere.[4] There is no doubt that China's Republican Revolution was in part led and informed by a new class in formation—a scholar-bureaucrat fraction transforming itself into an intelligentsia with connections to urban, rural, military and commercial elites—but it is not

---

4 Whether "bourgeois revolutions" were bourgeois or even revolutionary is a subject of debate. See Neil Davidson, *How Revolutionary Were the Bourgeois Revolutions?*, Chicago, IL: Haymarket, 2012.

evident that that means this class must be called a "bourgeoisie," or that the revolution is most appropriately understood as a class-based, bourgeois affair.[5] In a different idiom, the Republican Revolution has been claimed as a "Han-ethnic" revolution, where the Manchu-ness of the Qing is emphasized and the anti-Manchu nature of the revolutionaries becomes a paramount attribute. There were certainly a large number of adherents to revolutionary politics and activity of the time who construed the revolution in such mono-ethnic national terms. Sun Yatsen, for one, led a Japan-based Chinese revolutionary organization, the Tongmeng Hui (Revolutionary Alliance / 同盟会), formed in 1905, that explicitly espoused anti-Manchu sentiment and theorized the modern world of nations in ethnic terms. As cited in the epigraph to this chapter, a number of military songs mobilized troop support for the revolution in just this way. Indeed, it is an abiding curiosity of the Republican Revolution that its anti-imperialist/anti-colonial animus was aimed far more at the Manchus (construed as alien occupiers of China) than at the Euro-American or Japanese powers that were more recently settling into—and violently imposing themselves in—territorially conceded areas around the empire. By the same token, the relatively quick disappearance of mono-ethnicity in favor of a multiethnic flag and national-state rhetoric ought to give some pause over claims to too tight an enduring connection to Han-centrism on the part of most of the revolution's political and intellectual leaders.

It has also been claimed—with far better evidence from the outcomes—that the Republican Revolution merely replaced one patriarchal state form with another, and that in this, its class or ethnic character is entirely beside the point. Given how very quickly the new leaders turned to suppress their erstwhile female comrades, and given how very anti-feminist many leaders of the early ROC proved to be, the securing of a patriarchal state—even while it reluctantly opened certain social, professional, educational, and other opportunities to women—seems to have far more basis in fact than any of the other

---

5   For an argument about its global nature, see Karl, *Staging the World*.

claims. He-Yin Zhen, the anarcho-feminist cited at the opening of this chapter, saw this likelihood very clearly. The manifest continuity of patriarchy, however, masks the different ways in which that power operated in the new era: now, often by making common cause with socially progressive forces, some of which were led by women, patriarchal prerogative could partially conceal itself behind mildly feminist-seeming rhetoric and practice (the anti-footbinding movement and support for women's education are two such examples).

What also is quite clear is that the Republican Revolution of 1911 was one among many global nationalist revolutions of the first decade of the twentieth century that elaborated, in weak or strong fashion, an anti-imperialist and anti-colonial motivation to spark a political if not also a social upheaval. Although the Chinese version of that anti-colonial rhetoric was bent at this time to the particular historical purpose of anti-Manchuism rather than anti-Euro-American imperialism, without a prior understanding of modern global anti-colonial and anti-imperialist theory and practice, this Chinese historical re-narrativization of the Manchus-as-modern-colonizers would not have been possible. The modernity of the Republican Revolution is in part located in this global temporal and spatial simultaneity. In the 1911 Revolution we thus see the definitive redefinition of the Chinese concept for "revolution" (geming/革命) away from its previous containment to dynastic cycles—"severing" (ge/革) the (dynastic) "mandate" (ming/命) for the purpose of bestowing that mandate on a new dynasty—toward a modern global version connoting the fundamental transformation of political (if not also social) power from one form of polity to another—in this case, from dynastic empire to nation-state. At the same time, we also have, through this revolutionary process, a fundamental social redefinition of what constituted "politics" or the realm of the political, which now became an arena of potentially wide public contention rather than one contained wholly within the court/state. The social opening of the realm of politics was as consequential an outcome as any, as it was through this political rearticulation that China and the world were rethought, not separately but in necessary conjunction; and it was in this necessary conjunction that new classes came into political activity while global philosophies and practices of politics, society, economy, and culture became significant for and in China. It was, hence, when the relatively closed-circuit (though by now attenuated), intertwined Confucian logics of Chinese society, politics, economics, and culture crumbled that the social-ideological foundations of the dynasty collapsed and a new syncretic political possibility was established.

By the late nineteenth century, the accumulated domestic weaknesses of the Qing were sufficiently exacerbated by the increasing intrusions of Euro-American and Japanese capitalist-imperialism—as an economic imperative of competitive domination and internal social restructuring as well as an ideological temptation—to lead to a fundamental turn among the educated, who began to defect in ever-larger numbers from dynastic service and bureaucratic complacency. The Sino-Japanese War of 1894–1895 (also known as the Jiawu [甲午] War), fought in and over Korea and the nature of its sovereignty and ties to China and Japan, accelerated this trend. The Qing was badly beaten by an opponent long thought to be culturally and historically inferior. Japan—past borrower of the Han Chinese writing system, faithful emulator of Confucianism, piratical "dwarves of the East" in popular Southern parlance—destroyed China's new French-built navy before it even left harbor and humiliated Chinese troops on the Korean fields, where they met in face-to-face battle. Clearly, Japan had surged ahead, and, in stark comparison, the Qing seemed to have lagged behind. The Treaty of Shimonoseki ending the war was as punitive as any previously imposed upon the Qing by the Euro-American powers. Not only was Taiwan ceded to Japan, but the Qing was forced to pay for Japan's side of the war in addition to acceding to other major concessions. The humiliation was deeply felt.

In 1898, a number of aggrieved scholars, led by the reformist Confucian Kang Youwei and his disciples, launched a petition to urge the Guangxu Emperor to reform Qing state practices and to embrace a more progressive historical stance. After one hundred days of hopeful and urgent activity, the movement was suppressed by the Empress

Dowager Cixi, whose conservative advisors strongly counseled against all such destabilizing change. The emperor was placed under house arrest while Cixi, his adoptive mother, forcibly took over the regency and ruthlessly quashed any at court or elsewhere who might have supported Kang. Many of the most sought-after reformists escaped to Japan, enemy though it recently had been. Because Japan had new-style schools and political supporters of reform in Asia, as well as a written language still sufficiently close to Chinese, many stayed there, using it as a base from which to foment dissent against the Qing. Episodically pursued by Qing state agents abetted by Japanese police, the movement to fundamentally reform or oust the Qing nevertheless found a home in Japan.

The abandonment by a portion of the scholarly class of the tepid dynastically proposed solutions to China's historical and contemporary problems proved to be one major impetus behind the Republican Revolution of 1911. The exiled thinkers and political activists in Japan and Hong Kong—who used the nascent forms of journalism and pamphleteering, and who were themselves not even all revolutionaries but rather also translators, writers, philosophers, and reforming Confucians—were joined by socially situated on-the-ground organizers of the Qing military, and of general social discontent, in shaping the Republican Revolution over the first decade of the twentieth century. Other social forces were marginally involved: for example, many merchant and commercial elites were sympathetic to the critique of the dynasty's incompetence, and some even funded critical journals and publishing efforts that sponsored less dynasty-centric new forms of "universal history" (tongshi/通史) and advocated for new forms of knowledge. Nevertheless, the revolution was carried out by a military coup backed by an intellectual rationale substantially developed in exile abroad.

The dynasty itself did plenty to hasten this outcome. Indeed, aside from the military defeat by Japan, the routing from the court of reformist tendencies not controlled immediately by Cixi and her henchmen, and the related pursuit of progressive scholars into exile, the dynasty sustained a mounting fiscal crisis, a consequent increasing indebtedness to foreign banks and Euro-American-Japanese imperialist interests, and a last-ditch attempt to align with social forces of a rather atavistic sort. All of this spelled doom for dynastic survival.

The Boxer Rebellion of 1899–1901 indicates the desperation and growing irrelevance of dynastic governance to the imagined future of China and the Chinese state. In the north-central province of Shandong—birthplace of Confucius—a roiling discontent was brewing among local peasants, who saw their village lands occupied by Christian missionaries working in cahoots with local elites whose personal coffers were amply filled in return for their assistance. Forming a secret society known as the "Harmonious Fists" (ordinarily translated as "Boxers"), these locals, in a fit of murderous frustration, killed two German missionaries and went on a looting and killing rampage against local officials and those they called "rice Christians" (Chinese who became Christians allegedly only in order to obtain food). Through the end of 1899 into 1900, drawing adherents to their side with their mystical beliefs in their own invulnerability to bullets and their pledges to recover control over local affairs, the Boxers began to move toward Beijing. The wrath of imperialist gunboat retaliation fell swiftly and surely in Shandong. Yet, the Boxers moved quickly, growing in size and intensity as they swept into the North. They managed to reach Beijing with hugely swollen numbers of the frustrated and the faithful. The dynasty, seeing an opportunity to oppose the despised practices of Euro-American gunboat diplomacy in defense of missionary intrusion, seized the day and proclaimed their alliance with the rebels. The Boxer disruption of railway lines connecting Beijing to other parts of the country frightened the foreign community in Beijing enough to prompt them to send urgent telegrams to their various leaders seeking immediate assistance.

The Boxers and Qing military banners lay siege to the Legation Quarters, where diplomats, missionaries, and mercenaries from all the nations resided in the capital. After some brief moments of rousing success in isolating the foreigners, by June 20, 1900, the forces of world order came crashing down. In one of the first examples of a global "coalition of the willing," eight allied powers (Austro-Hungary, France, Germany, Great Britain, Italy, Japan, the United States, and Russia) marched upon Beijing. Led by the US Marines (whose leader was memorably played by Charlton Heston in the 1963 Hollywood epic *55 Days at Peking*), the Boxers and Manchu Banners were soundly defeated. By mid July a wholesale massacre of all suspected Boxer sympathizers was proceeding unimpeded upon a now-defenseless population. The Qing court, initially buoyed by popular rumors of Boxer success, was forced to abandon the capital, protected in its flight by the very foreign coalition then rampaging against Beijing's population. Cixi and her retinue waited out the events in the North.

Most elites—scholars, commercial merchants, bureaucrats, land-lords—were horrified at the court's support for the Boxers. In part, this was pure class hatred: How could the court throw in its lot with this motley, anti-modern, anti-progressive, mystical, uneducated crew of violent peasants? In part, this was connected to the increasing alienation elites experienced with relation to the dynasty, which could no longer pretend to represent a desired future path, or even a toler-able present, for the Chinese state. In part, there also were growing alliances between these domestic classes and foreign commercial and cultural power. Provincial leaders refused to declare solidarity with the court; indeed, in certain Southern provinces—Guangdong or Hunan, for example—irredentist sentiment became a subject of seri-ous debate in newspapers and journals. The massacres and conse-quent huge death toll in the wake of the Boxers, in addition to the extreme disruptions to transport, the economy, and social order occa-sioned by those fleeing the desperate remnants of the Boxers and the foreign pursuit, received little to no sympathy from elites safely out of range. The Boxer Protocol—the final punitive treaty imposed in 1901—was another devastating blow to the territorial sovereignty and fiscal capacities of the Qing court.[6] From this point on, the dynasty

---

6   Joseph Esherick, *The Origins of the Boxer Uprising*, Berkeley, CA: University of California Press, 1987.

attempted to promote a series of mild reform measures, intended to enhance the governing capacity of the state. These reforms closely mirrored those undertaken earlier by Japan. Yet, all this was too little, too late.

Sounding yet another death knell to the integration of knowledge and dynastic rule, in 1905 the civil service exam system that had secured the relation between education and appointment in the dynastic bureaucracy was abolished. The link between educated men, classical texts, and governing logics was severed. Some die-hard preservationists advocated the reconstitution of these connections in a cognate form; many more-progressive types proceeded to establish new schools to teach new knowledges, while yet others who would have taken the exams now found new forms of employment in book writing and publishing and/or in journalism. Meanwhile, political novels flourished, and translations from abroad of countless philosophies, world histories, biographies of great men (and a few women), scientific theories, and technological manuals were now sought after with huge enthusiasm by an urban reading public. New professional paths opened to educated men, and to a handful of educated women. The ideological and cultural sphere was invigorated and incredibly eclectic. Much of it contributed to the idea that the dynastic system was no longer a proper vessel or vehicle for the elaboration of a modern Chinese identity or polity in the twentieth-century world.

At the same time, social change was rampant as global and Chinese commodity markets became more integrated. Intensification of land use proceeded rapidly albeit unevenly, even as the handicraft production fueled by rural women's labor increasingly lost out to imported or urban-made manufactured goods. More and more, women from rural areas—whose productivity had been crucial to the economic survival of their households and who were now rendered surplus labor—were forced or lured into new urban-based manufacturing concerns—silk filatures, cotton mills, match factories—owned and operated by Japanese or Euro-American capitalists, or, more rarely, by local industrialists; other women and girls were sold by destitute households as prostitutes, concubines, or serving girls for richer families. With stiff competition from Japan, Italy, France, and the United States manufacturing similar commodities, women's wages were low, and they were easily preyed upon by gangs and other cohorts employed by bosses to keep them in the factories and obediently in line. Thus, as the rural economy deteriorated, there was an accelerating subordination of rural to urban space, helping to reorganize fundamentally the historical valence of social and spatial relations, even while many aspects of the outward appearance of continuity and stagnation remained.[7]

Widespread opium addiction—a problem that had begun to manifest in the early nineteenth century and that had rooted itself in practice up and down the urban and rural social ladders—facilitated international drug economies that were mercilessly exploitative, even while drug use and sale was outlawed domestically in Euro-America and Japan. These economies tied the Euro-American opium plantations and colonial states of South and Southeast Asia to China in close dependence. Colonial banks, whose capital funds were swollen and maintained in large part by opium revenue, controlled, to an ever-greater extent, the purse strings of the dynasty—even while powerful Chinese salt families, for example, started to transform their state-granted monopolies into dominance over other domestic economic spheres. These domestic concerns operated through the native Shanxi banking system that had for centuries facilitated inter-provincial trade through, among other modes, the verification of currency values (silver to copper valuation was one major issue, as copper was the currency in general use while silver was the currency of account). Yet, because colonial banks controlled the import and exchange value of silver, ultimately, financial affairs ended up running in and through that extraterritorially protected system. Throughout the late Qing

---

7 For a synthetic account, see the "Introduction" and "Historical Context" in Liu, Karl, and Ko, eds., *Birth of Chinese Feminism*. For debates over the rural economy in nineteenth-century China and its relation to women's labor, see Hill Gates, *China's Motor*, Ithaca, NY: Cornell University Press, 1996; Kathy Le Mons Walker, *Chinese Modernity and the Peasant Path: Semicolonialism in the Northern Yangzi Delta*, Palo Alto, CA: Stanford University Press, 1999.

period, in fact, the monetary situation became more and more muddled, as silver ingots, indifferently cast copper coin, paper currency, and other instruments of trade and exchange floated around the empire with varying, sometimes even arbitrary, degrees of value attached. There were times and places when opium served as the most stable medium of exchange. Only in the treaty ports, where currencies were strictly regulated by the colonial banks, was the monetary situation relatively clear.

Tied up with the weakening situation of Qing finances, the problem of railway construction flared into a major socioeconomic issue of the last decade of the dynasty. Initially undertaken by British, French, German, Russian, and Japanese companies granted territorial rights through treaty provisions extracted at gunpoint, railway construction was at first resisted by conservative Qing administrators (among other reasons, it was harmful to the dynastic-controlled system of horses and postal relays). After 1895, railways were understood to be both central to and significant for military, commercial, and governing purposes. In the face of exhortations by provincial leaders, who saw railway revenues sucked up by foreign concerns, the Qing began, in 1904 and 1905, to lend large sums to Chinese companies for the construction of trunk lines, several of which were built. However, these were not really economically viable, and by 1911 the indigenous lines had fallen into bankruptcy. The Qing proceeded to nationalize and then pledge them to foreign banks as collateral for loans. The discontent among merchant and commercial elites and their resulting restiveness directly contributed to the abandonment of the dynasty during the revolutionary events of October 1911.

Efforts at modernization—of institutions, of communication and commercial networks, of industry—went under the rubric of "wealth and power" (fuqiang/富强). Through the late nineteenth and into the early twentieth century, indifferent to labor and the socially disruptive impact of their various schemes, urban-based commercial and merchant elites operating under these initiatives grew in social power and even in cultural prestige. Landowners, the historical gentry and acknowledged dominant class of Confucian dynastic China, held onto their economic and social positions increasingly by making alliances with, marrying their footbound daughters into, or sending sons to engage in the previously despised spheres of trade and commerce. Theorizations of these and other developments became part of a budding disciplinary transformation in knowledge production, some of which tried to reconcile social changes with re-interpretations of Confucian texts, while others ditched those texts altogether to take up modern theories of state and economy emanating from Japan, Germany, Russia, France, Britain, and the United States. Scholar and publisher Yan Fu translated Herbert Spencer and Charles Darwin; Liang Qichao, Kang Youwei's student, introduced Jean-Jacques Rousseau, John Stuart Mill, Johann Kaspar Bluntschli (a now-obscure German statist political theorist and jurist), and Friedrich List (a German theorist of national economics); others made available in Chinese the rudiments of socialism, anarchism, Russian utopianism, and feminism, for example. Theories of "survival of the fittest" jostled with natural rights theory, which competed with liberal and anti-liberal statist positions, juxtaposed to modernist and anti-modernist anti-statism—some of which, in turn, was funneled into revolutionary and nonrevolutionary nationalist thought. The lines of debate were rarely clear—other than as marked between pro- and anti-revolutionaries—and the cauldron of thought was constantly stirred in the heated journalistic mediasphere of the day.

Sun Yatsen, not fully trained in Confucian texts or hampered by previous loyalties to one or another school of classical or foreign thinking, promoted in outline what he called the "Three Principles of the People" (*sanmin zhuyi* / 三民主义). A mild form of socialism intended to forestall the violence potentially produced by capitalist class division, Sun's Three Principles were aimed at helping realize the ideals of republican equality and democracy. Beginning from the principle of land redistribution (derived, eclectically, from the American agrarian reformer Henry George), Sun attempted to theorize and map out how, in a post-dynastic world, Chinese were to be made economically productive, politically democratic, and globally sovereign. Often understood to be the better road not taken in China, the Three Principles continued to be fleshed out from the 1910s onward and have remained a touchstone of Chinese political and economic thinking. They were ostensibly embraced by republican revolutionaries and their successors throughout the century, even as the Three Principles increasingly became more incantatory than real as goals of state practice. Nevertheless, the eclecticism of their political and theoretical sources demonstrates well the range of thinking that informed the revolutionary endeavors of the anti-dynastic republicans in the first decade of the twentieth century. It was this eclecticism that helped delineate the parameters and inevitability of Qing ideological collapse.

Among the first decrees of Sun's government in January 1912, men were enjoined to cut their queues, the pigtails symbolizing fealty to the Manchu Qing Dynasty that they had been forced to wear for 268 years. In the first years of the new republic, most Han men complied, keeping barbers busy all over the empire. (Men in Mongolia, Tibet, Turkestan, and other peripheral regions held out longer, perhaps leery of the durability of the new order.) In more than mere sartorial terms, queue-cutting marked a definitive end to Qing claims to ruling legitimacy. A new national flag was promoted, in which a five-ethnicity unity (Han, Manchu, Mongolian, Tibetan, Muslim) was proclaimed as a national state ideal, while a parliament was formed, extending voting rights to property-owning Han men. Women, who had fought the Qing in large numbers, had been promised full citizenship and a place at the political table; they were summarily booted from parliamentary proceedings. A particularly prominent appearance in the halls of power sealed the deal: as Song Jiaoren (Sun's deputy) was finalizing the terms of the republican constitutional charter in Beijing, Tang Qunying and two other women marched into the hall and slapped him with their fans in reproach for his/Sun's bargaining away of women's rights in exchange for conservative support. The betrayal of the promise of "equality and democracy" had, it turned out, been all but instantaneous.[8]

---

8   Gail Hershatter, *Women and China's Revolutions*, New York: Rowman & Littlefield, 2019, chapter 3.

Interlude: Post-revolutionary Disorder

> The capitalists do not plow the fields themselves, yet eat huge meals and drink beer by robbing the surplus of us workers. Yet we who plow the fields and work hard, day in day out, never have full bellies. Why does society tolerate these parasites, these rice buckets?
>
> —A mechanic (1921)[1]

Political, social, and economic disorder set in almost immediately after the 1911–1912 events deposing the Qing. This disorder mapped onto and was in part fomented by military power holders (conventionally called "warlords"), who quickly moved into competitive positions to claim economic and territorial prerogatives from each other and a crumbling center. Sun Yatsen, for his part, abandoned China for Japan in 1913, fearing for his life; he was to return and leave China repeatedly until his death from liver cancer in Beijing in March 1925. By late 1915, the ever-opportunistic Yüan Shikai declared himself emperor in an attempt to seize glory and reunify state power. Political and social opposition was comprehensive, stiff, and unrelenting; as it turned out, Yüan died of kidney disease in mid 1916, frustrated in his efforts. His death marked the end of the last serious bid to revive monarchy in China. Thereafter, the Republican Revolution, successful at finally banishing most vestiges of political support for dynastic rule (Qing or otherwise), yielded quite a political debacle. No social class was strong enough to impose its hegemony upon the Chinese state, and the constant demands by imperialist powers—now with Japan insistent and uncompromising—rendered the sovereignty of that shifting state often only nominal. China entered the second decade of the twentieth century in parlous condition, ripe for one

---

1 Cited in S. A. Smith, *Like Cattle and Horses: Nationalism and Labor in Shanghai, 1895–1927*, Durham, NC: Duke University Press, 2002, 120.

revolution after the next, through whose sequences the social relations of production and knowledge combined and recombined in unpredictable ways.

In January 1915, taking advantage of the European powers' preoccupation with the Great War, the Japanese government issued to China an ultimatum known as the Twenty-One Demands. These demands were designed to force the weakened Chinese state—such as it was at the time—to accede to Japanese requirements for political, territorial, and economic gains at the expense of the Europeans, the Americans, and of course, of China itself. Aimed in large part at wresting control of Manchuria from China so as to bind the territory to its colony in Korea, Japan's demands were articulated in the language of "protection" (that is, Japan protecting its yellow-race Asian neighbor from white-race imperialist depredation). As the Japanese put it, the demands were an "attempt to solve those various questions which are detrimental to the intimate relations of China and Japan with a view to solidifying the foundation of cordial friendship subsisting between the two countries to the end that the peace of the Far East may be effectually and permanently preserved."[2] After negotiations to soften a few of the provisions, Yüan Shikai signed the document in May 1915. In the early 1920s, the whole of part 5 of the document—dealing with economic matters—was vacated by negotiations forced by Britain and the United States, who wanted to curb Japan's growing control of the Chinese economy. However, the demands set the tone for the continued weakness of the Chinese state with relation to imperialist impositions.

A closely correlated aspect of the military, territorial, and economic expansion of Japan was the social scientific research—on traditions and customs, on politics and military, on social structure and economic systems—that came to undergird the colonial project. Of course, the derivation of knowledge about colonized peoples—the fixing of these peoples into categories, their relegation into

2   "21 Demands Made by Japan to China, January 1915," available at firstworldwar.com.

indigenous and congenital forms of "backwardness," the efforts to "civilize" them through the promotion of "advanced" knowledges and practices—was not unique to Japan; this had been a universalizing project of Euro-American colonizing powers for centuries. In the 1910s, after a trial run in Taiwan (which had been colonized in 1895), the Japanese colonial project in Korea, Manchuria, and China was defined explicitly as one of data and information collection in the interests of empire building. This was accomplished through an interlocking set of institutions, with both research and policy implications. A major current of Japanese scholarship on China emphasized sinological attention to ancient texts and thinkers: this was intended to demonstrate that while China had had a glorious past, that past was now forsaken and only recoverable through Japanese assistance in a pan-Asian cultural fraternity. Other currents included geographical studies, with attention to the diffusion of civilization across Asia, now defined as a Japan-centric Sinosphere; research into practical matters of military occupation, civilian pacification, and disease control; and trade and commerce research, through which the Japanese would penetrate, dominate, and create markets. A tight connection hence was made between the very design of research in the humanities and the social sciences, and the direction of colonial governance and military conquest.

Meanwhile, the provisions of the Treaty of Shimonoseki of 1895 had yielded the right to set up manufacturing and industrial concerns on Chinese soil to Japan, and by extension, to Euro-American imperialist powers.[3] By the 1910s, this had resulted in a wave of urbanized development in the treaty ports that pulled labor from the rural areas into factory work and discipline. From Canton to Fuzhou to Shanghai and Tianjin, male-dominated heavy industrial manufacturing centered on steel and shipbuilding, while female-dominated light industrial manufactures in silk filatures, match factories, and cotton

---

3 The 1842 Treaty of Nanjing ending the First Opium War had established the "most favored nations" clause, by which a concession ceded to one imperialist power was automatically extended to all the powers, to forestall any effort by the Qing to play one power off another.

mills busily produced refined raw materials and commodities for the world market, and hence surplus value for Japanese, British, American, and some Chinese factory owners. By the end of the Great War in 1919, there were over 1.5 million industrial workers in the country, with 300,000 concentrated in Shanghai alone. A fragmented urban proletariat came into being: men, whose guilds and unions excluded women, founded organizations that sometimes translated into political recognition;[4] and women formed informal "sisterhoods"—self-organized for personal protection against gang depredations—that often yielded strong bonds of labor solidarity and activism, as well as gendered identification.[5] Various other lines of fragmentation among the working classes also emerged: native place (corresponding to language divisions tied to birthplace); workshop specializations; skilled and unskilled; and so forth. Most of those lines of division were capable of disappearing in moments of great crisis, and the postrevolutionary period saw a number of such industrial labor crises develop. Yet, as difficult as the lives of these workers were, they had to be counted as the fortunate among those recently displaced from rural areas, for along with urbanization came widespread urban poverty and misery, including large numbers of impoverished children begging or working for pittances and women working as courtesans or streetwalkers, up and down the social ladder.[6]

A corresponding urban bourgeoisie incipiently formed, although it was more a type of multinational comprador class, comprised mostly of foreigners, along with some Chinese, many of whom had been educated abroad and were multilingual. This mixed elite resided in the colonial parts of the cities in grand mansions and spacious apartments, with in-home kitchens and hygienic facilities fully staffed

---

4   Jean Chesneaux, *The Chinese Labor Movement, 1919–1927*, tr. H. M. Wright, Palo Alto, CA: Stanford University Press, 1968.

5   Emily Honig, *Sisters and Strangers in the Shanghai Cotton Mills, 1919–1949*, Palo Alto, CA: Stanford University Press, 1986.

6   See Janet Chen, *Guilty of Indigence: The Urban Poor in China, 1900–1953*, Princeton, NJ: Princeton University Press, 2012; and Gail Hershatter, *Dangerous Pleasures: Prostitution and Modernity in Twentieth-Century Shanghai*, Berkeley, CA: University of California Press, 1997.

by recently migrated laborers from the countryside; from these homes, they were transported via rickshaw, pulled by impoverished men from the rural areas, to banks and offices along well-lit multilane macadam-paved roads. Dotted with gardens, parks, and pleasure palaces, the foreign concessions were spaces apart from the often-chaotic, under-regulated Chinese cities in which they were embedded and upon which they preyed for labor and service.[7] Here, the monied elites mediated financial and industrial relations among one another, as well as between the domestic Chinese setting and the global capitalist financial and commodity markets. Although Communists later were to distinguish between the "national" bourgeoisie (potentially part of a revolutionary alliance) and compradors (who were presumed always traitorous), the fact is that all capitalists in China (and elsewhere), no matter what their nationality, functioned as compradors, as mediators of capitalist relations. In that role, they were always prone to either support or betray any national state, depending on their own interests and capacities as well as on the national state's willingness to capitulate to their bottom lines.[8]

This incipient bourgeois class in China at times allied itself with a growing intellectual or petty bourgeois fraction of urban society, whom the capitalist elite often funded in their cultural endeavors. And a different fraction of the even-pettier bourgeoisie, men and women alike, moved into the professions, staffing the middle-administrative positions of the burgeoning bureaucracies of corporate, industrial, urban, and state institutions. These petty urbanites (*xiaoshimin*/小市民) gradually found a collective identity in the trappings of middle-class life: the nuclear family (rather than life in a multigenerational family), consumerism, hygienic living, love

---

7   See Nicholas Clifford, *Spoilt Children of Empire: Westerners in Shanghai and the Chinese Revolution of the 1920s*, Middlebury, VT: Middlebury College Press, 1992; and Leo Ou-fan Lee, *Shanghai Modern: The Flowering of a New Urban Culture in China, 1930–1945*, Cambridge, MA: Harvard University Press, 1999.

8   Rebecca E. Karl, "Compradors: The Mediating Middle of Capitalism in Twentieth-Century China and the World," in Joyce Liu and V. Murthy, eds., *East Asian Marxisms and Their Trajectories*, New York: Routledge, 2017, 119–36.

marriages, bank accounts, home economics, children's education, and more. Much of this was promoted through the exponential growth of a properly capitalist media and press environment—one where daily papers were now supported through advertising and subscription revenue. The new mass medium could reliably peddle pills, potions, and prescriptions; household appliances and conveniences; cosmetics and hygienic products; and opportunities to save for better living and educational activities for children. Alongside, there was a smaller political media presence, whose publications remained dependent upon the generosity of wealthy patrons and sponsors.

During the same years that dependent development intensified urban wealth and squalor, the overall conditions in rural China also worsened. While it is true that in the brief respite afforded domestic markets in China during the Great War, when imports from Europe were severely curtailed, certain sectors of the rural economy, such as coal mining, saw a temporary increase in profitability;[9] nevertheless, as the postrevolutionary political mess showed no signs of relenting, various warlords competed with the Republican state du jour to extract revenue from the rural population—either to support military operations, or for more general purposes of urban modernization and bureaucratization. The tax burden became unmanageable, and its arbitrariness sparked frequent resistance that, at times, grew into major regional peasant rebellions.[10] Meanwhile, landlords were busy converting themselves into direct arms of the state—either of the formal state, such as it was, or of whichever local warlord establishment—and through these alliances with revenue-extracting bodies, they became ever more predatory on rural production processes. These developments spread quite unevenly across the Republican Chinese territory, and their forms manifested differently in different geographical regions. North and South China, with different structures of relations of production (rice-based versus wheat-based, for

9 Jacob Eyferth, ed., *How China Works: Perspectives on the Twentieth-Century Industrial Workplace*, New York: Routledge, 2006.

10 Elizabeth Perry, *Rebels and Revolutionaries in North China, 1845–1945*, Palo Alto, CA: Stanford University Press, 1980.

example), experienced these changes in varying degrees. Nevertheless, the scholarly consensus points to a process of peasant immiseration, landlord empowerment, and increasingly sharp social and economic conflicts in the rural areas over land, taxation, and conditions of production. These trends were magnified and compounded over time.

In sum, in the postrevolutionary years, China saw massive fragmentation in every realm possible: state politics became an arena of strong-arm military factions, with those who happened to hold Beijing formally recognized as the Chinese state by the diplomatic conventions of foreign imperialist powers. Meanwhile, urban-based production spiraled into increasingly evident class divisions, whose conflicts now seemed to shape the contours of any present or projected future; gendered divisions of labor and social life, whose potential toxicity was sometimes muted and sometimes enhanced, moved women into public visibility in schools, factories, offices, streets, or department stores; and increased spatial unevenness within China was enhanced through the elaboration of urban/rural divides, and the relations between coastal regions—enriched by their connections with global markets in finance, commodities, and culture—and the hinterlands, now dominated by new extractive logics of urban and industrial modernization and militarization.

These developments sparked and informed a new round of revolutionary activity and thinking crystallized in the May Fourth Movement of 1919.

CHAPTER 3

The May Fourth Movement (1919) and Cultural Revolution

> What is the foundation of contemporary Europe lying so brilliantly before us? It is the gift of revolutions. The term revolution [*geming*] in Europe means change from the old to the new, which differs fundamentally from what we call the change of dynasties.
>
> —Chen Duxiu, "On the Literary Revolution" (February 1917)[1]

> What happens after Nora walks out? . . . What did Nora take with her apart from her awakened mind? . . . Dreams are fine, but otherwise money is essential . . . economic rights seem to be the most important factor in present-day society.
>
> —Lu Xun, "What Happens after Nora Walks Out" (1923)[2]

With disappointment rife about the political mess left in the wake of the 1911 Revolution, many intellectuals turned their attention to what they deemed the deeper substratum of Chinese social life: its culture. Critique moved from considerations of politics as state form—now a sphere condemned as endlessly corrupt and ineffectual—to an unsparing critique of the culture that underpinned the structures of everyday social hierarchy. The major target of this critique from the New Culture through the May Fourth period (1915–1925) was Confucianism—or the realm of what was called "man-eating ritual" (*chiren lijiao* / 吃人礼教)—which was imputed as the mode of the social reproduction of hierarchy in elevated and everyday behavior

---

1 Chen Duxiu, "On Literary Revolution," tr. T. Wong, in Kirk Denton, ed., *Modern Chinese Literary Thought: Writings on Literature, 1893–1945*, Palo Alto, CA: Stanford University Press, 1996, 140–5.

2 Lu Xun, *Jottings under Lamplight*, tr. Bonnie McDougall, ed. Eileen Cheng and Kirk Denton, Cambridge, MA: Harvard University Press, 2017.

alike. The basic social relations and bonds that this supposed all-encompassing Confucianism (*ruxue* or *rujiao*, 儒学/儒教) prescribed as the definition of a well-ordered state—the subordination of young to old, of sons to fathers, of women to men, of wives to husbands, of students to teachers, of ruled to ruler, and so on—were now exposed as the building blocks of Chinese "slavishness" and offered as reasons for the supposed inability of the Chinese to adapt to the modern world.[3] Soon enough, these were gathered into the catchall negative designation "feudal" (*fengjian*/封建) culture, which was said to be marked by blind obedience to and respect for authority. The feudal infestation had to be overcome.

From the mid 1910s into the 1920s, the claims made for culture (*wenhua* or *wenming*, 文化/文明) were totalistic. Everything was said to have a cultural root, and that cultural root was said to be not gently sinological nor quaintly traditional nor harmoniously uniting, but rather entirely rotten, toxic even. Cultural rot became an explanation for all manner of vice and ill and social problem—from the high-level corruption of officials through to the everyday gendered practices that sacrificed women's individuality (*renge*/人格) and men's freedom (*ziyou*/自由) to family honor on the altar of marriage. Indeed, the proliferation of what were identified as "social problems" (*shehui wenti*/社会问题) went hand in hand with what were understood to be the devolutionary properties of Chinese culture, where the insufficiencies of the latter were now said to subtend all failures of China's modern historical passage. This radical critique and condemnation of culture and of China not only characterized but animated the New Culture / May Fourth movement, an extended period of existential crisis in "Chinese-ness" that constituted the first of several cultural revolutions in China's twentieth century.

The New Culture / May Fourth movement has been called China's "Renaissance." Or, more frequently, its "Enlightenment." In these

---

3   Lu Xun is associated with the argument on slavishness, from his novella *The True Story of Ah Q*, published serially from 1921–1922; republished in his 1923 collection, *A Call to Arms*, tr. Julia Lovell, New York: Penguin, 2010.

designations, the period is defined as the exclusive historical possession of intellectuals. This is a paradigm of modernity that reinforces
an elitist ideological bias, rooted in a version of historical narrative
where popular mass movements are understood to be radically
disruptive of the more "rational" social transformation pursued by
the educated and the already empowered. Such a paradigmatic
containment privileges the liberal over the revolutionary momen-
tums behind the period's upheavals and has guided much research on
the period in Euro-American and Chinese Nationalist (Taiwan)
scholarship.[4] An alternative paradigm of the New Culture / May
Fourth—purveyed until very recently in PRC scholarship—holds that
this period led teleologically to the introduction of Marxism and the
formation of the Communist Party (1921), which is the true revolutionary successor to this (petty) bourgeois phase of culture critique.
Highlighting the role of the Communist Party in organizing and leading progressive historical initiatives, this PRC narrative turns the New
Culture / May Fourth into a mere transmission belt for Marxism; it
thus forecloses the more radical aspects of the culture critique (its
anarchistic tendencies, for example), consigns to historical oblivion
the competing liberal contribution (slated for inevitable historical
obsolescence), and emphasizes to the exclusion of much else the
coming-into-being of the Bolshevik-Communist nexus of political-
cultural social relations and knowledge production. In this party-
centered narrative, the Russian Revolution of October 1917 propels
history into motion in a linear unbroken line traced from Russia to
China to the founding of the Chinese Communist Party.[5] Each of

---

4   Vera Schwarcz, *The Chinese Enlightenment: Intellectuals and the Legacy of the May
Fourth Movement of 1919*, Berkeley, CA: University of California Press, 1986; Chow
Tse-tsung, *The May Fourth Movement*, Cambridge, MA: Harvard University Press, 1960;
Hu Shih, *The Chinese Renaissance: The Haskell Lectures*, Chicago, IL: University of Chicago
Press, 1934.

5   This narrative form was extremely prevalent until the 2000s. Exemplary is "Wusi
shiqi lao tongzhi zuotanhui jilu," [Record of round-table discussion by old Comrades of the
May Fourth period], in *Jinian wusi yundong liushi zhouniman xueshu taolunhui lunwen
xuan* [Collected essays in celebration of the sixtieth anniversary of the May Fourth
Movement], vol. 1, Beijing: Chinese Academy of Social Sciences, 1980.

these narratives contains elements of truth. But none of them covers the complexity of the historical questions raised (and never answered) at the time about modernity, Chinese-ness, and China's modern revolutionary histories.

In 1917, Chen Duxiu, later one of the founding members of the Chinese Communist Party (CCP) but at this point still just a professor at Beijing University with a reputation for radicalism, wrote a rallying call to the youth of China to cast off the old and create something new. The youth—a category of Chinese social life just emerging into relevance, as elders had hitherto been venerated to the exclusion of others—were, according to Chen, still relatively unsullied by blind adherence to tradition and thus the only ones capable of challenging commitments to hierarchy so as to produce new social values. Chen's argument proceeded as a call for a literary revolution, where revolution is named—as cited at the opening of this chapter—the tide of modern times. His exhortation is comprised of three positions. The first is encapsulated in the slogan "Down with the ornate, obsequious literature of the aristocrats; up with the plain, expressive literature of the people!": a wholesale attack on what he considered the formulaic, dead classical mode of writing characteristic of ancient Chinese texts, with a concomitant call for a writing style and system closer to the everyday lives of living human beings. The former type of writing, in his estimation, perpetuated the reproduction of a social hierarchy of the classically educated and the elders, whereas the latter would be productive of new values ideally rooted in "the people." Second and relatedly, Chen called for an end to "the stale, ostentatious literature of the classics; up with the fresh, sincere literature of realism!" Realism, at that time in China and Japan, as well as in Euro-American literature, was understood to be an advanced form of literary expression: it was unadorned, clean, socially useful, and devoid of the show-offy and imitative flourishes required of "good" classical writing. Realism was imbued not with timelessness but with the timeliness and dynamism of rapidly changing social life itself. Chen's third position was expressed as: "Down with the pedantic, obscure literature of the

recluse; up with the clear, popular literature of society!" In juxtaposing the recluse to popular society, Chen indicated that literature could
not be created by and for individuals insulated from society, but rather
had to be a politically and socially democratic creative act.[6]

Chen's focus on the literary/cultural sphere signaled a retreat
from politics in its state form. However, in its invocation of "the
people" and its totalistic critique of the hitherto-accepted intertwined
reproductive relation of textual practice and social hierarchy, Chen's
call exhibits the elements of the conjunctural moment of New Culture
in China, when the arrival of the working class and social division,
along with the emergence of the intelligentsia, became a potential
social and political alliance that could transform China.[7] This is when
socialism—as well as anarchism, syndicalism, feminism, nationalism,
and patriotism, among others—became visibly and viscerally relevant
to social life, as well as an urgent matter of intellectual investigation
and practice. The realm of the cultural, from this time forward,
became a primary sphere in which many "isms" were battled into
shape and debated into everyday parlance.

In a less radical mode than Chen Duxiu, the philosopher and
literary scholar Hu Shi—educated at Cornell and then under John
Dewey at Columbia University, and newly returned to China in the
mid 1910s—wrote of his own "modest" sense that literature should be
reformed. In an early 1917 essay on the topic, Hu's proposals revolved
around linguistic matters: What language should be used for literary
writing? For him, the problem was shaped by the extreme imitative
formalism characterizing Chinese writing, an imitative ideal inimical
to a creative style or timely content. For Hu, the turn to the vernacular—a written language that in one way or the other would reflect,
create, and give literary form to a spoken language—was necessary
and yet also fraught with the threat of vulgarity. Neither politically
revolutionary nor imbued with any sentimental notion of the "the

---

6   Chen Duxiu, "On Literary Revolution."
7   Arif Dirlik, *Revolution and History: Origins of Marxist Historiography in China,
1919–1937*, Berkeley, CA: University of California Press, 1978, 59.

people," Hu understood that the trend toward vernacularization, begun already in the late Qing and now gaining traction with the growth of urban literacy and the increase in popular writing for profit-seeking journals and publishing houses, required careful management by elite intellectuals, lest such writing become so debased that the vernacular itself would have to be abandoned as a "high" literary proposition. In Hu's proposal, safeguarding the vernacular for the literary required it to be properly regulated and channeled, by and through the intellectual elite. In pursuit of this endeavor, Hu chose to praise earlier vernacular writers, such as the authors of the *Dream of the Red Chamber* or *Water Margin*, who "faithfully write about the contemporary situation," thus entering the halls of "true literature"[8] rather than the far bawdier (and actually more popular) narratives of the Ming-Qing marketplace, such as *Jin Ping Mei* (The Golden Lotus). Hu's call for the vernacular as a literary language sparked enormous backlash, with conservatives, including the prolific translator Lin Shu, accusing the foreign-educated Hu of having lost his Chinese-ness and been enslaved by foreign thinking, and with radicals accusing him of snobbish elitism. (No one at this point culturally defended the wildly popular and profitable "lowbrow" novels classified as "mandarin duck and butterfly" literature.)

Ever since, the battle over what constitutes "the vernacular" (*baihua*/白话) has been continuously waged. As China has a huge number of spoken languages, often corresponding to very specific locations, the question of which of the major languages was to constitute the "standard" spoken vernacular to be reflected and refined in "high" literary form was a cause for much debate. The issue is still not completely solved, although the imposition by strong states after 1949 of a "national language"—in Taiwan called *guoyu* (国语, language of the state), and in the PRC called *putong hua* (普通话, common speech)—foreclosed some possibilities, while leaving the door open

---

8   Hu Shi, "Some Modest Proposals for the Reform of Literature" (1917), in Denton, ed., tr., *Modern Chinese Literary Thought*. The two named works are from the Ming dynasty (1366–1644).

for others. In post-1949 Nationalist-ruled Taiwan and Communist-ruled PRC alike, the national language ultimately was modeled on the Northern Chinese dialect that had become the spoken language of the dynastic bureaucracy ("Mandarin"); and yet, most people in China did/do not speak this language as a matter of daily life, or at all. Thus, while various geographical-linguistic forms were offered as possible contenders for literariness (Cantonese, Fujianese, Shanghainese, etc.), until recently, they were excluded a priori. With the rise of regional media empires, however, these languages have staged somewhat of a comeback. The problem of language in today's China is still part of a struggle over how to be Chinese. The question was systematically raised for the first time in the mid 1910s.

The most ambitious of the language revolutionaries of the New Culture / May Fourth period, Qu Qiubai, advocated not the endorsement of a particular regional language but rather the creation of an entirely new language, to be pieced together from the ongoing and contemporary comingling of the multilingual, rural-derived proletariats working in urban factories.[9] Instead of what he called the "mule language" (neither horse nor donkey) of a Europeanized Chinese / Mandarin vernacular that conformed to foreign-educated elites and their lifestyles in the treaty ports but was not spoken by regular folks, Qu's proposed language was to be based in the very daily practice of the proletariat that came closest to the ways that ordinary people from different language groups found to speak to one another. In Qu's theory, language was to be a class attribute rather than a national one. Ultimately Qu's radically democratic advocacies were dropped from discussion.

With the successive arrival of radio, recordings, talkie cinema, popular music, and other modes of sound reproducibility, the question of language and form continually (re)imposed itself as a political, social, and market problem. It also became completely intertwined

---

9   Qu Qiubai, "Puluo dazhong wenyide xianshi wenti" [The practical questions of proletarian mass literature], *Wenxue* [Literature], 1932; followed by his more precise statement on the question, "Dazhong wenyide wenti" [Questions of mass literature].

with the intractable issue of the written form itself, the *hanzi* (汉字, characters) that were distinctive to China's historic expressive system. European language experts, who, through the nineteenth century, had come up with immutable (colonial) taxonomies of world languages, had long since decided that China was hampered by the *hanzi* form of writing, and that this "pictographic" or "ideographic" form could never be flexible enough to express modern thinking or conceptual matters properly. On this view, Chinese were imprisoned in and by nonalphabetic backwardness. After considering and discarding Esperanto as a possible solution, Chinese language experts in part accepted European theories and tried over many decades to find an adequate linguistic logic for the transformation and/or simplification of *hanzi*: using alphabetic equivalents, inventing new pronunciation symbols and guides, and ultimately reducing the number of strokes required for the writing of any given character (the 1950s PRC solution to the problem). With the telegraph and then the advent of computers, the issue was rejoined from yet other angles.[10]

The difficulty of writing/reading in the process of learning redounded immediately to the sphere of education and textbooks. The explosive expansion of schools and literacy helped to redefine the purpose of education. From a tool of gentility, good breeding, or male access to state power, education for boys and girls became, on the one hand, a form of training for individual fulfillment and/or creating activists to lead the fight for social justice; on the other hand, as education came under the control of agents of a would-be state and the conservative forces of textbook publishing, it became a way to produce citizens as patriots and servants of a putative (still nonexistent) national state. Grammar texts became one key to producing whatever sense of citizenry could be wrought from the disunified territorial

---

10 The problem of language reform—written and spoken—has been taken up recently by Lorraine Chi-man Wong, "The Chinese Latinization Movement: Language, History and Politics: 1917–1958," PhD diss., New York University, 2014; and Zhong Yurou, "Script Crisis and Literary Modernity in China, 1916–1958," PhD diss., Columbia University, 2014. Typography and the computer are addressed in Thomas Mullaney, *The Chinese Typewriter: A History*, Cambridge, MA: MIT Press, 2017.

whole. Meanwhile, emulating Germany and Japan, physical educa-tion was incorporated into the new-style schools, based on the convic-tion that the old separation of effete scholarship (*wen*/文) from brawny military pursuits (*wu*/武) was outmoded and inimical to an all-round ideal militarized citizen of the nation. Even the young Mao Zedong was captivated by the practice of physical exercise, although he was hugely critical of the mechanical, rote way in which it was taught in schools.[11]

Thus it was that from the earliest phases of the New Culture movement's calls for a radical transformation in language, literary form, and the social purpose of culture, the issues raised went to the core of how "Chinese" or "Chinese-ness" was to be practiced, incul-cated, experienced, and understood in modern terms. Over the course of the 1920s, 1930s, and 1940s, these issues were repeatedly debated and re-raised, in ever-deeper and ever more expanded form. They remain at issue today.

In late 1917, the Russian Revolution did not wash across Chinese radical circles in a wave of clarity. In the immediate aftermath, the October Revolution was understood as a "victory of anarcho-communism."[12] Indeed, through the 1910s and well into the 1920s, the major language of radicalism in China was that of anarchism: Peter Kropotkin's mutual aid, Leo Tolstoy's agrarian utopianism, Mikhail Bakhunin's laborism, Pierre-Joseph Proudhon's collectivism, Emma Goldman's radical feminism, Daoist eremetism, and of course, with even less theoretical rigor, various advocacies for assassination and nihilism. There was little to distinguish Bolshevism or Marxism from anarchism as an anti-state and pro-labor form of socialism.[13] It was only in late 1918 through 1919 that the various "isms" started to

---

11 Mao Zedong, "A Study of Physical Education," *Xin Qingnian* [New youth], April 1, 1917, in Stuart Schram, ed., *Mao's Road to Power*, vol. 1, New York: Routledge, 1992, 113–27.

12 Dirlik, *Origins of Chinese Communism*, 28.

13 Dirlik, *Anarchism in the Chinese Revolution*, Berkeley, CA: University of California Press, 1991.

get separated out and elaborated more clearly in relation to one another. Yet even as the intellectual scene was muddled, Chinese state agents and foreign authorities were not confused about the potential dangers of the revolutionary appeal of Russia; large numbers of journals, whether merely liberal or more radical, were shut down while what was called "Bolshevist" activity was sought so as to be rooted out of foreign concession areas. Most of the captured activists were in fact anti-Bolshevist anarchists, but that mattered to no one in power.

By late 1918, Li Dazhao, a professor at Beijing University and soon to be one of the founders of the CCP along with Chen Duxiu, was lauding the victory of Bolshevism in Russia in the pages of the quintessential journal of the time, *New Youth* (*Xin Qingnian* / 新青年); by 1919 he was writing more about Marx and Marxism than Bolshevism. Meanwhile, Qu Qiubai, temporarily sidetracked from politics by a love of the Russian language and nineteenth-century Russian literature, was called upon to translate Russian political tracts and to participate in the new Beijing University–based Marxist Research Society reading groups. In these groups, basic tenets of Marxism and Bolshevism were discussed with reference to a meager number of translated texts. By early 1920, Qu was sent by the *Beijing Morning Post* to Moscow to report directly on the Russian revolution and its messy aftermath. His travelogue, *History of the Heart in the Red Capital* (*Chi du xin shi* / 赤都心史), published in 1922, was rigorous in its reflections on the promise and problems in postrevolutionary Russia; for its honesty, it has been called "one of the most influential pieces of 'red propaganda' ever written."[14]

When confronted from an anarchist perspective, several of the difficult aspects of an acceptance of Bolshevism/Marxism included the prominence accorded by Bolshevism to a centralized disciplined party in the organization and leadership of political and ideological activity, as well as the centrality given in Marxism to the inevitability of class struggle and the victory of the proletariat in the era of

---

14   Elizabeth McGuire, *Red at Heart: How Chinese Communists Fell in Love with the Russian Revolution*, New York: Oxford University Press, 2018, 5.

industrial capitalism. On the latter issue, anarchists tended to see things in the binary terms of authority/non-authority, where authority was embedded not merely in state / society or class antagonisms, but also in families, the cultural realm, everyday routines, labor regimes of all varieties, gender relations, and so on. Thus, unlike liberals, who believed China's social structure did not have class conflict but was merely backward (as compared to Euro-America-Japan), anarchists saw class, but could not accept it as the primary way through which people lived their social subordination. Moreover, anarchists could not accept that an authoritarian institution such as the party or the state could be used to transform social relations in an equitable direction. The mismatch between ends (social justice) and means (state or party authority) was too great. This, then, led them to suspect that the discipline of a centralized Bolshevist party, whose role was to coordinate activity and police acceptable ideological parameters of political understanding, would lead to the imposition of the party over social and political life more generally. In their refusal to accept these premises, anarchists, through the 1920s, became anathema to the CCP, and the party—once formed—diligently purged them from the ranks, as had Lenin in postrevolutionary Russia.

Meanwhile, difficulties ensued in Chinese understandings of Marxism in its own terms. For example, the materialist conception of history—in which "pre-capitalism" was merely a past prelude to the present—was perceived as too mechanical and bloodless for early Chinese Marxists. Li Dazhao, for example, argued strenuously that "we cannot rely on material change alone," and that any view of history requires an ethical and spiritual component that seemed to be absent in the Marxism he had available to him.[15] The fact that the past lived on prominently in the present—capitalist social relations were unevenly dominant in parts of China, where older relations ruled— also made the relevance of historical materialism less evident. Indeed,

15   Maurice Meisner, *Li Ta-chao and the Origins of Chinese Marxism*, Cambridge, MA: Harvard University Press, 1967, 93.

an investigation of the ways in which Marxist historical materialism could or should be used to interpretively re-narrate Chinese history or to understand the global Chinese present was a challenge undertaken only in the 1930s, once a large number of Marxist texts had been translated (from Japanese, English, German, and some Russian) and were being absorbed. The social history debates of that decade were wide ranging and of huge intellectual and revolutionary consequence, ideologically clarifying the historical premises of the Chinese Communist Revolution.[16] For the moment, in 1917–1919, radicals in China cheered the success of the Russian Revolution in deposing the tsarist regime without fully understanding what it connoted, were encouraged that it seemed to show a new way through and out the other side of modern global capitalism and the imperialist world that capitalism had wrought, and strove to understand what the revolution meant, not only for culture critique but for China's modern political and social future.

At the end of the Great War in 1918 and 1919, the victorious powers met in Paris and Versailles to hammer out the provisions of the peace. The Chinese, who had joined the allies early and had supplied over 150,000 peasants (mostly from Shandong) to dig trenches and clear battlefields on behalf of the British and French armies, sent a delegation to the negotiations with high hopes of having their German-occupied territories in Shandong returned to them. Woodrow Wilson's "Fourteen Points" and rhetorical commitments to colonial self-determination seemed to indicate that the United States, at least, would be sympathetic to the Chinese cause (as well as to that of Japanese-colonized Koreans, British-colonized Egyptians, and so on). The Chinese—along with all other colonized and semi-colonized people—were shocked at how quickly their aspirations were betrayed and how thoroughly Wilson's rhetoric was demonstrated to be empty.

---

16   Arif Dirlik, *Revolution and History: Origins of Marxist Historiography in China, 1919–1937*, Berkeley, CA: University of California Press, 1978.

Back in Beijing, now held by the Beiyang government led by the warlord Duan Qirui, news of the betrayal at Versailles hit at the height of the ongoing cultural ferment, discussions about the Russian Revolution, industrial conflicts in Shanghai, and ongoing domestic warlord competition. Accustomed to critical reading, drafting of proposals, campus-level activism, as well as the occasional call to "go to the people" (in the manner of the nineteenth-century Russian *narodniki*, who idealized village peasant life as the wellspring of all that was pure and good), activists at Beijing University were enraged by the compromises being foisted upon the Chinese delegation in France. On May 4, 1919, under the coordination of the Beijing University group, over 3,000 students from thirteen universities poured onto the streets and into Tian'anmen Square, fronting the Forbidden City, in peaceful protest against signing the treaty advocated by alleged Japanese collaborators within Duan's government. Transforming themselves for the first time into a bloc of political activists while claiming, also for the first time, the public space of urban streets and squares for an incipient mass politics,[17] students— joined by petty urbanites of various backgrounds—marched to the home of one of the alleged collaborators. When he refused to answer their petitions, the crowd turned violent and proceeded to assault and burn the house. Several students were arrested, although they were later released. The treaty was not signed by the delegation in France, even though its provisions to transfer German-held Shandong to Japan went into effect without Chinese acquiescence.

The humiliation and betrayal at Versailles and the courage of the Beijing activists sparked a larger movement through May and June of 1919 that engulfed many of the semi-colonized urban spaces of coastal China. Under banners proclaiming the urgent necessity to embrace "Mr. Science" and "Mr. Democracy" (thus continuing the critique of Confucianism), accompanied by calls to boycott Japanese merchandise as well as that of the other imperialist powers; and with

---

17   Fabio Lanza, *Behind the Gate: Inventing Students in Beijing*, New York: Columbia University Press, 2010.

condemnations of domestic politicians who would compromise with rather than confront foreign powers, the May Fourth Movement welded together urban classes into activist solidarity, giving some material form to the previous abstract calls for culture and class critique and the transformation of social life in China. It was, in short, the first modern mass political movement in China's history, and it was as anti-imperialist as it was culturally revolutionary, as anti-capitalist as it was internationalist.

Toward the end of 1919, Mao Zedong was in his native province of Hunan tending to his mother's ill health and death. He had observed the May Fourth events from afar and published dispatches from Beijing and Shanghai about them in his *Xiang River Review*. A small news item now caught his attention: a certain Miss Zhao—of no fame and no name—had committed suicide by slitting her throat in the sedan chair transporting her to an arranged marriage, a common-enough occurrence in the prevailing social world of the time, where marriage was controlled by families and matchmakers, and where young women and men were routinely sacrificed to family need and ritual propriety. Mao decided to make of the ordinariness of this event a cause for critical intervention. Transforming the suicide from merely an individual woman's tragedy, Mao inserted Miss Zhao into the broader May Fourth–era discussions on the "woman question," in which the new totalizing category "woman" was understood to be embedded in a set of repressive ritual and social relations rooted in the everyday life of family. Mao characterized these relations as "iron nets" that bound youth in patterns of everyday violence—he called home life a daily trial of "direct rape" for women—that could only be perpetuated if the family system remained intact.[18]

Mao's commentary on Miss Zhao fell on receptive ears, as a certain form of feminism was by then embraced by many intellectuals, male and female. Much of it focused on the demand for freedom

---

18   Mao Zedong, "Commentary on the Suicide of Miss Zhao" (1919), in Schram, ed., *Mao's Road to Power*, vol. 1, 421–49.

in marriage. In Shanghai, Henrik Ibsen's play *A Doll's House* was just then taking everyone by storm. Suffering from a stifling marriage, the heroine, Nora, leaves her husband and children in order to find her own self and her own way. Nora's leaving home was actually a bad fit for China at the time: most cultural radicals were agitating *for* precisely the type of free love bourgeois marriage that Nora found intolerable. Nevertheless, Nora became an icon, a beacon, a symbol of hope: a woman could leave her marriage and realize herself. Until Lu Xun, at that time already a famous writer, threw cold water on the Nora phenomenon by pointedly querying: What happens after Nora walks out? As cited at the beginning of this chapter, Lu Xun, picking up on some of Mao's earlier points from the Miss Zhao suicide commentaries, remarked that would-be Chinese Noras of the time simply had no social or economic place to go if they left their families. They would be faced with starvation, prostitution, or death. In spite and because of these reservations, a good deal of feminist literature was launched in Nora's wake, developing and indigenizing her and her milieu. Slightly later, Ding Ling's scandalous short story "Miss Sophie's Diary" (1928), in which a sickly, bored young urban woman attempts to figure out her sexuality and whether love was a way into autonomous personhood, is one particularly notorious example.

For Lu Xun, as well as for Mao, Ding Ling, and many other cultural radicals of the May Fourth generation, the "woman question" needed to be more thoroughly elaborated through the general question of social transformation. In most cases, that elaboration began with the family as the basic repressive structure of social authority through which everyday life was lived. And yet more broadly, the issues of subjectivity, agency, personality, individuality, autonomy, and freedom all arose in expanded form through the question of women. Indeed, it was in the theoretical maturation of the "woman question" that the crucial theoretical revolution of these years came to revolve around the conviction that the demand for "liberation"—of class, gender, nation, whatever—had to be a demand for an inauguration of an entirely new order of social relations. Feminism and women were the key lenses through which these demands were rendered visible and comprehensible.

In 1920–1921, the Soviet government, still fighting an international civil war for its own survival, sent emissaries via the Comintern (Communist International) to China and other places, to help transform loosely organized Marxist reading groups into Communist Party cells. The group at Beijing University led by Chen Duxiu and Li Dazhao became one of several chosen for this purpose; another group in Shanghai was also contacted by Gregory Voitinsky, chief of the Far Eastern Bureau of the Comintern in Irkutsk. The perceived relevance of a potential Communist Party in China clearly owed a good deal to the New Culture / May Fourth movements that preceded the arrival of Voitinsky. Nevertheless, the founding of the CCP in response to the Comintern's encouragement must be seen as opening a new chapter in the organization of Chinese radicalism and socialism as sociopolitical activity and ideological tendency. The First National Congress of the Chinese Communist Party was held in July 1921 in Shanghai's French Concession and then moved to a barge in the middle of the Huangpu River after the twelve members attending were hounded out by foreign police tipped off by Chinese agents. At that congress, Chen Duxiu was named chairman, Li Dazhao was unofficially designated the leader of the Beijing branch, and Mao Zedong became leader of the Hunan branch. None of the branches actually existed, and some of the named were not even in attendance, but each leader was tasked with building the party in their region. With the Second Congress in July 1922, the party gained both definition and stability, and the project of clarifying party discipline gained steam. Through the 1920s, not only were anarchists purged, but Trotskyists and many other kinds of so-called "deviationists" were also sidelined or eliminated. In this environment, Marxism developed in China more as a handmaiden to party organizational discipline than as a critical, independent mode of socioeconomic analysis.

The CCP was still too small to make real political or widespread social headway in the chaotic environment of early 1920s China.

Instead, it was the reorganized party that had emerged from Sun Yatsen's late-Qing Revolutionary Alliance that became China's first mass political entity. This was the Nationalist Party, known as the Guomindang (GMD, 国民党). The GMD's major ideological platform was based upon an elaboration of Sun's "Three Principles of the People," a form of non-Marxist, mild socialism that called for a strong state to ensure that social conflict was forestalled and managed in the socially divisive rush to capitalist modernization and development. While essentially the party of capitalists and landlords, the GMD in the early 1920s also was broadly sympathetic to and political home to liberal critiques of Confucianism that took certain forms of social hierarchy as inimical to the proper development of productive life. Yet, as Sun's health deteriorated, and particularly after his death in 1925, the party drifted toward militarism and right-wing advocacies, positioning itself finally as the only obstacle to China's descent into barbarism (Communism) and as the defender of the Confucian values that were to define true Chinese-ness.

The May Fourth Movement, having originated in a culture critique and crescendoed in mass urban demonstrations, subsided in the mid 1920s back into a cultural mode, through which critique was expanded and deepened. The cultural counterrevolution also dug in and gained some traction. In the latter mode, and especially after the massive destruction of the Great War and the Versailles betrayals, a good number of liberal and conservative intellectuals turned their backs on European claims to the superiority of their civilization. If Europeans could slaughter each other with such abandon, how could such a society possibly be civilized or attractive? Now these intellectuals often looked to a totalized Asian past for new inspiration. Japanese advocated a culturally unsullied pan-Asianism with a muscular Japan at its center; the Indian poet Rabindranath Tagore lectured in China on the benefits of an Asian spiritual unification supposedly harking back to some distant past; and Buddhist mystics attempted to promote the ideal of a primordial Asia connected through belief and practice that could be resurrected in the present to save China and the world. These positions came to be lumped together under the rubric of putative pan-Asian "Eastern values," "Eastern spirituality," or "Eastern civilization" and, in that guise, were counterposed to the supposed unified category of "Western materialism" or "Western civilization." Large-scale debates filled the journals of the day, with discussions that ramified into every possible realm of social life. Indeed, every issue that had been raised since 1915 got re-debated in the 1920s in the now-renovated East/West binary culturalist idiom.

On May 30, 1925, a combined force of British-colonial Sikh and Chinese police commanded by a British officer opened fire on a crowd of protesting students in the International Settlement area of Shanghai. Four were killed immediately; five others died soon thereafter; scores were injured. The students had arrived at this location in an effort to free their classmates, who had been arrested several days earlier when they had attempted to form a phalanx of solidarity during the public funeral of a cotton mill laborer, shot by a Japanese foreman and now transformed into a martyr by left-leaning groups. The factory in which the laborer worked, #8 Cotton Mill, was notorious for its poor treatment of Chinese labor by Japanese owners and managers; the situation there had worsened, particularly in the first months of 1925, and with the growing presence of Communist-led labor unions in Shanghai and elsewhere, the maltreatment was not ignored. The shock, however, of students being slaughtered in Shanghai by the combined forces of the imperialists and collaborating Chinese police was enormous.

The next day, May 31, Chinese students were fully mobilized, along with workers and others infuriated by the impunity with which imperialist police operated. Posters were posted, speeches were offered, solidarity marches were organized, and a list of demands was delivered to the Chinese Chamber of Commerce, whose regulatory power stopped at the border of the International Settlement. A final rhetorical flourish in the demands was the following: "Death is preferable to tame submission to such oppression. Close your ranks and make war on imperialists."[19] On June 1, the foreign-dominated Municipal Council declared martial law and began a monthlong sweep of raids and cleansings of the foreign concessions, intended to root out radicals and all those supporting the students and their now-burgeoning social movement. Over that month, businesses closed and workers went on strike, tramways were destroyed, shops were looted, and other destructive acts took place. Up to 200 students and workers in Shanghai lost their lives to the protection of vested foreign property and commercial interests. Meanwhile, riots, boycotts, and strikes spread around the country in sympathy with the Shanghai students and workers, in rage and shock over the violence visited upon the young activists. Anger was directed against the Japanese, and then, even more fulsomely, against the British. The Canton–Hong Kong Strike of this period was directly aimed against British colonizers.

Various warlords took advantage of the situation, with some, such as Feng Yuxiang, siding with the activists and demanding a formal apology from Britain; others, such as Zhang Zuolin, who controlled the area around Shanghai, cooperated with the British in their pursuit of Communists, suspected Communists, and anyone else who was purportedly dangerous. Meanwhile, in the aftermath of Sun Yatsen's death in March that year, a wholesale scramble for power within the GMD was raging. By the summer of 1925, the militarist Chiang Kaishek had beaten back most contenders and seized leadership of the GMD. The situation was no longer ripe for continued revolutionary activity. The movement petered out in China, even though it continued into 1926 in Hong Kong.

The immediate and enduring upshot of the May Thirtieth Movement was to bring anti-imperialism and mass pro-laborism to the front and center of subsequent activism and theorization. In literary works, May Thirtieth and its mass political mobilizations became a frequent plot device, "jolting heroes and heroines from their

---

19   Andrew Fields, "Aftermath of the May 30th Incident of 1925," *Shanghai Sojourns: A Shanghai Flaneur's Website*, January 22, 2019, shanghai-flaneur.com.

romantic complacency" and allowing them to "awaken" and "see" reality in all its messy "bloodshed, horror, [and] poverty."[20] Ding Ling's two-part novella *Shanghai, Spring 1930* famously does just that: one of its female heroines realizes, with a clap of recognition, the insufficiency of bourgeois romantic love during her encounter with demonstrations that recall exactly the May Thirtieth Movement. Staging a showdown between the two prevailing icons of May Fourth liberated woman—the radical/realist "new woman" versus the bourgeois/romantic "modern woman"—Ding Ling fleetingly indicated that the only way out of this dilemma is a third version of woman, embodied as the proletarian who is sexed and gendered, yet who is also classed.[21]

The May Thirtieth Movement clarified two social and political facts. First, that students and youth more generally were a political force to be reckoned with and, relatedly, that their comparatively elite social status did not make them immune to state violence. Second, mass politics was here to stay, and any political movement would require at least lip service to "the masses." But who were "the masses"? How the question was addressed and answered would condition what the future of "China" was to be, and in whose name and serving whose interests "China" was to be unified as a national state. This became one task of the 1920s and 1930s.

20 John Fitzgerald, *Awakening China: Politics, Culture, and Class in the Nationalist Revolution*, Palo Alto, CA: Stanford University Press, 1996, 337.

21 Ding Ling, "Shanghai, Spring 1930," tr. Shu-ying Ts'ao and Donald Holoch, in Tani E. Barlow, ed., *I Myself Am a Woman: Selected Writings of Ding Ling*, Boston, MA: Beacon Press, 1986, 112–71.

Interlude: Uneven and Combined— China in the 1920s

> On the fringes of big Chinese cities the shadows of lofty factory chimneys fall across fields still tilled with wooden ploughs . . . In the streets great trucks and jangling trams roar past carts drawn by men harnessed like animals to their loads. Automobiles toot angrily at man-drawn rickshaws . . . On some of these streets are huge mills run by humming dynamos.
>
> —Harold Isaacs (1938)[1]

> Miss Liu Hezhen, one of the more than forty young people killed, was my pupil . . . She is no pupil now of one dragging on an ignoble existence like myself. She is a Chinese girl who has died for China . . . The valor shown by Chinese soldiers in butchering women and children and the martial prowess of the Allied troops in teaching students a lesson have unfortunately been eclipsed by these few streaks of blood . . . But Chinese and foreign murderers are still holding their heads high, unaware of the bloodstains on their faces.
>
> —Lu Xun, "In Memory of Miss Liu Hezhen," (April 1926)[2]

The problem of foreign imperialism in China was pressing, yet it remained intractable at this point. By contrast, the disunification of the Chinese state—with big and small warlords vying for power—and

---

1 Harold Isaacs, *The Tragedy of the Chinese Revolution*, Palo Alto, CA: Stanford University Press, 1951 [1938], 1. Isaacs, a Trostkyist, was involved in the aftermath of the 1927 Revolution. His and Trotsky's *Problems of the Chinese Revolution* are two important accounts of China's 1920s.

2 Lu Xun, "In Memory of Miss Liu Hezhen" (April 1926), available at *Marxists Internet Archive*, marxists.org. Liu Hezhen was one of the forty students killed in Beijing as they attempted to deliver a petition to the Duan Qirui government and guards opened fire.

the perilous circumstances of economic production—whose benefits were often repatriated to foreign coffers, and whose costs were displaced unto burgeoning numbers of dispossessed, immiserated, and exploited urban and agrarian laborers—were issues that could be addressed, monumental though they were. To find an adequate way forward, a state with territorial range, military capacity, some mass appeal, and ability to extract revenue would need to be formed. To that end, the two major political parties—the already-large GMD and the small but growing CCP—were to be induced to cooperate, even though their visions of social relations, their conceptualizations of China's problems, and their analyses of solutions were diametrically opposed.

On the latter point, briefly, in the GMD analysis based on Sun Yatsen's "Three Principles," China's major problem was its "backward" national economy, the only resolution to which was to modernize under the aegis of a strong state by encouraging capitalist investment and production, while privileging finance and urban industry over rural or any other sectors. Property ownership was to be strongly protected, while rural usury was to be incorporated into a regulated banking system; in this way, the landlord-dominated rural economy was to be tied and subordinated more clearly to the urban imperative, and the conditions of agrarian production would be regulated and harnessed more tightly to finance capital and the industrial economy. Only upon the basis of a stronger capitalist-oriented economy, more parts of which were to be controlled by ethnic (Han) Chinese rather than foreigners, could China compete its way out of colonial subordination. Social division was to be managed and addressed through ameliorative state policy. GMD prescriptions for achieving these goals were highly contested within the party, vacillating between militarist and civilian versions, yet the basic analytical tenets of the problem were clear.[3]

By contrast, the CCP was convinced that the problems of China's "backward" economy stemmed from domestic class division and

---

3   Margharita Zanasi, *Saving the Nation: Economic Modernity in Republican China*, Chicago, IL: University of Chicago Press, 2006.

uneven relations of global domination in the economic sphere. The only way forward was to expel the imperialist-colonial dominance over the Chinese economy and society and simultaneously to revolutionize through class struggle the unjust social relations of production upon which imperialism was preying for its own benefit. The uneven and combined formation at the foundation of China's current weakness, in CCP analysis, was an unstably explosive formation whose benefits accrued only to the most rapacious. It needed to be uprooted. This would be accomplished by overthrowing landlords and supplanting the landlord economy—prop of imperialist and bourgeois extraction in the rural areas—with a peasant-led economy, whose logic would be national provisioning rather than profit and commodity export. At the same time, a revolution was needed to overthrow the dominance of global finance and industrial exploitation over the lives of the urban laboring classes and over the national economy more generally so as to eliminate the material bases for the growth of a hegemonic bourgeoisie. The specific modalities of achieving these goals were endlessly debated within the CCP, but the premises were agreed upon.

In the mid 1920s, these opposing views were sidelined—they never disappeared—in the interest of achieving a unified Chinese state. The mediating body to broker the inter-party cooperation was the Comintern. The Dutch agent Henk Snievling (aka Maring), along with Voitinsky and soon the Indian Marxist M. N. Roy, were tasked with forming and supporting a revolutionary United Front, so as to join the parties with the goal of unification. This was the immediate outcome of two developments outside of China. First, with its long border with the Soviet Union, China was to be rendered a frontier bulwark for the Soviet state, recently victorious in its international war of survival but fragile because of domestic food shortages, ideological infighting, and a leadership crisis in the wake of Lenin's death in 1924. For this bulwark to be strong, the Chinese state had to be unified. Second, China was to be a testing ground for the Comintern hypothesis that anti-colonial or nationalist revolutions needed to be pursued through a class alliance between the progressive proletariat, led by Communists, and the capitalist-landlord-petty bourgeois-led Nationalists.

This latter problem had been raised in the course of debates between Lenin and Roy during the 1920 meeting of the Second Congress of the Comintern in Moscow. The debates took place within the context of the just-concluded Great War, where proletariats of the various nations had accepted, enthusiastically, the proposition that they had to slaughter each other in war; where the right to self-determination of the colonized had just been betrayed; and yet where empires, such as the Ottomans, were being broken up into national fractions and placed into semi-colonized mandates overseen by capitalist imperialist powers. Thus, on the global Communist revolutionary agenda was the need to clarify the historical question of the relationship between Communist and nationalist movements in the colonies. The particular features of capitalism in these social formations posed analytical complications. In China and elsewhere, capitalism was deeply intertwined in uneven and combined form with noncapitalist social and economic domination, and the majorities of populations were involved in agrarian formations that were neither urban nor "advanced." From these conditions arose a central political question: What was to be the role of the peasantry, as a noncapitalist ("backward") class, in the imperialized/colonized global situation where everyone is unevenly incorporated *into* global capitalism but is not necessarily *of* capitalism? And then, how does the global Communist movement—born of industrial society, now materialized in the Soviet state—relate to this situation? How, then, to conceptualize and provide support for bourgeois-led nationalist (anti-imperialist) movements while infusing those movements with anti-capitalist content and securing the outcome for Marxist Communism?[4]

The question was ideological, but the Comintern's solution for China was tactical: to establish a United Front between the two

---

4   John Riddell, ed., *Workers of the World and Oppressed Peoples, Unite! Proceedings and Documents of the Second Congress, 1920*, 2 vols., New York: Pathfinder, 1991; vol. 1, 211–90; vol. 2, 846–55.

existing mass parties as a way to vanquish the warlords, so as to unify the country under one national state. For the immediate purpose, the CCP was to instruct its individual members to join the larger GMD in a "bloc within" structure, where the CCP was to be subordinated to the GMD. Within the CCP, the discussions about compromise and the nature of political hegemony and mass organizing were acrimonious. In their Third National Congress, held in 1923 in Guangzhou (Canton), Chen Duxiu, then party chairman, agreed that individual CCP members should join the GMD in order to effect the unity of the parties demanded by the Comintern; Zhang Guotao, the party's organizational secretary, objected. The contested upshot was party support for Chen and the Comintern, a decision that came to haunt everyone within a few years. By the same token, GMD leaders were hugely opposed to letting Communists into leading positions in the GMD. After heated debate, Sun Yatsen acquiesced and requested that the Comintern assign a permanent advisor to the GMD; this advisor was the former Jewish Bund member Mikhail Borodin (born Mikhail Gruzenberg).

Both parties' misgivings were set aside temporarily, even while relations with the right wing of the GMD and the left wing of the CCP led to endless fraying and tensions between and within the respective parties. There was a relatively clear division of labor: the CCP was strongest in the urban factories and in Southern rural villages, and after the May Thirtieth Movement, its membership rose exponentially as the number of CCP-led strikes and peasant actions increased. At the same time, however, cultural matters on the left remained in contention: for example, the 1923 formation of the Crescent Moon Society under the aegis of the Bloomsbury-connected poet Xu Zhimo, made common liberal cause with Tagore and Hu Shi to dispute the radicalism of May Fourth culture critique. Meanwhile, the United Front military was dominated by the GMD's Chiang Kaishek, who had gone to study military matters in Moscow in 1923. Upon his return to China, he became the first commandant of the Whampoa Academy in Guangzhou, newly founded to train a modern military on the model of the Soviet Red Army. There Chiang solidified his credentials and proceeded to link major elements of the GMD organizational structure to the military and thus to himself.

Through the middle years of the decade, two United Front organizations were dominated by a Communist-inspired agenda; both faltered when the United Front fell in 1927. One was the Women's Bureau, headquartered in Shanghai, with Xiang Jingyu as leader; and the other was the Peasant Movement Training Institute in Guangzhou, led by Peng Pai and Mao Zedong.

Xiang Jingyu was one of the first women to join the Chinese Communist Party. After a childhood in Hunan shaped by and through anti-Qing activism, she studied in France as part of a postwar anarchist-inspired work-study program. In Montargis, she married Cai Hesen, an early enthusiast of Marxism, and worked with him and others to introduce and organize radical political activities among Chinese students in France and elsewhere. According to her friend Ding Ling's account, Cai and Xiang's wedding photo features them holding Marx's *Capital*, volume 1.[5] Xiang wrote about women's liberation and communism for *New Youth*, the iconic journal of the May Fourth era edited by Chen Duxiu, and by the time she returned to China in 1921, she was well known in radical circles. By 1924, now the mother of two children, whom she left with her own mother in Hunan so that she could continue her political work unencumbered, Xiang had been elected into the Communist Party leadership and was installed in Shanghai at the head of the joint Women's Bureau. From this position she organized women in the silk filatures for strikes in 1924 and for participation in the events surrounding the May Thirtieth movement in 1925. She also published a good deal about social reproduction and the relation between education, class, and gender oppression in *Woman's Weekly* (*Funü zhoubao* / 妇女周报), the supplement to the *Republican Daily* (*Minguo ribao* / 民国日报) that she edited.

---

5 Adriana McElderry, "Woman Revolutionary: Xiang Jingyu," *China Quarterly*, March 1986, 104. Ding Ling and Xiang were old friends from Hunan, where they had been in school in the last decade of the Qing.

However, her appointed task, to reconcile Communist class-based organizing with Nationalist political unification activity, ultimately put her on the wrong side of both parties. Sidelined by the CCP, she was captured and publicly executed by the GMD in early 1928 as a warning to would-be radical women all over China. The bureau was disbanded. Yet, for all its putative marginalization from the Communist or Nationalist mainstreams, the history of Xiang and the Women's Bureau illustrates how gendered social reproduction was already in the 1920s an unavoidable and vital analytical element in mass revolutionary mobilizing.

As for the Peasant Movement Training Institute, Mao Zedong had originally been tasked with work in Shanghai in 1924, where he battled endlessly with the GMD. Frustrated, he summarily left his position and returned home to Hunan. From there, he went south to Guangzhou, where he took on the task of organizational instruction through the institute already established by Peng Pai, a longtime rural activist. The institute, set up to train peasant mobilizers for the national revolution, had few students who knew about agrarian life or production, so Peng Pai brought them on Sundays to villages near Guangzhou to learn from peasants. By the end of 1924, GMD stipulations notwithstanding, peasants were being armed to support the national revolution, and institute organizers were at the forefront of such developments.[6] From institute activity, a new journal was founded, *Chinese Peasant* (*Zhongguo nongmin* / 中国农民), and a notional (rather than empirical) class analysis of the peasantry and Chinese society was undertaken; by late 1926, Mao wrote an article addressing the relation between the national revolution and the peasant movement, asserting that the two were one and the same insofar as they depended upon one another for resolution. Within the year Mao revised his position, now asserting the primacy of the peasant movement over the national one. This he published in his famous early 1927 "Report on an Investigation on the Peasant Movement in

---

6   Fernando Galbiati, *Peng Pai and the Hai-Lu-Feng Soviet*, Palo Alto, CA: Stanford University Press, 1985, chapter 8.

Hunan," a dramatic departure from the theoretical perspective of the CCP and the Comintern.[7]

By early 1926, the formal aspects of the national revolution were being prepared in what was called the Northern Expedition. At their Second Congress in Guangzhou, the GMD, with one-third of the delegates Communists, affirmed that the core problem of the national revolution was state unification. And yet, already in March 1926, Communists in key spots and roles were being arrested and disappeared by GMD forces. A simultaneous campaign was carried out in the countryside, as peasant associations so carefully nurtured through the institute in Guangzhou were attacked, disarmed, and dismantled by landlords supported by GMD military elements. Borodin, the GMD's Comintern advisor, refused to intervene in the decimation of CCP-led social organizations. Mao abandoned the institute and began working with the active peasant movement in Hunan, despite Stalin's orders via the Comintern to stop such activities. Peng Pai held on into 1928, with the establishment of the Hai-Lu-Feng Soviet, a bulwark of peasant organizational autonomy. Peng Pai was betrayed to the GMD, arrested in Shanghai, and executed in 1929. (The traitorous comrade would be assassinated soon enough by underground CCP elements at the behest of Zhou Enlai, later the first premier of the PRC.)

In late 1926, the Northern Expedition was launched as a military operation intended to defeat warlords on the battlefield or induce them to lay down their arms. Many smaller warlords made common cause with landowners and the GMD, in order to tamp down peasant activism and retain their personal and class privileges. The South fell relatively quickly into line. Chiang Kaishek still needed the Communists to win over the urban workers, so his purges remained for the moment focused on rural areas. In February 1927, Chiang's troops were close to Shanghai, having swept through southern China in approximately the same pattern as had the Taipings seventy years previously. With warlords signing fealty or being defeated, the

7   Mao Zedong, "The National Revolution and the Peasant Movement," in Schram, ed., *Mao's Road to Power*, vol. 2., 387–92.

Communists rushed to control mass movements within the newly occupied territories, while the GMD rushed to control the levers of government and administrative power.

In March 1927, the Shanghai General Labor Union called a general strike finally to chase Shanghai-based warlords out of the area and to prepare the ground for the triumphant entry into the city of the Northern Expeditionary troops. By then, Chiang had already secretly entered Shanghai, where he engaged in negotiations with the consuls from various imperialist powers, with Shanghai bankers, and with the supposedly underground (but actually quite open) criminal gangs who held street-level social and economic power, for example, over lucrative opium sales and dens. By April 12, with labor unions openly lining the streets to hail the triumphant GMD military, all was ready for an attack against radicals. The army, the police, and the gangs set upon the factory areas and union strongholds, massacring any before them who were actual or suspected Communists. Women with short hair were caught up in disproportionate numbers, suspected, because of their hairstyles, of harboring radical ideas and engaging in radical political activities. The order to turn against and slaughter Communists (real or suspected) was conveyed, throughout the South and Southeast, to those areas through which the Northern Expedition troops had just marched with support from Communist-organized peasant, women's, and labor movements.

The White Terror had been launched; it would not abate for many years. The Nationalist revolution, successful at the expense of the Communists and their allies, attempted to consolidate itself in the South and Southeast, and it soon abandoned the North to warlord and Japanese activity. With the movement of the GMD capital to Nanjing, the Nationalists became the internationally recognized government of the Republic of China. The uneven and combined economic and political landscape was now the explicit terrain upon which the competing revolutionary movements of the GMD and the CCP took shape.

CHAPTER 4

Competing Revolutions in the
Nanjing Decade (1927–1937)

Military force can only eradicate banditry that has an objective form, and only politics can cleanse banditry that does not . . . Because the banditry that has an objective form is relatively scarce, eradicating it is relatively easy, while formless banditry is more prevalent, and extinguishing it comparatively difficult, for it breeds the most quickly.

—He Zhonghan (1931)[1]

Political power comes out of the barrel of a gun.

—Mao Zedong (1927)[2]

From 1927 until the full-scale Japanese invasion in 1937, the GMD engaged in an open battle with the CCP over revolution and ideology. Conventionally known as the "Nanjing Decade," one of the major determining features of social and political life of this period was the emergence of two would-be state entities, each vying to control the meaning and trajectory of revolution and the future in China. One entity, the GMD, was recognized as the national state of the Republic of China; the other, the CCP, was recognized by no one. While recent mainstream assessments of the Nanjing Decade positively evaluate the GMD's efforts at modernizing state and society,[3] a small number

1 Cited in Maggie Clinton, *Revolutionary Nativism: Fascism and Culture in China, 1925–1937*, Durham, NC: Duke University Press, 2017, 102. He Zhonghan was a leader of the fascist faction of the GMD called the Blue Shirts.
2 Originally recorded in the August 1927 emergency meeting of the CCP, repeated in a 1938 CPC plenary meeting; Mao Zedong, "Problems of War and Strategy," *Selected Works of Mao Tse-tung*, vol. 2, Beijing: Foreign Languages Press, 1954, 224–5.
3 See Brian Tsui, "Introduction," *China's Conservative Revolution: The Quest for a New Order, 1927–1949*, Cambridge, UK: Cambridge University Press, 2018.

of scholars has broken with this formalism to emphasize the fascist ideological bases of GMD practices. Treating the GMD and the CCP not as equivalently modernizing states but as ideologically opposed adversaries helps underscore the very different historical claims on the past, the present, and the future at stake in their competition for social hegemony and power.

During the Nanjing Decade, the GMD concentrated on state building, collecting revenue, suppressing and managing mass movements, and, finally, vanquishing militarily as well as ideologically their Communist nemesis. GMD theorist Dai Jitao's influential rearticulation of Sun Yatsen's "Three Principles" in a Confucian mode—purging all aspects of socialism therefrom—served notice that the GMD's bid for hegemonizing power would be in the mode of what Engels called a "conservative revolution,"[4] a narrowly self-interested preservation of class privilege. The Communists, for their part, concentrated on survival, on remobilizing and refining from a now-rural base the ideological and organizational premises of the anti-capitalist, anti-colonial, anti-imperialist, and anti-feudal socialist revolution in China, and on building the kind of mass movement that could support a protracted struggle and withstand future GMD attacks. Mao Zedong's rearticulation of Marx's historical materialism to feature the peasantry as the leading revolutionary class served notice that the CCP's bid for hegemony would break both with Stalinist orthodoxy and European Marxist insistence on the primacy of the industrialized world and the urban proletariat as leader of global anti-capitalism.[5]

From the vantage of mid 1927, however, the consolidation of the state around the GMD and the ouster of the CCP from the ruling coalition represented a victory for the GMD and a total defeat for the CCP. The terrain of politics was redrawn. Urban centers throughout the South and Southeast became GMD strongholds, forcing radicals

---

4   Tsui makes this point. Engels, "On the Polish Question," *Collected Works*, vol. 6, London: Lawrence Y. Wishart, 1976, 550.

5   Rebecca E. Karl, *Mao Zedong and China in the Twentieth-Century World: A Concise History*, Durham, NC: Duke University Press, 2010, chapter 2.

and their critical energies to burrow deeply into a diffused underground. Police, gangs, and censors worked hand in hand to pursue, suppress, and eliminate perceived textual, spiritual, and material threats to GMD rule; foreign-governed concessions in the treaty ports became far less tolerant of harboring political refugees from Chinese state violence. Meanwhile, certain rural areas, namely those that became bases for the rebuilding of the party-led Communist movement, were hotbeds of social transformative activity and thus targets of unrelenting GMD military assault. The spaces in between were alternately neglected, super-exploited, or imagined anew by folklorists and rural reconstructionists as foundation for the regeneration of a primordially better China. The nominal unification of the state under the GMD hence led to the absolute fragmentation of politics and social life. And imperialists went nowhere, other than to strengthen their grip on profitable sectors of the Chinese economy, while cheerfully building embassy quarters in the new GMD capital of Nanjing, blessedly close to Shanghai and thus more comfortable for easy circulation between political and financial sectors, between the pleasures of "the Paris of the East" and the drudgery of diplomatic work.

The failure of the Chinese United Front also led to the reimagining of revolutionary possibility globally. Stalin, having consolidated power in the Soviet Union, proceeded to purge his internal enemies. Trotsky, who had warned and worked against the Comintern strategy in China—foreseeing that the GMD were far from reliable allies for the CCP—fled to exile in Mexico, where he was ultimately assassinated by Stalin's henchmen. M. N. Roy escaped China with his life, and in his peripatetic travels thereafter, he moved away from organized Communist politics toward other forms of worldly radical thought. Less mobile dissenters in the USSR were exiled to Siberia, imprisoned, put on trial, or executed. Like nothing before it, the Soviet-led Comintern's role in the Chinese national revolution marked an end to most utopian hope that the Russian Revolution would yield a new path to global peace, progress, and social justice. What remained was strategic alliance. After 1927, the Comintern nakedly acted as the international arm of the Stalinist Soviet state. Occasionally challenged strongly or weakly by the Trotskyist Fourth International, the Comintern's support for anti-colonial nationalism was sometimes motivated by revolutionary internationalism and at other times by realpolitik. Yet, while many radical or nationalist leaders—African, Asian, North American, Latin American (black, white, and brown)—looked to the Comintern for assistance, they also tried to push the Third International toward more race-conscious and less instrumental positions. For example, the Guyanese Marxist Walter Rodney departed from Stalinist orthodoxy on historical "stages" to argue that promoting socialism had to be part of the very decolonization of Africa.[6] Meanwhile, the League against Imperialism, launched in Germany as a connective thread between the Comintern, Europe-based anti-colonialism, and anti-colonial movements in Asia and Africa, ended up driving a wedge between the Comintern and anti-colonial movements when the latter did not align with the former.[7] In China after 1927, the Comintern remained involved with the Chinese Communist Party, although its dictates became ever less relevant to Mao Zedong's evolving rural-based revolutionary strategy.

In the year after the GMD seizure of state power, over 300,000 people lost their lives to the Nationalist-sponsored White Terror. The leadership of the CCP was decimated. Li Dazhao, having taken refuge in the Soviet embassy in Beijing, was captured therefrom by the warlord Zhang Zuolin, cooperating for the moment with Chiang Kaishek. Zhang had Li and eighteen other Communists hanged at the end of April 1927. Chen Duxiu was scapegoated for the disaster by

6   Jesse Benjamin and Robin Kelley, "Introduction: An African Perspective on the Russian Revolution," in Walter Rodney, *The Russian Revolution: A View from the Third World*, ed. Robin D. G. Kelley and Jesse Benjamin, London and New York: Verso, 2017, xix–lxxiii, lix.

7   Fredrik Petersson, "'We Are Neither Visionaries nor Utopian Dreamers'": Willi Münzenberg, the League against Imperialism, and the Comintern, 1925–1933," PhD diss., Turku, Finland: åbo akademi, 2013.

remaining members of the CCP; he was banished from the Party and later became a Trotskyist. He was arrested and imprisoned by the GMD for eight years and ultimately died in Sichuan in 1942 of ill health. His two sons were executed by the GMD. Mao Zedong escaped, while his wife, Yang Kaihui, stranded in Hunan, was executed in 1930 for her persistent refusal to denounce her husband. The overlapping political elite, up to now drawn from the same well of educated society, split irrevocably. Yet the vast majority of those killed in the reign of terror were peasant association members, union activists, and strike participants. Villages and factories were further polarized.

The cultural sphere, after a brief silence, lurched to the left, finding in the right-wing turn of the GMD and the indiscriminate use of violence a form of state power many found repulsive. Acrimony and antagonism built to new heights. Huge literary talents—such as the poet Hu Yepin, Ding Ling's husband—were executed, as were a host of less well-known figures. Lu Xun soon helped organize such Shanghai-based associations as the League of Left-Wing Writers, five of whose members were executed publicly in 1931. Others, such as Hunan-based short story writer Shen Congwen, Beijing-based Zhou Zuoren (Lu Xun's brother), or Shanghai-based Eileen Chang, tried to find a middle ground, yet their liberal political neutrality smacked of complicity and they were shunned by leftists. Mass-market fiction avoided political engagements and continued in a pure popular entertainment mode. These writers were looked down upon by both left and right. Conservatives were emboldened; such figures as Liang Shiqiu and Mu Shiying launched attacks on the nihilism of May Fourth radicalism that they blamed for the current violent impasse, instead advocating a return to Confucius and tradition. The CCP, regrouping out of urban sight, did not yet have power to control leftist cultural production. That would come. For the moment, a good number of intellectuals, writers, artists, filmmakers, and songwriters, as well as journalists, teachers, educators, and cultural critics took a sharp left turn, often at great personal risk. Political polarization led to the fragmentation of the cultural elite: one now had to choose sides.

*   *   *

The GMD's primary ambition after 1927 was to govern a hitherto-fractured territory and unruly population while also recalibrating the national economy to serve capitalist development and build statist strength. The GMD's reorganization of the state was hampered initially by its relative paucity of revenue and its only partial territorial reach; it was also shaped by the huge proportion of the budget sucked up by the military—in hot pursuit of the remnants of the Communist Party and their sympathizers—and the secret services—hunting down putative Communists, domestic and foreign spies lurking in the porousness of urban centers.

One of the first tasks at hand was the purification of the party-state so as to root out the polluting infiltration of Communist ideology. Dai Jitao, the theoretician with the most influence on Chiang Kaishek, was a believer in mass mobilization, yet the masses, in Dai's vision, had to be mobilized from the top for docile production. They were to be fashioned into a disciplined phalanx of rural and industrial producers, obediently contributing to and guarding the national economy against depredations both of imperialists and the Communist cancer. Class was dismissed as an irrelevant analytic—it was divisive rather than unifying. Instead, the analytic center of ideology focused on the "nation" and its hyphenated partners, the GMD and the state. The social inequality and disruption produced by capitalist development was a perspective to be suppressed, even while individuated social problems were acknowledged to exist and require remediation. Most centrally, by theoretically reorienting the concept of "people's livelihood" (*minsheng*/民生), one of Sun's Three Principles, away from an ambition to transform uneven *structural conditions* of life toward the national development to which all productive activity needed to tend, Dai Jitao and other GMD thinkers bent Sun's vaguely socialist philosophy to a more conservative purpose. As historian Brian Tsui argues, the turn from emphasizing *sheng* (生, life) to *yu* (育, cultivation) signaled and mirrored a turn away from class struggle against unequal relations of production toward a top-down, state-led program for tutelage.[8] While elements

---

8　Tsui, *China's Conservative Revolution*, 41–3.

of this ideology were in place by 1925, the 1927 seizure of state power rendered it a governing ideal.

Having banished the Communists, the conquest of the state still was not complete. The Northern warlords remained in place, yet even in the South, the powerful Sun Chuanfang, erstwhile dominator of the Shanghai region, continued to hold out against Chiang's military. With internal party dissension rife, Chiang Kaishek left his colleagues to contemplate their options while he went to Japan to marry Song Meiling—the sister of Sun Yatsen's wife, Song Qingling, and the daughter of one of China's richest men, T. V. Song, a financier and banker. Now linked by marriage to the father of the nation (dead though he was), with a Christian wife educated at Wellesley, fluent in English and all things United States, and with the financial backing of the well-connected and hugely wealthy Song family, Chiang returned to Nanjing considerably strengthened. He shook down Shanghai's richest Chinese families by forcing them to "contribute" to his GMD coffers, and then proceeded to subdue remaining warlords with the purchased cooperation of Feng Yuxiang and Yan Xishan, two power-ful Northerners.[9] Zhang Zuolin, ousted from Beijing, died when his Manchuria-bound train was bombed by the Japanese; his son, Zhang Xueliang, made temporary peace with Chiang and became a warlord in Manchuria.

By the beginning of 1928, with the ideological purge ongoing and the social connections to finance capital secured, Chiang's biggest concern was for the GMD state under his iron rule to remain as autonomous from social pressure as possible. This required manipu-lations of ever-forming factions; a large investment in symbols of power and the tools of propaganda, including the inauguration of "National Day" as a holiday (October 10) and of "humiliation days" that reminded people of the wrongs perpetrated upon China by impe-rialists; the relocation of Sun Yatsen's embalmed body from Beijing to a final resting place in Nanjing; the welding of the military closely to

---

9   Peter Zarrow, *China in War and Revolution, 1895–1949*, New York: Routledge, 2005, chapter 13.

Chiang's personal rule; the devising of mechanisms for the reliable gathering of revenue through taxation; and the territorial expansion and consolidation of GMD rule. The GMD's national unification claimed the frontiers of Tibet, Eastern Turkestan (today's Xinjiang), and Inner and Outer Mongolia for Chinese sovereignty, although the government's ability to enforce this territoriality was limited. And, despite the anti-imperialist rhetoric of the regime, foreign debt ballooned, and bond sales or bank loans became frequent ways to finance the state.

Not content with grand policy, even sartorial aspects of the new state were taken up: clean-cut professional and political men were encouraged to wear the "Sun Yatsen suit," a neat, military-inspired short jacket with buttons down the front, four pockets, and pleated pants in blue, tan, or black; and urban professional women, school-girls, and proper wives were encouraged to style their long hair in braids or buns, have natural (unbound) feet shod in sturdy leather or cloth shoes, and wear modest clothing—below-the-knee pleated skirts and buttoned-up blouses became one urban uniform of sorts—that was feminine but demure. The *qipao* (or *cheongsam*), a high-collared, thigh-high, slit-up-the-sides slinky dress that swept into urban fashion during these years, was deemed characteristic of disreputable entertainers; yet, in loosened contours it became desirable as a form of modest native dress for women.

The GMD government was organized by *yuan* (branches), although during the Nanjing Decade some of the branches worked better than others. Whatever their efficacy, institutions were not intended to enfranchise the population, but rather to facilitate party control over society and the economy. A strong police force was one such institution, even as the police in Shanghai, for example, remained tied inextricably to the fearsome Green Gang criminal organization and its wide-ranging extortionist activities.[10] Opium sales, nominally illegal, flourished under the protection of gangs and

---

10   Frederick Wakeman, *Policing Shanghai, 1927–1937*, Berkeley, CA: University of California Press, 1995.

police. Indeed, without opium, the peasant economy likely would have collapsed, and GMD tax revenue certainly would have shriveled. In fact, it was during these years that Chinese-produced opium finally surpassed, in volume of consumption, British-produced imported opium from India and Malaya. Meanwhile, under the Judicial Yuan, the system for civil and criminal law grew. Legal codes were rewritten—for example, monogamous marriage became a legal ideal, although far from a practiced reality—and courts were reorganized, although along already-existing Qing dynastic lines, under which judicial procedures were dominated by the discretion of judges. While extralegal punishment—assassinations, political retributions, and so forth—was a prominent feature of life under the GMD, at local levels, a functioning judiciary was able to investigate and bring people to justice for wrongdoing. Seemingly prosaic aspects of criminal investigations, such as forensics, became routinized and encoded as procedure and norm.[11]

Despite the censorship and intimidation of critical journalism, daily newspapers, tabloids, and periodicals flourished, as did radio and cinema, with competing studios producing popular Hollywood-style and martial arts films of varying quality. From the early 1930s onward, a left-wing cinema tendency—walking a tightrope between censorship, market viability, and radicalism—also took root. The growth of communication networks linked by telegraph allowed for swift transmissions of information, news, commercial notices, and social scandals across a larger geographical range. Whether or not such media contributed to a more unified "imagined community" of the nation, as Benedict Anderson might have claimed,[12] it is undoubtedly true that these circulatory mechanisms allowed for the formation and exploitation of a mass market and mass consumer base.

Transformations in China's political economy under the GMD were both less dramatic and more devastating than before. The

---

11   Daniel Asen, *Death in Beijing: Murder and Forensic Science in Republican China*, Cambridge, UK: Cambridge University Press, 2016.

12   Benedict Anderson, *Imagined Communities: Reflections on the Origins and Spread of Nationalism*, London and New York: Verso, 1983.

economy essentially stagnated, and with military expenditures eating up the GMD budget, funds for economic development were scarce. The great depression hit at essentially the exact moment of GMD consolidation, and agrarian economies along with commodity prices the world over collapsed. Japan attempted to take advantage by tying the Chinese rural economy more tightly to Japanese-controlled industry in Japan and Shanghai. To that end, the research arm of Japanese imperialism, linked to the Southern Manchurian Railway, undertook large-scale surveys of the Chinese countryside in order to devise more efficient ways to exploit and control it. Under these multi-sided pressures, existing relations on the ground—agrarian and industrial—became more and more exploitative, as taxes, rent, and wages were squeezed to yield profits and revenue. It might be true that the Shanghai capitalists and financiers became weary of Chiang's frequent shakedowns, but it is also true that Chiang's economic and social policies remained friendly to capitalism and landlordism as modes of production, if not always to individual capitalists and landlords.

Meanwhile, the production of raw materials hit major snags. The sources of cotton and silk remained, for the most part, embedded in the household economy, diffused across provinces and growing conditions and dispersed into households, where women's labor was central. Among other issues, cotton thread could not be standardized in these conditions, and yet machine weaving in the urban factories, where the thread was now being aggregated to be woven into cloth, required standard thicknesses and tensile strengths. A similar problem emerged with silk: the variability of household production conflicted with the requirements of machine filatures. Foreign imports of cotton and silk thread, as well as of finished garments, accelerated the trend toward the displacement of household production. GMD economists and policy makers attempted to bridge agrarian and urban economic gaps by forcing rural producers into managed cooperatives and top-down credit societies, with the object of breaking the back of agrarian elites by directing a redistribution of wealth to the

industrialized coasts.[13] None of this dealt with the uneven structures of production or with the ways in which the household economy and women's work were being destroyed. In these conditions,
economic stagnation meant actual immiseration.

The unilateral US Silver Purchase Act of 1934—an attempt to
jump-start the US economy by remonetizing silver and recalibrating
the relation of silver to gold—pushed the price of silver, long China's
metallic monetary standard, into the stratosphere. In historian
Tomoko Shiroyama's words, "The sudden and massive rise in the
price of silver caused by heavy U.S. purchases just as suddenly raised
the price of silver abroad. This precipitated a massive flow of silver out
of China and upset the silver standard Chinese economy."[14] This
monetary crisis spiraled into the collapse of the real estate market and
many other forms of economic activity through the mid 1930s: land
values plummeted, credit dried up, banks struggled, and the GMD
was forced into a ruinous round of currency reform and economic
intervention in the urban finance markets. Much of this was effected
by further squeezing revenue from the depressed agrarian economy
and floating loans from foreign banks.

At the same time, testing the waters of Chinese nationalist fervor,
the Japanese, using as pretext the 1931 Mukden Incident—a staged
bombing near a Northeastern railroad depot—invaded Manchuria so
as to annex its raw materials, peasant labor, and territories to their
colonial empire in Korea. With his military bogged down in attempts
to dislodge the Communists from their bases in Jiangxi Province,
Chiang Kaishek would not contest the Japanese over Manchuria, and
Zhang Xueliang ordered his troops to lay down their arms. By 1932,
the Japanese had installed a puppet regime in the newly renamed
Manchukuo, governed by the last Qing emperor, Pu-yi, who had been
deposed in 1911 when he was three years old and now had grown into
a dissolute young man. Manchukuo remained a pariah state,

---

13   Margharita Zanasi, *Saving the Nation: Economic Modernity in Republican China*,
Chicago, IL: University of Chicago Press, 2006, chapter 5.

14   Tomoko Shiroyama, *China during the Great Depression: Market, State, and the
World Economy, 1929–1937*, Cambridge, MA: Harvard University Asia Center, 2008, 156.

unrecognized by any other than Japan itself, leading Japan to withdraw from the League of Nations thus helping provoke the League's collapse. While Zhang Xueliang took the brunt of criticism for nonresistance, Chiang's preoccupation with annihilating the Communists was also critically questioned. Japan escalated its attacks. At the end of January 1932, another manufactured pretext resulted in the Japanese bombing of Shanghai followed by a long siege, during which the city was defended by hard-pressed GMD troops. In late February, the Chinese were defeated and a cease-fire was brokered; China was prohibited from garrisoning troops in or around Shanghai, essentially leaving that city to the Japanese and other imperialist powers.

Through these chaotic years, urban life flourished. Dance halls remained well stocked with Chinese women from the rural areas, whose livelihoods had disappeared and who were now forced into the urban service economy at its lowest rungs; they were joined by other women reduced in circumstance by global capitalist displacement, as well as by white Russians who had fled the Russian Revolution without the wealth they had once possessed. Shanghai- and Guangzhou-based cinemas produced one starlet after the next, who captured public imagination, became enmeshed in tabloid-level scandals, and were swept aside by newer public conquests. Chefs in major urban areas turned regional dishes into national cuisine served in opulent settings accompanied by famous Chinese opera singers catering to Chinese and foreign palates, while noodle houses and smaller urban eateries employed women as service workers to waitress for the lower-level office denizens on lunch or dinner breaks. Opium dens designed for upscale or downscale consumption proliferated. Churches, Buddhist temples, and other places of religious life prospered. Bathhouses, brothels, horse and dog racing . . . many forms of amusement and legal or illegal gambling thrived. Langston Hughes and other luminaries of the Harlem Renaissance arrived in Shanghai, where African American musicians were eagerly hosted on stages in the French Concession, where American race laws did not apply. Hughes, upon his return to the United States, wrote and published an anti-colonial poem famously entitled "Roar, China:"

Roar, China!
Roar, old lion of the East!
Snort fire, yellow dragon of the Orient,
Tired at last of being bothered.
. . .
Stand up and roar, China!
You know what you want!
The only way to get it is
To take it!
Roar, China![15]

Many of these urban pursuits were in fact racially segregated, with Chinese in paid servile relation to white foreigners and Japanese inhabiting an ambiguous position in the racial hierarchy; but some of them, particularly the more illicit types, were open to all. The cultural dynamism of Shanghai and urban life of the time has been celebrated by recent scholars as the cosmopolitan product of a specifically hybrid Chinese modernity. This characterization superficially captures something, yet it erases the foreign-dominated imperialist, immiserated capitalist, and politically authoritarian materiality of its conditions.

By the early 1930s, a Sun Yatsen memorial was being planned and built in the purple mountains on the outskirts of Nanjing on a monumental scale aiming to impress all with its permanence and national significance. Constructed in a pleasing blue-and-white color scheme, with stairways sweeping up the mountainside and archways inscribed with repurposed Confucian adages, the memorial was a magnificent homage to the endurance of a timeless "China" in the name of the timeliness of the "father of the nation." Urban planning, architecture, roads, and street lighting all boomed around the country. Nanjing, the national capital, saw streets widened and a number of government buildings and ministries designed and built in a "Chinese modern"

---

15 Tina Kanagaratnam, "Roar, China! Langston Hughes in Shanghai," *Historic Shanghai*, historic-shanghai.com.

idiom, with upturned roofs. In Xiamen (Amoy), remittances from overseas Chinese labor and wealthy merchants alike helped transform the cityscape, producing a distinctive look to housing, streets, and commercial space that came to characterize Southern Chinese urban style.[16] In Beijing, the ancient inner city was partially remade to connect the now-diminished erstwhile capital to other places, even while older spaces of chaotic street life persisted and occasionally were endowed with new "folk" meaning, despite their "vulgar" performers.[17] Much of this urban transformation was funded by merchant subscription and overseas Chinese investement, and was undertaken by local governments.

In an attempt to breathe vitality into their postponed ideological and spiritual conservative revolution, in 1934 GMD theorists and propagandists came up with a scheme to remake the everyday in the image of disciplined workerism. Called the "New Life Movement" (NLM), this initiative was launched to infuse unity and uniformity into a fragmenting and ever more divisive social situation. As historian Maggie Clinton has characterized it, the NLM was a form of "Taylorized modernity," an attempt to weld together an understanding of the nation, Confucian at its core, "as natural and class-cooperative," even as the NLM was also an "aestheticized response to issues of social difference . . . in which capitalist dynamism was cemented by feudalistic hierarchy."[18] Intended to instruct everyone on knowing, occupying, and performing their proper places in society, the NLM was a series of injunctions to clean up sloppy behavior, regulate and regiment life, and cultivate obedient and, above all, productive modes of citizenship. It aspired to generate a healthy individual body that would produce and reproduce for the accumulation of wealth in the name of the nation-state. To this end, in its propaganda and

---

16 James A. Cook, "Reimagining China: Xiamen, Overseas Chinese, and a Transnational Modernity," in Madeline Yue Dong and Joshua Goldstein, eds., *Everyday Modernity in China*, Seattle, WA: University of Washington Press, 2007, 156–94.

17 Madeline Yue Dong, *Republican Beijing: The City and Its Histories*, Berkeley, CA: University of California Press, 2003.

18 Clinton, *Revolutionary Nativism*, 129.

presentation, the NLM linked selective aspects of Confucian social hierarchy—expressed in the four virtues, *li, yi, lian, chi* (礼/义/廉/耻; propriety, righteousness, honesty, integrity)—to Dai Jitao's already-selective interpretation of Sun Yatsen's "Three Principles of the People," thereby creating a timelessly natural-seeming national cultural foundation, expressed by the particular Chinese state manifested in the GMD. At first directed from party headquarters, the NLM was taken over by Song Meiling (aka Madame Chiang Kaishek), in a public expression of feminine virtue and modest womanhood.

Ubiquitous in expressive presence, the NLM ultimately was not effective as a mass movement. Yet for all its trivial-seeming concerns—Chiang Kaishek's list of proper behaviors was disseminated across the mediasphere in 1934[19]—the NLM was a serious bid for a conservative reconceptualization of life in modern China. Cognate movements had been or were being launched in fascist Japan, Nazi Germany, Franco's Spain, and soon, Mussolini's Italy. In the conditions of wartime contingency characterizing the ongoing GMD attempts to oust Communism as a material and a spiritual ("formless") threat to the body politic, the movement was initially aimed at winning over the rural population in Jiangxi from the contamination of the CCP, who had recently been based there. Spreading from Jiangxi to the GMD-controlled part of the nation at large, the NLM often worked through schools or such organizations as the Girl and Boy Scouts—founded in China in 1934, with Dai Jitao as vice president—to patrol, surveil, and edify. By inscribing the everyday as the basic unit for the reproduction of the conditions of life and livelihood, and by conservatively repurposing the established categories of "youth" and "newness"—linked since May Fourth with radicalism and collective action—the NLM proposed a top-down mass movement to encourage cultivation and "self-improvement" at the level of the individual embedded in the patriarchal family, who could then be welded to the national body. In such a fusion, the socially "useful" body was counterposed to the poisonous body of

---

19   "Outline of the New Life Movement" [*Xin shenghuo yundong gangyao*].

"vermin" (*duchong*/毒虫)—Communists—idle non-(re)productive aliens in the national midst, slated for annihilation.[20]

The GMD's effort to define and mobilize a conservative revolution in a nationalist mode was a fascist response to the radical reshaping of politics and life in modern China. As with contemporaneous fascisms elsewhere, this response emerged from the same structural conditions as the Communist revolutionary movement—industrialization and class antagonism; imperialist domination and capitalist control; uneven social and economic formations yielding modern sectors in combination with and preying upon pre-modern modes of organizing life and production; and cultural critique and innovation that was inextricably linked to global trends. The GMD's attempt to impose its version of top-down revolution was designed to quell any move toward the structural reorganization of the social conditions of life and to seize the definition of China's modernity for a statist fascism, characterized by military rule closely allied with urban capitalist and rural landlord production. This was thinly overlaid with an anti-imperialist rhetoric that masked deep dependence on global finance capital for survival and that was underpinned by a deeply conservative cultural primordialism.

At the same time, Communists were regrouping, elaborating their version of revolution.

April 1927 represented an almost complete defeat for the Chinese Communists. The brief moment during which the left wing of the GMD, headquartered in Wuhan, seemed able to hold the line against total disaster soon collapsed. After a quick meeting of remaining leaders in August 1927 in Hankou, next to Wuhan, the CCP dispersed, pursued by right-wing GMD forces. It was at this meeting that Mao Zedong articulated the view that political power can only be secured with the backing of military might, as cited at the opening of this chapter. It was a lesson he never forgot. For the moment, upon escaping Hankou, he and others ended up on the Jiangxi-Hunan provincial

---

20 Tsui, *China's Conservative Revolution*, 96.

border, where they embarked on a wholesale rethinking of the premises of the Communist revolution in China. Building a Marxist-
inspired modern revolutionary movement in such poverty-stricken
and backward places seemed a preposterous proposition. And yet
that is what was done, through massive ideological compromise and
creativity, huge bloodshed, constant infighting requiring enormous
ruthlessness, and an iron will to salvage whatever could be saved for
the present and future from the debacle.

Mao Zedong's base in Jinggangshan was at first neither the only
nor even the most successful Communist refuge from GMD pursuit.
Yet, because Mao became the unquestioned leader of the CCP after
1935, his Jiangxi base became historically iconic and contemporane-
ously instructive. Situated in an under-governed, rugged periphery
similar to the type of location that had nurtured Hong Xiuquan's
Taiping movement eighty years earlier, what was to become the
Jinggangshan base was populated by bandits, desperados, local
despots, struggling peasants, lineage groups, and various ethnicities
(mostly Hakka/客家人). There were also some local elites, radicalized
in schools of the nearby cities Changsha (Hunan) or Nanchang
(Jiangxi), who had returned to their native place to foment social
transformation. Thus, before Mao arrived, there was already a small
but persistent revolutionary impetus. One node of such activism
became famous because it was led by He Zizhen, who became Mao's
next wife. He Zizhen was well educated and physically adept, unusual
for a woman of her elite background. From age sixteen, riding on
horseback, she had participated in the peasant movement, in addition
to being tasked with "women's work" by virtue of being female. In the
1926 wave of peasant mobilizations in support of the Northern
Expedition in her region, He Zizhen's group played a central role.
When the crackdown came in April 1927, she and others went underground. She would surface later that year, as Mao and 700 or so
soldiers retreating from the Autumn Harvest Uprising reached
Jinggangshan.

After the clandestine CCP meeting in August in Hankou, Mao
had mobilized a military action in Hunan. With the assistance of Li

Zhen, who rallied proletarians from the mining towns under her command to Mao's cause, the Autumn Harvest Uprising had battled landlords and GMD troops in September 1927. The uprising failed, and Mao retreated with those who remained, among them Li Zhen— who was to become the first woman commander in the Communist army. From then on, Mao was leery of putschism, preferring to painstakingly build a movement away from the militarist adventurism beloved by Stalin, and by certain CCP leaders now lodged clandestinely in the relative safety of Hangzhou and Shanghai. This was when Mao started to formulate his distinctive revolutionary theory of the countryside surrounding the city. From late 1927 until early 1929, when he was dislodged from Jinggangshan by the GMD military and elite-led local militias, Mao, along with a shifting roster of others, reorganized the remnants of local revolutionary activism into a coordinated party-led movement to redistribute land, smash the power of landlords, and mobilize the peasant masses; in the process, they began to elaborate institutions, procedures, laws, and ideologies appropriate to the new historical obstacles and opportunities. In the words of the late anthropologist Stephen Averill, what the Jinggangshan moment demonstrates is how Mao's movement came to "assimilate . . . strategies and actions to the structures, practices, and recent historical experience of local inhabitants."[21] The successes and failures shaped subsequent Communist revolutionary ideologies and strategies.

The year 1928 found Mao on a mountaintop, mostly cut off from central CCP and other sources of party discipline. Yet, he was not isolated. As his movement gained notoriety—in large part because of the resistance it called forth from landlords and established members of the social hierarchy whose ways of life and privileges were being attacked and transformed—he drew to him various supporters, including rudiments of what later would be called the Red Army commanded separately by Zhu De and Peng Dehuai.

---

21   Stephen C. Averill, *Revolution in the Highlands: China's Jinggangshan Base Area*, New York: Rowman & Littlefield, 2006, 147. This discussion of Jinggangshan is based on Averill and on Karl (2010).

Welded together from a number of armed groups, what was then called the Zhu-Mao Army grew into the "guns" backing Mao's political power. And yet, the army was not merely brawn to Mao's brain. The precepts eventually guiding the army's actions were highly evolved in political consciousness, and they became integrally theorized aspects of what later emerged as Mao Zedong Thought or Maoism.[22] The army was called upon to be attentive to the environment in which they operated, among ordinary civilians whose sympathy and support they needed to win and retain; to be mindful of their modes of comportment (theft, rape and pillage, gambling, opium use, and so forth were to be eradicated); and to be careful about the structures of obedience upon which any army relies (such hierarchy as was retained was accompanied by plain living and frugality for all). These precepts were encapsulated in an exemplary code of conduct, for whose provisions and actualization the Red Army became famous.

The Red Army also became known for its tactics—what we call today "guerilla" or "asymmetrical" warfare. Theorized by Mao slightly later under the strategy of "luring the enemy deep," these tactics were developed during 1928 to account for fundamental weapons and troop weaknesses in relation to enemy (GMD) strengths. What were counted as those strengths—urban bases, hierarchical structures, weapons systems, highly rigid formations—were turned by these tactics into weaknesses, as the Red Army operated in a mobile and flexible manner, using local knowledge and sympathy to trick, trap, and subdue many an enemy foray. The topography informed the tactics, and the tactics shaped how the topography was used to advantage. In this way, the Red Army was able to defeat larger, better-equipped armies and keep the GMD and landlord-backed local militias at bay, for a time.

Meanwhile, social transformation proceeded, even though the Jinggangshan laws for the distribution of land to peasants were

---

22 In China, this philosophy is not called "Maoism" [*mao zhuyi* / 毛主义] but Mao Zedong Thought [*Mao Zedong sixiang* / 毛泽东思想].

characterized more by idealism than reality. Land was thought of as the source of value production, and peasant labor as the mode through which value was realized; landlords were treated as a barrier to the full actualization of this relationship. And yet, Mao's group was to find that rural society was not just about land and labor, because social relations of production were far more complex. Moreover, in land redistribution, the logic of per capita labor (one person as one unit of labor) was posed against labor power, with the family and other factors such as farm implements and animals as the unit of aggregation. The latter seemed to preserve already-existing advantages, and the former seemed far more equitable and yet incongruent with how people lived their productive and affective lives. In the event, peasant collectives were formed out of the destroyed remnants of what had been the peasant associations, while commercial activity was regulated to conform to peasant marketing needs rather than to urban elite accumulation desires. By mid 1928, these peasant collectives paved the way for efforts to redistribute land. Mao's brother Zetan was deeply involved in this initiative. But the mechanisms of land seizures and the means through which the seized land was to remain seized constituted one realm of problems; another realm was the principles upon which whose land was to be seized on whose behalf and according to what logic it was to be distributed. Kinship ties, the lineage structures of ownership and production, the fact that some of Mao's local military was comprised of sons from the families whose land was being seized—all of this and more became part of an experiment that was neither successful nor, in actual fact, very long lived. However, all of the problems confronted at this time fed into a larger theorization of the relation between theory and practice, and, several years later, once Mao's group was resettled in the Ruijin region, they rethought the premises of their social revolutionary endeavor. In this process, it became clear that practice and theory had to be far more dialectically linked, and thus was born Mao's radical Marxist practice of "investigation" (diaocha/调查).

Investigation, as independent scholar Marcelo Hoffman argues, has been a powerful form of social inquiry in the service of radical transformative struggle all over the world.[23] Mao's version was announced embryonically in his 1927 "Report on the Investigation of the Hunan Peasant Movement," in which, among other things, he lambasted urban Communists for wringing their hands in despair over the then–peasant movements' so-called "excessive violence." Indicating that the charge of "going too far" was an anti-revolutionary theory of bourgeois conciliation, and further, that class struggle was not a refined dinner party but a violent overthrowing of one class by another, Mao claimed that political opinions on proper action could only emerge from eye/I-witness investigations, not from faraway finger pointing and theoretical abstraction. Beginning in the early 1930s, this view of the relation between investigation and transformative activity was deepened and more thoroughly realized and theorized in the Ruijin base area and beyond. The point was that dogmatic theory—for instance, about the necessary urban proletarian bases of Communist revolution—or what Mao called "bookism" (*benben zhuyi* / 本本主义), was inadequate to the revolutionary task of China's present. Starting from the specificity of the present—as a given *and* a created urgency emerging from the dialectic between human activity and found materiality—was the only viable option for true revolution. The emphasis on practice that subsequently became a hallmark of Maoism thus was born of Mao's experience with and insistence on investigations. Without investigation, Mao famously was to repeat, there is no right to speak[24]

Ruijin, the capital of the Jiangxi Soviet, was where Mao, Zhu De, and the Red Army were instructed to set up their base in 1931, when Jinggangshan was no longer tenable. This was the place where far-flung nodes of Communist activity in the general region were to be amalgamated into one movement, and where Mao's renegade operation was to be reined back in by the now-reconstituted Shanghai-based, Moscow-directed CCP leadership under Li

---

23   Marcelo Hoffman, *Militant Acts: The Role of Investigations in Radical Political Struggles*, Albany, NY: SUNY Press, 2019.

24   Mao, "Oppose Bookism," May 1930, *Selected Works of Mao Tse-tung*, vol. 6, marxists.org.

Lisan.[25] Here, the Chinese Communist movement was able to more fully elaborate its agrarian revolutionary ideology, to develop new approaches to land redistribution, and to pioneer the use of literature and drama for peasant revolutionary mobilization. In the almost three years during which the region functioned as an alternative state within GMD-ruled territory, the Jiangxi Soviet became a laboratory of Communist experimentation. It also was host to and perpetrator of a number of bloody internal party purges that alienated supporters, alarmed friends, and ruthlessly set limits on lines of correct ideology and proper leadership.

Despite living in and among the peasantry, CCP leaders struggled to understand the society in which they were embedded. While some of the leaders—Mao included—had come from peasant families (although Mao's was a rich peasant family, not a poor one), a good number of the CCP leaders were of urban origin, often foreign educated, and thoroughly unfamiliar with and indeed suspicious of the vulgarity and poverty of the countryside. At the level of personal habit, Mao already had cultivated a lifestyle closer to the rhythms of his poor rural environment, and he condemned those who clung to bourgeois habits. Nevertheless, the complexities of rural social relations often thwarted the most sincere attempts at transformation. The investigations with which the CCP advanced their land policies started from a conviction that class struggle existed and that classes were constituted in the form of social scientific categories—landlord; rich, middle, and poor peasant; farm laborer; lumpenproletariat— loosely derived from Marx, and secondarily derived from what historian Tani Barlow has called "vernacular sociology." The categories did not map easily onto Chinese rural society; therefore they needed to be substantiated in the course of social transformation. Land reform, in other words, unfolded simultaneously with the categorical elaboration of the land relations they sought to upend.

---

25   For other bases and leaders, see G. Benton, *Mountain Fires: The Red Army's Three-Year War in South China, 1934–1938*, Berkeley, CA: University of California Press, 1992.

This created complications among and between families, villages, and the simultaneously horizontal and vertical ties of clan and class. It also created complications in theory and interpretation. And yet, during the three years of the Ruijin-headquartered Jiangxi Soviet, landlordism was more or less eliminated, debts incurred through rapacious usury were wiped out, ordinary peasants gained control over land, and the tax/rent system was unified under CCP administration. The CCP also issued its own currency, bought seed and fertilizer and other necessities in bulk for distribution, and circumvented the GMD blockades to obtain salt. The purchase and sale of girls as child brides and women as reproductive chattel were prohibited, and women's labor was mobilized in the fields to help produce staples for their own livelihood and the growing CCP bureaucratic and military requirements. Far from a utopia, the Jiangxi Soviet was nevertheless a functioning society that strove toward egalitarian and nonhierarchical social relations; more successful in some realms than others, it was a social experiment from which the CCP would, yet again, learn crucial lessons for the future.

Throughout the period, the realm of culture—overseen in part from Shanghai by Qu Qiubai, who only arrived in Ruijin in 1934, and in the Soviet itself by Zhang Wentian (pen name Luo Fu)—was a vital arena of ideological work.[26] As Zhang made clear, cultural work could not be merely about enlightenment—the liberal May Fourth model—but had to combine the organization of clubs and reading groups with performance and entertainment to foster active participation and instruction. To this end, Li Bozhao, a dramatist, introduced the "living newspaper" (huobao/活报) format into her troupe performances, creating the type of agitational drama that became ubiquitous later in Communist cultural work.[27] But the creativity of the time was not primarily even about new forms or new contents; more important, it was about pioneering new social relations of cultural production that

---

26   Ellen Judd, "Revolutionary Drama and Song in the Jiangxi Soviet," *Modern China* 9:1, 1983, 127–60.

27   Judd, "Revolutionary Drama," 135.

could account for and incorporate unevenness or asymmetries between cultural producers, including performers, and those traditionally called "audiences." These new relations were concretized in the context of reading clubs. In this mode, as anthropologist Ellen Judd has explored, Red Army "cultural evenings" were devoted to singing, dancing, or performing to create a common political understanding and unity among soldiers from different militaries, while the mass version of these evenings involved, for example, cooperative script writing and other activities. From 1931 to 1934, the Red Army School in Ruijin became a center of cultural and ideological creativity.

In mid 1934, the CCP finally was forced by repeated GMD encirclement to consider leaving the Jiangxi Soviet. The decision to abandon the area was not taken lightly, and it was well understood that landlords and previous practices of social hierarchy would make a roaring return in the vacuum left by CCP withdrawal. Those left behind would be subject to the White Terror of reprisal. Mao's base withstood four "extermination" campaigns devised by the GMD military; in 1934, with Nazi German assistance, the GMD finally was able to break through the base's defenses. The Red Army was overwhelmed, and by mid October the evacuation began, even while a rearguard was left behind to do mop-up work, with the hope of getting smuggled to Shanghai afterward. Qu Qiubai, tubercular and too ill to go far, stayed behind; he was captured and shot in 1935 after a brief imprisonment. Many CCP-affiliated women, men, and children were left behind and lost their lives, yet it was again true that the brunt of the terror fell on locals who had participated in the social transformations. Landlord reprisals were particularly vicious.[28]

The occupation of the Soviet by the GMD was ruthless; as Chiang exhorted, "The true nature of the bandit [Communist] is that of a beast. Our bandit suppression is therefore akin to a struggle against beasts, the same as exterminating beasts. It is to save the citizens of the Chinese Republic, to allow them to live as humans and not be

---

28   For who left and who stayed, see Benton, *Mountain Fires*, 14–68.

turned into beasts!"[29] By April 1935, as one GMD report proudly proclaimed of the Jiangxi Soviet area:

> There is not a dwelling that has not been burned, there is not a tree that has not been felled, there is not a fowl or dog that has not been killed, there is not an able-bodied man remaining, no smoke rises from the kitchen chimneys in the alleys and the lanes, the only noise in the fields is the wailing of ghosts.[30]

The crisis of 1934–1935 was demoralizing for the CCP; it represented yet another defeat so soon after the 1927 debacle. The evacuation of Jiangxi—later mythologized as the Long March—took the party and its followers on a circuitous journey through some of the most difficult of China's terrains, with no evident destination. The CCP was looking for a relatively safe haven from GMD harassment and extermination. This finally was found in the Northwest, in one of the poorest and most destitute environments of China. Only 7,000 of the original 100,000 evacuees made it there; large numbers were killed along the way by the pursuing GMD military, the wounded were left along the route, and others dropped out because of fatigue, illness, pregnancy, or disillusionment. Children were left behind in farm households, some were found and reunited with their parents, others were lost in the ensuing chaotic years. In the course of the retreat, Mao secured his position as paramount leader after a series of internal battles that, among others, sidelined Li Lisan and the Moscow clique, thus solidifying the rural revolutionary strategy Mao favored.

In October 1935, over one year after their ouster from Jiangxi, several Red Army fronts met in Shaanxi Province, near Yan'an. In a flourish of good humor and to honor Peng Dehuai, who had led his Red Army front into an alliance with the Northwest-based "Ma family clique" of Muslims who together finally vanquished remnants of the pursuing GMD cavalry, Mao wrote the following classically metered poem:

---

29   Cited in Clinton, *Revolutionary Nativism*, 110.
30   Cited in Benton, *Mountain Fires*, 68.

The mountains are high, the roads are long, the gullies are deep
Huge forces gallop through in every direction.
Who is it dares to ride on horseback with drawn sword?
None but our great General Peng![31]

In Yan'an, Mao and the Long March survivors settled into loess caves to rebuild, yet again, the CCP membership, the movement, the momentum, and the semblance of a political presence in China.

Then, the Japanese invaded.

---

31   Cited in Stuart Schram, ed., *Mao's Road to Power*, vol. 5, New York: Routledge, 1998, 37.

Interlude: The War of Resistance against Japan

Life is the root [*genben*/根本] of spirit; if life lacks rationality, spirit lacks vitality and wholesomeness.

—GMD's Guiding Principles[1]

When the season changed, so changed the strategy
We took off our uniforms and put on the old cotton cloth . . .
A shout of KILL! and we'll fight back
Rakes and spades will be mobilized:
This time our army will come out from the fields
They will be like storms and hurricanes.

—CCP guerilla song (1939)[2]

On July 7, 1937, the Japanese provoked an incident at Marco Polo Bridge, known as the "7/7 incident." With forces already surrounding Beijing and Tianjin—Boxer Protocol provisions of 1901 allowed the powers to station their troops along rail lines—the Japanese had engaged in military maneuvers on July 6, during which one of their soldiers went missing. The Japanese demanded permission to go look for him and were denied; while the Japanese soldier showed up in camp a little later, a battle already was under way. The tiny Chinese garrison at Wanping was overwhelmed. Conventionally known as the beginning of the War of Resistance against Japan, the 7/7 incident led

---

1 Tsui, *China's Conservative Revolution*, 138. These principles were part of the GMD's spiritual mobilization campaigns to gain national support for resistance against Japan.

2 Tr. Mr. Zin-may Zau, cited in W. H. Auden and Christopher Isherwood, *Journey to a War*, London: Faber & Faber, 1973 [1939], 195.

to the full-scale invasion of China, an event that fascists and militarists in the Japanese government had long desired.

Indeed, prior to July 1937, uncontested Japanese aggression in the North already had so enraged the Manchuria warlord Zhang Xueliang that he and others used the occasion of Chiang Kaishek's December 1936 visit to Xi'an to kidnap him and coerce him into turning GMD attention away from "bandit extermination" and toward the Japanese threat. The kidnapping forced Chiang into negotiations with Zhou Enlai, Mao's closest comrade and the CCP representative sent from Yan'an, on the formation of a new United Front. This Second United Front was to be structured differently from the first, which had ended in such bloodshed a decade earlier. Formed on the principle of a "bloc without," each entity was to retain its own integrity, and the unity between them was to be achieved based on negotiated rules of cooperation. Chiang agreed under captive duress, was released, and returned in Zhang's company to Nanjing. (Zhang was condemned to house arrest for his role in the kidnapping.) There was relief in Nanjing over the changed priorities; and meanwhile, Zhou returned a hero to Yan'an.

The Second United Front, whose terms were finalized only well into 1937, meant many things. For one, it treated the GMD and CCP as equally lawful entities. This was no small concession on Chiang's part, while it also required the CCP to modify their virulently anti-GMD stance. Mao felt it necessary to explain this modification over and over to a CCP military nurtured on hatred of the GMD; and Chiang, too, had to engage a good deal of ideological work to convince his military that the CCP was no longer the target of annihilation. Second, the United Front also loosened travel controls to Yan'an through GMD-policed territories, allowing thousands of leftist intellectuals and others to come and go far more freely than previously possible. Third, this United Front required the GMD and the CCP to each operate in their own spheres, thus conceding territorial control to each party's claimed geographical scope around a putative war front. Yet the definition of whose sphere was where was not always clear: styles of warfare were entirely different—the GMD engaged in positional battles and the CCP mostly in mobile or guerilla war—so the "front" was not stably identifiable. The United Front, while fragile, nevertheless ensured for a time that the militaries under each party's direction would concentrate on combating the Japanese rather than on slaughtering each other.

As the Japanese practiced it, the war in and for China was a total war against a population and a nation-state, a crucial step in an envisioned global war, whose resolution would carve the world into culturally racialized spheres of influence and extraction: Japan was to rule Asia on behalf of the yellow and brown people, and the white people would rule elsewhere. In Japanese estimation, a quick victory in China could be secured through the complete demoralization of the Chinese people; this, they thought, would induce the GMD into unconditional surrender. From there, it was postulated, the GMD would join Japan in eliminating the Communists. In the first years, it certainly looked as if China would fall to Japanese occupation. With inferior arms, a factionalized military, ongoing political division, a population far from unified or even ideologically primed for a defense of the motherland, and a weak economy dominated for a century already by foreign powers, China did not present as a formidable foe. After the Japanese invasion, no allies came to China's aid. The European powers, dealing with the Nazi threat and soon German territorial advances, had nothing to spare for their Asian colonies, which, from Indochina to Indonesia and Hong Kong to Singapore and Malaya, were relinquished to the Japanese with nary a fight. The Soviets provided advice and direction to the CCP—often ignored by Mao—but stayed on the sidelines. The United States remained smugly ensconced in its isolation, proclaiming the Japan-China affair to be a regional matter that concerned it not while continuing to supply Japan with crucial materiel until the late 1930s. The Japanese were able to convince one wing of Chiang's GMD to form a collaborationist government, set up in 1940 in Nanjing under the leadership of Wang Jingwei, a former close associate of Sun Yatsen, who now believed Communism to be the most dangerous domestic and global threat and who thus was willing to accept Japan's offer of anti-Communist pan-Asian fraternity. Despite all, the GMD-CCP United Front held just long enough to allow the Chinese a chance to organize themselves. Instead of a quick victory, then, what Japan got was an eight-year-long slog that sucked up men and treasure while laying waste to huge swaths of China and Asia generally.

The main Japanese assault rushed down the Northeast corridor, then inland along the Yangzi and by navy along the coast. The CCP had no presence in this area, and thus the brunt of the first assault waves fell completely on the GMD military and areas under their rule. By December 1937, the Japanese armies had arrived at Nanjing. They entered the GMD's capital city, now abandoned by Chiang's military, which was in full-scale retreat toward Shanghai. Upon a defenseless civilian population, Japanese troops there perpetrated what is known as the "Nanjing Massacre," during which an estimated 200,000 Chinese civilians were butchered and countless women raped and, if they survived that, turned over to sex slavery organized in what the Japanese labeled "comfort stations." While hardly unique in its barbarism—the British in South Africa, the Belgians in the Congo, and the Americans in the Philippines and during their own continental expansion, among many others, had long since practiced tactics of mass civilian brutalization—the terror was nevertheless breathtaking. It established brutality as an official Japanese military policy, covered by the pithy slogan Three Alls: "kill all, burn all, loot all."

The GMD, with a traditional military hierarchy and structure, recruited young men from villages by a draft requiring men to volunteer or to be dragooned into the forces. With spiritual exhortations like the one cited at the beginning of this section, recruits were thrown into battle after minimal training. Women were encouraged to support their men and nation with productive economic activities and to exhibit the virtue and comity expected of good wives and wise mothers. The professional army—a portion of which had been trained under Nazi German guidance during the Communist extermination campaigns of the early 1930s—were comparatively better off, although their commanders were often competitively uncooperative with one another, and the troops were neither well-enough equipped nor well-enough led to be entirely effective against a stronger enemy. In retreat from Nanjing, GMD troops defended Shanghai as long as possible, but they ultimately were defeated. It is estimated that almost 60 percent of Chiang's troops were lost in the first six to eight months of the war.[3]

The GMD withdrew to Wuhan in early 1938. When the strategic city of Xuzhou was lost in May, panic ensued. In June, Chiang ordered the dykes along the Yellow River to be blown up, in a bid to slow Japanese advances toward Wuhan. The river flooded the region, leaving 800,000 Chinese dead and 12 million refugees wandering the countryside; meanwhile, the soil was rendered infertile for decades, and the river was redirected hundreds of kilometers out of its original path.[4] A great famine in the area ensued. Japan's army was barely importuned. By late 1938, the GMD was in orderly retreat inland, arriving finally at the new wartime capital, Chongqing, in the mountains of Sichuan Province, where geographical features could keep party and government headquarters relatively safe for a time (even though it was bombed ceaselessly by the Japanese). The eastern coast and Yangzi River delta were substantially abandoned to Japanese occupation.

Following the troops' lead, dismantled munitions and steel factories, art treasures from the coastal museums, university libraries and archives, and many things of productive and cultural-patrimonial value were transported westward by oxcart, shoulder pole, and the occasional train or truck. Civilian refugees streamed there too, seeking sanctuary, remunerated work, and relief. Factories were rebuilt into mountainsides—hollowed out by men and women wielding nothing more than shovels, hands, and woven straw baskets—to keep the productive forces safe from Japanese air assaults; leading universities combined their faculties into one "unified university" (lianda/联大), to continue the education of elite youth in the far Southwest city

---

3   Zarrow, *China in War and Revolution*, 306.

4   Diana Lary, "Drowned Earth: The Strategic Breaching of the Yellow River Dyke, 1938," *War in History* 8:2, April 2001, 191–207.

of Kunming.[5] A number of liberal and conservative cultural figures followed the GMD westward, while many others remained in the temporary safety of Shanghai's foreign concessions, which came under Japanese rule only in late 1941 with the declaration of war against the Allies announced with the bombing of Pearl Harbor.

With the threat of the fall of Wuhan in 1938, Mao had suggested to Chiang that the United Front take the form of mass mobilization to assist in the city's defense. He cited as a precedent the recent defense of Madrid by the Republicans against Franco. At the time, a number of leftist European cultural figures, some of whom were recently relocated to China from Spain, and many of whom were waiting to go to Yan'an or to be attached to Mao's New Fourth Army, were gathered in Wuhan. They were sympathetic to Mao's position.[6] Yet, leery of leftists and ever suspicious of uncontrollable masses, Chiang refused Mao's suggestions. In the event, Wuhan fell, Chiang went inland to Chongqing, and Mao consolidated in Yan'an. The European contingent departed.

With a reprieve from GMD pressure, Mao and the CCP were able to build a society in Yan'an that put into practice a good number of socialist principles, all the while devising a war strategy that, while seemingly hopeless, was commensurate to the conditions of the China they governed and hoped later to rule. This strategy was called "protracted war," and it was an elaboration of "total war"—not as pure destruction, but in the opposite idiom, as a people's war of creative construction.[7] Militarily modeled on the "luring the enemy deep" tactic used during the GMD encirclements of the Jiangxi Soviet, in its simplest form, the idea was that China had two unambiguous advantages with regard to an invading enemy: its expansive territory and

---

5   John Israel, *Lianda: A Chinese University in War and Revolution*, Palo Alto, CA: Stanford University Press, 1998.

6   *Journey to a War* evokes the atmosphere of 1938 Wuhan. Martha Gelhorn and Ernst Hemingway also made their way to China at the time; see Gelhorn's *Travels with Myself and Another*.

7   Mao Zedong, "On Protracted War" (1938), available at *Marxists Internet Archive*, marxists.org.

large population. The method of protracting the war through time and in geographical space would allow the Chinese to unify and gather force: it thus called not for direct confrontation with the enemy but rather for luring the enemy deep into territory and populations they did not know and could not trust. Once there, the enemy could be harassed, dispersed, and conquered by guerilla fighters embedded in familiar places among sympathetic people, as the song cited in the epigraph indicates. Hence, unlike the GMD's retreat inland under the slogan of "trading space for time," the CCP did not move through and abandon places so as to strengthen elsewhere; rather, it called for troops to melt into the population, live and produce among them, learn from them, and educate them, as well. "Protracted war" was a people's war, not merely as military method but as a theory of history and a practice of intervening in the present. As historian Wang Hui puts it, "People's war was a process that created a new political subject with its own political structure and forms of self-expression."[8] That is, the very process of popular mobilization produced subjects of a new politics, through which "the people" would become an empowered political mass with expressive and active potentials.

The War of Resistance against Japan raged to great destructive effect. With the bombing of Pearl Harbor in December 1941, the "orphaned islands" (gudao/孤岛) of the foreign concessions in Shanghai were overtaken by the Japanese. Shanghai was swollen with refugees: Jews from Germany, refused entry elsewhere, landed in Shanghai, where they were put in squalid urban camps, soon to be joined by the hugely wealthy Baghdadi and Iranian Jews, who had long since made Shanghai their home and source of fabulous fortune, but who were abandoned by their white non-Jewish brethren to their fates as now-despised Jews. Meanwhile, civilians jammed the city, prompting the foreign powers to defend the exclusivity of their concessions with growing racist belligerence. Through it all, Soviet, Korean, and Chinese Communist, Nationalist, and collaborationist

---

8   Wang Hui, *China's Twentieth Century*, ed. Saul Thomas, London and New York: Verso, 2016, 136.

spies created cosmopolitan havoc. By early 1942, leftist intellectuals streamed out toward Yan'an, where they were welcomed with ambivalent ardor; foreign nationals on the wrong side of the Allies/Axis divide were interned. Shanghai became Japanese and remained utterly decadent.

And yet, the bombing of Pearl Harbor also brought China into the globally recognized ambit of the Western war, called World War II. With that, the United States needed China to continue to pin down Japanese troops in ever-greater numbers, so as to buy time to rebuild its Pacific Fleet and put itself on a wartime footing. Madame Chiang was sent to lobby the US Congress—her 1943 speech in Washington, DC, is justly celebrated for its elegance and oratorical achievements— until supplies, assistance, and advice started flowing to Chongqing, even if at an extortionist lend-lease cost that forced the GMD into ever-heavier indebtedness. The USSR, betrayed in the Nazi-Soviet Nonaggression Pact when Germany invaded in June 1941, was pinned down, fighting for survival. The CCP got nothing in terms of aid. Nevertheless, slowly but surely, the tide of war changed. And the United Front frayed beyond repair.

The Second Sino-Japanese War was not just an invasion, an occupation by a foreign power, a would-be colonization, or a state resistance to those. Rather, the war provided the conditions for a fundamental disordering of China's social world that led to the potential for different kinds of reorderings.[9] Unlike the social disorderings since the mid-nineteenth-century Taipings, the anti-Japan war for the first time socially and politically inscribed a highly contested ideological sense of "China" as a national state that could mobilize a popular defense against a foreign enemy. In the aftermath, the GMD's failure to secure China has been seen as evidence of its failures in the war, while the CCP's victory in the postwar civil conflict has allowed it to bask in the glory of the defeat of Japan. Yet, as historian Brian Tsui

---

9   Diana Lary, *The Chinese People at War*, Cambridge, UK: Cambridge University Press, 2010; Rana Mitter, *China's War with Japan, 1937–1945: The Struggle for Survival*, London: Allen Lane, 2013. For contextualization, see Aaron Moore's review, "China's War with Japan, 1937–1945: The Struggle for Survival," *Reviews in History*, history.ac.uk.

points out, at war's end in 1945, both the GMD *and* the CCP were potential beneficiaries of the historical opportunity to reorder China.[10] However, the ways that each turned the postwar into revolutionary capacity took utterly different paths.

---

10   Tsui, *China's Conservative Revolution*, 115.

CHAPTER 5

The 1949 Revolution

> We have closed our ranks and defeated both domestic and foreign oppressors through the People's War of Liberation and the great people's revolution, and now we are proclaiming the founding of the People's Republic of China . . . Ours will no longer be a nation subject to insult and humiliation. We have stood up. Our revolution has won the sympathy and acclaim of the people of all countries. We have friends all over the world.
>
> —Mao Zedong (1949)[1]

> To tell the truth, never, in China or abroad, has there been a revolutionary party as decrepit and degenerate as we [the Guomindang] are today; nor one as lacking spirit, lacking discipline, and even more, lacking standards of right and wrong as we are today. This kind of party should long ago have been destroyed and swept away!
>
> —Chiang Kaishek (1948)[2]

The Chinese Communist Party and the Guomindang built different societies during the war. After the war, their respective approaches yielded different results. Through its "people's war" approach, the CCP had managed to gain the wary hope and conditional trust of large swaths of China's ordinary people—those they had already governed in the North during the Yan'an and war years and those they were newly encountering as the civil war dragged on from 1946 to 1949. By contrast, although the GMD had secured in 1943 the full renunciation of the post–Opium War "unequal treaties" signed at gunpoint with the various imperialist powers, the Nationalists gained

---

1   Mao Zedong, "The Chinese People Have Stood Up!" (September 21, 1949), available at *Marxists Internet Archive*, marxists.org.

2   Cited in Lloyd Eastman, "Who Lost China? Chiang Kai-shek Testifies," *China Quarterly* 88, December 1981, 658–68.

only weary acquiescence after the war and, soon, popular revulsion—from those already in their Chongqing ambit and those they returned to rule in the East. To be sure, the postwar conditions of the country were disastrous. Some 15 to 20 million Chinese—civilian and military—had been killed, and over 95 million were displaced as refugees. The productive capacity of the country was destroyed or severely compromised, and social order was in a deep state of collapse. After a brief moment when a political commitment to unity was reaffirmed by both sides, the final fratricide could no longer be postponed. The ensuing civil war would add 2.5 million more casualties and yet further mass displacements to the wartime totals.

In 1945, the GMD was assisted by the United States military in receiving the surrenders of Japanese troops around the country. Rushing to reclaim and exploit the major resources of Manchuria, among other places, they commandeered the factories, mills, and other sites of production hitherto run by the Japanese, privately pocketing the profits and continuing slave-like labor conditions, albeit now in the name of Nationalism. Strikes and street protests were violently suppressed. At the same time, the GMD also continued conscriptions of rural manpower from decimated villages to rebuild their military strength. The CCP, for its part, hurried into the Manchurian hinterlands and other locations, attempting to install its own administrative hegemony, focusing on organizing peasants for land reform against collaborator and rapacious landlords. The GMD recovered the cities, including Shanghai and Nanjing; the CCP remained headquartered in remote Yan'an, as guerilla activists spread through the countryside. The US-sponsored Marshall Mission attempted to broker a peace, with Zhou Enlai negotiating on the CCP's behalf in Nanjing. But in 1946, the GMD insisted on convening the National Congress with delegates elected before the war (thus without CCP participation), and the Communists refused to recognize the Congress as legitimate. Tensions rose. When General Marshall left China in mid 1947—forced to retrench by US domestic politics—hope for political unification evaporated.

Clashes across the country resumed. With their better-equipped troops, the GMD was expected to win easily. However, these battles more and more often resulted in mass defections of GMD troops with their weapons to the CCP side, soon changing the balance of forces. Symbolically, Yan'an was captured by the GMD in March 1947, but by then the CCP was far along in its "countryside surrounding the cities" strategy, gaining rural adherents because of its land reforms and pro-peasant practices. As Deng Xiaoping, then a commander in the People's Liberation Army (PLA), summed up the situation in 1948:

> We had worked only in some of the guerilla areas, yet all the people supported us, digging half the ditches, for example . . . They gave us every bit of grain they could spare, saying it did not matter if they suffered from hunger so long as they could help us. To help us solve the problem of firewood, people even pulled down their houses without hesitation and gave us the wood. The people also undertook other arduous tasks for the campaign, including repairing roads and transporting grain.[3]

Meanwhile, the GMD increasingly was isolated in islands of unsustainable urban occupation.

The final civil war years were marked by endemic urban and rural chaos, as well as widespread GMD corruption marked by such extreme individual and systemic bureaucratic venality—for example, wholesale prices in Shanghai increased 7.5 million times in the space of three years, forcing ordinary people to fill wheelbarrows with worthless cash to make purchases, while GMD-aligned merchants and bureaucrats enriched themselves by hoarding and manipulating markets—that even Chiang Kaishek was disgusted, as cited at the top of the chapter. No matter how terrified the liberal petty bourgeoisie or the big capitalist bourgeoisie might have been of the CCP's anti-capitalist policies of dispossession and redistribution, the GMD had lost

---

3   Cited in Delia Karamouzis, *The Shanghai Campaign of 1949*, website, arcgis.com/apps/Cascade/index.html?appid=eb9435f82a484efcbf11fba5d9ea1acd.

urban dwellers' confidence. Young people of all classes flocked to join the CCP's underground organizations, despite the GMD security forces' regular violent roundups of suspected leftists and activists. By the same token, rural landlords—whose assets were immovable and who feared the force of peasant retribution—as well as the city-based opium/criminal gangs and high government officials, continued to hitch their wagons to the GMD, knowing that for them, there was no real alternative.

In April 1948, Yan'an was retaken by the CCP; by September, major ports along China's eastern coast were in CCP hands; by October, most of North China was CCP territory; and by December 1948, Nanjing and Shanghai were being evacuated and the GMD capital relocated to Guangzhou. In May 1949, after a series of masterful military victories, the PLA took Shanghai. The rout was all but complete. GMD soldiers, officers, dependents, as many liquid assets as could be gathered (gold bars, currency reserves, and so on), the cultural patrimony of museums, the archives of libraries: all were collected at various sea and air ports to be transported on available ships and planes to the newly recovered territory of Taiwan, where the GMD chose to retreat in hopes of one day retaking the mainland (*guangfu dalu* / 光复大陆).

Those on Taiwan, having endured fifty years of Japanese colonization, were not immediately unwelcoming toward the GMD; however, the GMD looked upon Taiwan residents as tainted Japanese subjects and treated them as an occupied enemy people. Taiwan's working classes, peasants, intellectuals, and others, hoping to gain some measure of participatory political role in determining their own futures after the Japanese withdrawal, were incensed. In one uprising after another—most spectacularly, in the "2/28 incident" of 1947[4]— they made their opposition to GMD occupation known. The GMD,

---

4   The incident, on February 28, 1947, involved the GMD police killing of an itinerant peddler for selling cigarettes illegally, which sparked demonstrations and ongoing protests that snowballed into an all-out movement of political and social opposition to GMD high-handedness. The GMD responded by sweeping up, imprisoning, and executing a generation of intellectuals and by violently suppressing all others.

however, demonstrated their characteristic intolerance of bottom-up mass mobilization and proceeded to perpetrate what became a decades-long White Terror against those who dared to voice opposition to their rule. The multiple Chinese civil wars—GMD versus CCP, GMD versus Taiwan—that are legacies of 1949 are still not over. They came to an uneasy stalemate in 1949, latently ready to flare in the ensuing seventy years.[5]

There were elements in the CCP who cautioned that an all-out ousting of Chiang's GMD from China was not wise, that it would further destabilize a precarious situation. They were outnumbered by Mao Zedong and the PLA under the leadership of Lin Biao, who argued for a fight to the end. With this position, Mao and his supporters consolidated their strength in the party. All were astonished at the rapidity of the GMD collapse. The CCP, however, also recognized that, having been absent as a political force from cities for almost two decades, they were largely unprepared to administer urban complexities or a national economy. Coming to an accommodation with those technocratic types who did not flee, but who were also not necessarily Communist sympathizers, was necessary. Sociologist Joel Andreas evokes one kind of situation CCP revolutionaries confronted as they entered the cities:

On December 15, 1948, Communist troops advancing on Beijing arrived at the vicinity of Tsinghua University . . . Most members of the Tsinghua faculty were from families of more than modest wealth and social standing, and many were certainly apprehensive about the Communists' declared aim of radically redistributing wealth . . . After years of war, however, many were also hopeful that a new regime would bring order and more honest government . . .

On December 17, a delegation of Communist soldiers came to the Tsinghua campus . . . On one side of the meeting were erudite,

5   Odd Arne Westad, *Decisive Encounters: The Chinese Civil War, 1946–1950*, Palo Alto, CA: Stanford University Press, 2003.

well-groomed intellectuals; on the other side were battle-hardened peasant revolutionaries. The Communist delegation was headed by Liu Daosheng, a peasant from Hunan Province who had joined the communist movement in 1928 and had served as a revolutionary soldier through the grim days of the Long March and the epic guerilla war against the Japanese ... The Tsinghua delegation was headed by Zhou Peiyuan, scion of a wealthy landowning family ... [who] had graduated from Tsinghua in 1924 and had studied physics at the University of Chicago and under Albert Einstein at Princeton ... The delegations ... were in many ways typical of the two very distinct groups who would face each other in the top echelons of Chinese society.[6]

At times somewhat smooth and at other times quite stormy, the mutual accommodations between the revolutionaries and the representatives of elite urban society are part of the story of how the CCP hoped to revolutionize Chinese social relations and fulfill the political-economic expectations of die-hard and ambivalent supporters alike.

In an immediate sense, at the level of everyday life, peasant revolutionary troops entering the cities were greeted by an urban lifestyle that, however compromised by wartime disruption, was more comfortable, more wealthy, more decadent, more "advanced" than anything they had experienced before. In a relatively benign manifestation, as Yuan Xiqin, a CCP soldier, remarked upon her entry into Jinan, no one knew how to turn on the electric lights or how Western-style toilets functioned.[7] In a less benign fashion, CCP troops, accustomed to privations of all sorts, could be lured into the excesses of city life and could claim these as the deserved spoils of war. Aware of the deep danger posed by these temptations, Mao reminded the PLA: "I hope that the revolutionary personnel of the whole country will

---

6   Joel Andreas, *Rise of the Red Engineers: The Cultural Revolution and China's New Class*, Palo Alto, CA: Stanford University Press, 2009, chapter 1.

7   Cited in Feng Keli, "Seeing Red: China's Communist Revolution Captured on Camera," *Sixth Tone*, April 7, 2018, sixthtone.com.

always keep to the style of plain living and hard struggle maintained for more than a decade by the working personnel in Yan'an and the Shaanxi-Gansu-Ningxia Border Region."[8] His warnings were not entirely successful.

At the level of economic policy, the hyperinflation left by the fleeing GMD, achieved by the endless printing of money to finance the war, had to be brought under control. Meanwhile, workers had to get back to work, teachers and students had to return to the classroom, social order had to be reestablished, demobilized soldiers had to be employed, profiteers had to be stopped, opium addiction had to be addressed, and the real and imagined sabotage of productive forces by remaining GMD supporters had to be ferreted out and suppressed. Destitute women—some of whom worked as prostitutes—and children were to be relocated, educated, and given a chance to lead "wholesome" productive lives. This all was to be accomplished even as the gold reserves and other liquid financial assets of the country had been carted off to Taiwan or transferred to safe havens in the United States and Hong Kong.

Already in late September 1949 at the opening of the newly convened People's Congress, Mao had announced, "We have stood up." A few days later, on October 1, 1949—thereafter celebrated as "National Day"—Mao proclaimed: "This government is willing to establish diplomatic relations with any foreign government that is willing to observe the principles of equality, mutual benefit, and mutual respect of territorial integrity and sovereignty."[9] Only the USSR and the Eastern bloc countries established relations with and offered aid to China. Within a year, the Korean War broke out on China's border, and the United States intervened in the civil war on the side of the South. Chinese volunteers were sent to assist the North, leading to pronouncements in the US that China should be nuked and that Chiang Kaishek should be reinstalled in mainland China by

8   Mao Zedong, "Always Keep to the Style of Plain Living and Hard Struggle," *Selected Works of Mao Tse-tung*, vol. 5, Beijing: Foreign Languages Press, 1977.

9   Mao Zedong, "Proclamation of the Central People's Government of the PRC," *People's Daily*, October 2, 1949.

the force of US arms. The Korean War was fought for three long years before a truce was struck at the forty-eighth parallel. The US threw a military cordon around Chiang's Taiwan, offering aid and open markets while patrolling the strait with its navy and stationing troops on the island; it also reversed course in Japan, to make of Japan an ally rather than enemy country. In the gathering storms of the global Cold War—actually a series of hot wars in Asia—Mao's China was embargoed by the US and Europe, and any hope of gaining access to foreign investment or even peaceful coexistence for rebuilding the country was lost. Tensions outside and inside China mounted, while threats—real and imagined—to CCP consolidation and rule made for a poor political climate in 1950 and 1951. Mao was forced to go to Moscow to beg for assistance from Stalin. The aid was meager and came at a high price, yet Mao was in no position to bargain for better. On February 14, 1950, the Sino-Soviet Treaty of Friendship, Alliance and Mutual Assistance was signed. Yet, despite all, the momentous fact remained: the removal of imperialist control from China's territory and institutions marked the first time in over a century that Chinese were in charge of China's territory, polity, and economy.

While the consolidation of a central government and control over the cities were the CCP's first priorities, land reform campaigns were launched and deepened to distribute land to the peasants in accordance with CCP promises and the necessity to get agrarian production back into gear. Indeed, without productive rural stability, food supplies would remain scarce, raw materials could not flow to urban industries, and no future "socialist abundance" could be glimpsed on the horizon. The troops fighting in Korea also needed to be provisioned with food and warm clothing to withstand the brutal Northern climate. The principles of land reform were debated and contested. Ultimately, the question was: Upon what basis should land and tools be distributed? Political economist Lin Chun summarizes:

> The principle of equality drove the project of land reform, in which all farming families and individuals of both sexes held equal rights to land. Achieving this meant categorizing all farmland by size, quality,

and distance for the purposes of distribution and compensation, with the goal of equalizing possession and tax burdens . . . Meanwhile, the process involved a highly charged undertaking of class identification designed to "rely on the poor and landless, ally and stabilize the intermediate, neutralize rich peasants and target the landlords," as the policy slogan went.[10]

Characterized in some areas by huge violence against landlords and rich peasants, the process of land reform resulted by 1952 in 300 million peasants gaining productive control over their own land, with tax burdens decreased by more than half. Grain production soared. Having learned the lessons of Jiangxi (1930s) and of Yan'an (1940s), the basis of the reforms skewed toward the preservation of a "rich peasant economy." Indeed, as Mao put it in March 1950, "If we leave the semi-feudal rich peasants untouched for the time being and deal with them a few years later, we will stand on stronger ground, that is to say, politically we will have more initiative."[11] Another round of reforms would later eliminate the "rich peasant economy."

In addition to its class basis, the land reform was founded upon the principle that the heteronormative family was the basic unit of rural social life. One of the first laws the PRC promoted upon its accession to power was the Marriage Law—allowing women to divorce abusive or unloved husbands and prohibiting child brides, among other provisions; it was considered one of the most progressive pro-woman laws of its time in the world. Nevertheless, the explicit expectation was that happy (hetero) families would produce more efficiently. A closely correlated principle, then, was that the social reproductive functions of rural life were to be fixed in the family, with women's labor enlisted in unremunerated domestic tasks to be

---

10   Lin Chun, "Rethinking Land Reform: Comparative Lessons from China and India," in Mahmood Mamdani, ed., *The Land Question: Socialism, Capitalism and the Market*, MISR Book Series, vol. 5, Kampala: Makerere Institute of Social Research, 2015, eprints.lse.ac.uk/59697.

11   Mao Zedong, "Request for Opinions on the Tactics for Dealing with Rich Peasants," March 12, 1950, available at *Marxists Internet Archive*, marxists.org.

performed in addition to the productive labor they also were expected to engage. In this sense, embedded in the very logic of China's rural socialism—as an integrated economic, social, and ideological system—was a heteronormative form of gendered social relations.[12] In many ways pro-woman, the CCP's socialist state nevertheless was built firmly on patriarchal principles.

The legitimacy the CCP gained in rural society through its thoroughgoing land reform was underscored by the attention it paid to the ideological dimensions necessary to any revolutionary process. For this purpose, Mao exhorted artists to go to the countryside to depict peasants' idealized everyday lives in vibrant color and vigorous activity. The artist Shi Lu produced work exemplary of the trend: the prominence of rural women in his paintings—as objects of gaze, as classed political subjects, as emancipated laboring women—became ubiquitous and contributed to his being sent in 1955 as a socialist cultural ambassador to India.[13] Other cultural workers—journalists, novelists, poets, filmmakers, film projectionists, dramatists, choreographers, dancers, opera singers, and so on—also fanned out across the country to promote socialist values through the creation of new forms of art that were both of and for the revolutionary people. Songs were written to extol collective labor and the new socialist everyday. For example, "The Little Swallow" (*xiao yanzi* / 小燕子), a children's ditty sung in nursery schools to this day, invites the bird to alight upon newly built factories as an advantageous perch from which to celebrate the spring; or "In That Distant Place" (*zai na yaoyuan de difang* / 在那遥远的地方), based on a Kazakh folk tune, became a popular song performed by student groups sent to the countryside to help in land reform and the other mass campaigns of the period.

The Patriotic Health Movement (*aiguo weisheng yundong* / 爱国 卫生运动) also was launched in the early 1950s, to help vanquish

---

12 Tithi Battacharya, ed., *Social Reproduction Theory: Remapping Class, Recentering Oppression*, London: Pluto Press, 2017.

13 Wang Yang, "Urban Subjectivity in Representations of Peasant Women in the Early PRC," paper delivered at CHANGE conference, Brussels Free University, February 15, 2019.

malaria and other hygiene- and disease-related causes of shortened lifespans and crippled bodies. Rural women were trained as midwives, as well, to help infants and mothers survive childbirth.[14] As with most efforts in the postrevolutionary years, the scarcity of resources required creative solutions to problems. In the arena of health and disease control, therefore, basic medicine for the masses was promoted above specialization and fancy technologies.[15] Life expectancy rose precipitously.

Along with the health and cultural-ideological work were mass campaigns to tackle illiteracy. For if the revolutionary people were to take charge not only of their own lives, but of building socialism in China and globally, they would need to read and write and speak and understand at a level of sophistication hitherto unavailable to them. Illiteracy elimination classes (*saomang ban* / 扫盲班) were inaugurated in factories and villages, among grannies and young people, among women along with men, with adults and children attending classes together in the interstices of working hours and domestic labor. Those who knew something taught those who knew less. The 80 percent rate of illiteracy was slowly whittled down, and a simplified Chinese writing system, along with an alphabetic pronunciation scheme (*pinyin*/拼音) based on Mandarin, were standardized and inscribed in all PRC printed matter from the late 1950s onward. (Taiwan and Hong Kong retained traditional forms of writing and different pronunciation notations to maintain their claims on China's true patrimony.)

During the land reform, CCP power was extended down into the smallest hamlet of the country. This was done by mobilizing the peasants themselves in an effort to overthrow not only the economic but the deep cultural power that the landlord-gentry had held for millennia over social life in the villages. "Speaking bitterness" (*suku*/诉苦) meetings were held in every village, encouraging peasants to give

---

14   Gail Hershatter, *The Gender of Memory: Rural Women and China's Collective Past*, Berkeley, CA: University of California Press, 2014.

15   Bu Liping, "Anti-Malaria Campaigns and the Socialist Reconstruction of China, 1950–80," *East Asian History* 39, 2014, eastasianhistory.org.

voice to and find in their individual experiences a collective and systemic source of oppression. Women, who had often understood their suffering as "fate," came to understand gendered oppression as the result of a historically situated, classed patriarchy. While these sessions certainly introduced a standard political vocabulary and repetitive narrative form into the recitals of "before liberation" (pre-1949) suffering and "after liberation" (post-1949) freedom, they also empowered individuals to take charge of their lives through collective action. Having peasants drive the transformations in their own lives socially inscribed the idea that revolution was not removed from rural society, happening far away at the level of the state alone; rather, the revolution was to be lived in the processes and routines of quotidian practice itself. The revolution was socialist life; if it could not be that, it would be nothing. These campaigns were the process through which "the people" (renmin/人民) were created as revolutionary political subjects and a political subjectivity.

The form of state established at this point was called the "people's democratic dictatorship," where "the people" were understood to be the allied revolutionary classes that included everyone except GMD reactionaries/counterrevolutionaries, imperialist supporters, and landlords. As Mao wrote in his 1940 "On New Democracy"—an essay establishing the idea of a mixed economy and united class society that guided much CCP practice in the early 1950s—democracy was reserved for the resolution of problems among "the people" (revolutionary classes), while dictatorship was to be exercised over "reactionaries," or the non-people. "The people"—not a citizenry inscribed in a state-territorial sense, not a cultural category of blood, language, or history, but a category of active revolutionary practice—became an exceedingly important designation. In the early 1950s, "the people" was capacious; it was to narrow and expand and narrow again many times over the course of the Mao years and beyond. Being part of "the people" meant having a role in revolutionary society; being a "non-people" meant being cast out of society, to be reeducated, disciplined, or purged.

*   *   *

From the very beginning of the CCP's accession to power, major ideological and thus practical problems were presented by the contradictions between the revolutionary aspirations of the Communist Party and its developmentalist goals. Mao certainly was pledged to economically develop China, but he wished China to develop without the vast systemic inequalities that capitalism inevitably introduces and reproduces. Development for its own sake was never on Mao's politico-economic horizon. Yet, there were very real policy differences within the Communist Party on this question. Those advocating rapid development at any social cost—the resurgent Moscow clique—were still quite powerful, and frequent intra-party struggles were waged over substantive ideology about the meaning of socialism itself. These conflicts erupted with great consequence very soon after the 1949 conquest of the state. One of the most acute contradictions revolved around the reliance upon extracting resources from the peasantry, whose lives the CCP had pledged to revolutionize and yet whose productivity was crucial to accumulations of surplus necessary for urban industrialization. This posed a theoretical and thus practical impasse all but impossible to overcome. By the same token, the necessity for the urban proletariat to increase production while revolutionizing social relations within the factory to become more democratic also became a contradiction that haunted industrial life. Imbalances in urban/rural relations became an enormous problem, not only because surpluses were exploitatively extracted from the rural to supply the urban, but because the cultural and social advantages of urban life were also thereby enhanced. Even though primary schools were established in the lowest rural villages, higher and better educational opportunities were reserved for urban children, and the best was offered to children of intellectuals and CCP cadres. The reproduction and deepening of inequality in social and spatial terms increasingly appeared to be a consequence of socialist policy, and not only a holdover from the previous system.

Meanwhile, the desire to politically and culturally-ideologically transform the country and its people through the instrumentality of the Communist party-state very quickly began to clash with the transformation of the party into a technocratic bureaucracy that imposed itself on society rather than being organic to it. The danger that CCP cadres would become a privileged class reared its head early. Indeed, the contradictions between the CCP's bureaucratic role and its historical role as the bearer of social-cultural revolution informed and subtended the whole Maoist period. These questions ramified into another arena of insoluble social contradiction: the need for the educated classes to help build the scientific, technological, techno-cratic, creative, literary, and other bases of socialism, even as the inde-pendence and elitism of intellectuals thwarted party discipline and social equality. Sometimes the issues were addressed through mass movements launched to enable or to force intellectuals to be "reedu-cated" in programs designed to culturally and ideologically remold them into "new socialist personhood" (*shehuizhuyi xinren* / 社会主义新人); at other times the issues were left to fester, only to burst into anti-intellectual campaigns later. However it was handled, the contra-dictory space intellectuals occupied—as reproducers of elite knowl-edge, as arrogant and enlightened urban-based cosmopolites, as cultural preservers of traditional and modern forms of class privilege, *and* as necessary contributors to socialism—was intensely fraught and fought.

By 1953, the CCP opted to follow the Soviet path of development: a forced-march modernization plan based on urban-located heavy industry, to be presided over by a centralized state that would allocate and distribute resources according to purely economic, not social, dictates. From 1953 to 1956 the first Five-Year Plan installed this Soviet model, chosen for three reasons. First, it was the only socialist experience then extant; second, the Soviets, providers of the only aid China received, supplied many advisors; and third, the economic weaknesses of China were so huge and China was so globally isolated that rapidly building industrial capacity seemed to be the only answer. After all, industrialization had brought capitalist societies great riches and power; it had assisted the Soviet Union in becoming a superpower; it appeared to be the only possible method of economic development at the time. Due to the embargo on China by the United States and its allies, the Chinese essentially had to produce everything they needed, which led to relative autarky as well as a policy of affirming China's one advantage—its huge population—as a positive economic force rather than a negative economic drag. However, the Soviet centralized "commandist" model created enormous tensions in the revolutionary goals of the CCP by the mid 1950s, and as agricultural production stagnated in the rural areas when the limits of productivity on small plots of land were reached, the CCP began to seek ever-newer methods of increasing agrarian surplus. This led to the amalgamation of the very same plots allotted during land reform into cooperatives and collective farms from 1955 onward. While most peasants did not yet oppose this move—the cooperatives and collectives were voluntary and were based not in production but in distribution—there were holdouts against the trend, as rich peasants who had re-emerged since the land reform began to reassert their economic and cultural prerogatives. Indeed, not only in rural areas but all over the country, as social order stabilized through the 1950s, there was an increasing hierarchization of ranks, salaries, and position that reproduced inequality. The CCP attempted to deal with these mounting material problems through ideological reeducation and coercive exhortation.

Despite problems, social optimism was high. Many cultural figures enthusiastically joined the experiments on the historical and aesthetic possibilities opened by creating a culture adequate to the socialist transformation of China. These experiments took seriously the legitimacy of socialism and attempted to pioneer a set of cultural practices that could give adequate expression to its aspirations. If a previous emphasis in China on new culture in the May Fourth period had located the source and catalyst of China's and the world's cultural renewal in the petty-bourgeois urban literate sphere, and if in Yan'an the turn was toward the mass rural sphere (peasants) as source and catalyst for social transformation and national unity, then by the 1950s, the rural emphasis was enhanced and complicated by the urban proletarian realm. The post-1949 political and cultural environment thus presented new possibilities for petty-bourgeois intellectuals (*wenren*/文人), shaped by and through the May Fourth and Yan'an periods, to transform themselves into new-style culture workers (*wenhua gongzuozhe* / 文化工作者) for socialism.

The challenges of such a transformation were largely articulated through the problem of "massification" (*dazhonghua*/大众化), first developed in Mao's 1942 lectures "Talks at the Yan'an Forum on Art and Literature." Massification included not merely representational issues, although who was to be the protagonist and how she was to perform her role as a new gendered/classed subject was a very important problem. It was not merely about inclusiveness, although the sociological principle of giving voice to different social types was of obvious concern. It was even less about "dumbing down" or "making accessible," although fulfilling reader expectations and selling/surviving in the socialist marketplace were clearly vital points to be considered. Massification, most importantly, was about establishing a dialectical relation between form and content, culture producer and audience. That is, to the extent that peasants and proletariat needed to learn new cultural habits from culture workers, those same workers needed to learn new political and social habits from the peasants and proletariat. This was no one-way street; it was not an enlightenment project undertaken by awakened intellectuals, bestowing the benefits of their erudition upon a benighted population. Rather, writers and other culture producers had to enter into a constantly changing social situation. Indeed, as Mao enjoined in the "Talks," every transformation in the social relations of production required the development of a new consciousness of and in society itself. The task of socialist literature, then, was not merely to reflect but to produce culturally this consciousness and this new society; the changing social situation was not merely the raw material for a crude representational practice, but also the ground upon which the production of a socialist culture adequate to the ever-changing situation had to be engaged as a practice. Narrative—Which facts?

Which stories? Whose voice?—became an overriding concern of this practice.[16]

At the global level, the promise of a non-Soviet, non-sclerotic socialism was an animating feature of the appeal of China's Maoism abroad. Leftists from all over the world—some defying their national governments' bans—streamed to Mao's China to be dazzled not by material plenty or fancy living but by the spiritual-ideological practices of collective life. Simone de Beauvoir visited in late 1955, invited by Zhou Enlai to stop in on her way from the Bandung Conference of nonaligned nations just concluded in Indonesia. Her book *The Long March: An Essay on China* was published in French two years later, and in English a year after that. Knowing nothing of China, de Beauvoir nevertheless managed to convey her appreciation for what she called the "Chinese scenario of a progressive and peaceful disappearance of capitalism."[17] With a blindness to authoritarian practices that is structurally mirrored in generations of Chinese intellectuals' writings about the "freedoms" of the "West" (which pervasively ignore historical and contemporary race, class, gender, and colonial oppressions), de Beauvoir's account of China was characteristic of European leftist enthusiasms of that time.

At the same time, many African leaders allied their racialized anti-imperialist, anti-colonial movements with Mao's China. Egypt recognized China in 1955, and China financially assisted Egypt in the Suez Crisis of 1956; indeed, Cairo was home to the Afro-Asian People's Solidarity Organisation, and a CCP delegation attended its first conference in late 1957.[18] Radical Asian leaders, too, were attracted to Mao's Third World socialism, which posited that formerly colonized countries with uneven economies did not need to pass

---

16 The above paragraph is adapted from Cai Xiang, *Revolution and its Narratives: China's Socialist Literary and Cultural Imaginaries, 1949–1966,* tr. and ed. Rebecca E. Karl and Xueping Zhong, Durham, NC: Duke University Press, 2016.

17 Cited in Julia Kristeva, "Beauvoir in China," tr. Susan Nicholls, kristeva.fr/beauvoir-in-china.html.

18 Joshua Eisenman, "Comrades-in-Arms: The Chinese Communist Party's Relations with African Political Organisations in the Mao Era, 1949–76," *Cold War History,* March 2018.

through a capitalist stage of development in order to leap into social-ism; rather, what socialism required was a strong Communist Party, a mobilized revolutionary people, and a commitment to anti-capitalist justice and equality outside the domination of the United States or the Soviet Union. Placing itself as first among equals in this newly minted "Third World," China became friend and ally to many a postcolonial leader or would-be socialist revolutionary.

Domestic tensions building in the early 1950s served to separate revolutionary theory and goals from social practice in more and more obvious ways. By mid 1955, Mao, disturbed by this separation, gave a speech on agricultural issues, to reset the economic agenda but also to bypass the collective CCP structures of decision making. In Mao's view, the relationship between agriculture and industry was so imbal-anced that it was now time to reignite the revolutionary fires so as to redress the divide. In 1956–1957, the rural collectivization campaign was launched; facing deeper opposition than the cooperatives move-ment that had just concluded, this campaign required a good deal of coercion on the ground. Unlike cooperatives, where each family retained its own means of production, higher-level collectivization and later communization required families to pool all productive resources—including land, animals, implements, and labor—and use them collectively. Administrative structures needed to be put in place to manage these new rural productive formations. Despite opposi-tion, collectivization was completed relatively quickly. With the second Five-Year Plan under discussion, the stage was set for a show-down between Maoists—opposed to continued reliance on the Soviet model—and the Moscow clique—intent to push on with heavy indus-trialization. Enormous battles within and outside the party ensued, soon leading to the ultra-radicalization of the Great Leap Forward of 1958–1961.

In 1957, preparatory to those battles, the Hundred Flowers Campaign was announced. This urban movement was intended to mobilize and encourage intellectuals to offer sympathetic albeit not sycophantic critiques of the party's bureaucratic tendencies. Slowly, intellectuals took the CCP up on the invitation to voice critique: they let one hundred flowers bloom. Criticisms were serious but almost always based on the premise that the CCP was the legitimate ruling party of China and that socialism was the correct path of development. Soon, however, intellectuals were made to regret their boldness, as the party initiated a crackdown against "rightists"—critics of the CCP. It proclaimed the flowers to be weeds, harboring snakes poised to dispense venom on an unsuspecting populace. Intellectuals were rounded up and forced into scripted self-criticisms; they were shipped out to reeducation camps; their careers stalled, they and their families marked as politically untrustworthy from then forward. Whether this was a deliberate strategy to draw out and slap down intellectuals or the contingent outcome of intra-party struggles over ideology and policy remains an unresolvable historical question. What can be noted is that Mao, in this process, managed to mobilize people *against* the CCP precisely as he was trying to push through an economic plan that flew in the face of the Soviet model to which China's central planners were committed. Mao was trying to split and make an end run around the party.

Mao's early 1957 speech "On the Correct Handling of Contradictions among the People" is located at the convergence of his failed attempt to bend the party bureaucracy and turn economic plans toward the new goal of deepening the social revolution. In the speech, Mao says, first, that there is a contradiction between the "leadership and the led"—that is, between the party and the people. An extraordinary statement, by implication this put Mao on the side of the people against the party and appeared as a declaration of war on behalf of the people against the party itself. Second, Mao declared that class struggle, far from being eliminated by socialism, in fact remains and mutates form under socialism. Socialist class struggle was not based in ownership or private property, which had been eliminated by the revolutionary transformation of social relations after 1949. Socialist class struggle was based in ideology, where class was more a question of revolutionary consciousness and activism than a socioeconomic category. In locating class in ideology, the category was more malleable and potentially revolutionary, as well as more arbitrary and potentially dangerous. In this instance, Mao's intention was to curb party prerogative and re-establish socioeconomic goals in contradistinction to the technocratic developmentalists. This is the context in which the radical—and disastrous—Great Leap Forward (GLF) was launched.

The GLF was a theoretical experiment and a practical failure. As a theoretical endeavor, the GLF was based in an attempt to find a theory for a specifically socialist economics that uses categories derived from capitalism—value, price, tax, and so on—but does not replicate the necessary imbalances and produced inequalities of capitalism. What the mechanisms of the socialist economic laws were to be—state, market, virtue—was never resolved. However, the search for a socialist economics was animated by Mao's theory of "disequilibrium." The antithesis to planned economies, "disequilibrium" calls for revolutionary leaps rather than linear progress. A rejection of plodding Soviet-style urban industrialization, the theory of leaps requires not only heightened productivity but heightened ideological commitments. Consciousness was to lead production: "More, quicker, better, thriftier" (*duokuai haosheng* / 多快好省) and "Dare to think, dare to act" (*ganxiang gangan* / 敢想敢干) were two of the more ubiquitous slogans of the time. Leaps were to emerge from the rural areas, as Mao reaffirmed his belief that "the true sources for revolutionary social transformation reside in the peasantry and that the countryside is the main arena where the struggle to achieve socialism and communism will be determined."[19] At the level of practice, the GLF transformed the organization of production into integrated communist forms and put production on a militarized footing so as to shock the country into higher productivity. The major practical point was to even out the rural/urban imbalances through what was called "the urbanization of the countryside and the ruralization of the cities."[20]

19   Maurice Meisner, *Mao's China and After: A History of the People's Republic*, 3rd ed., New York: Free Press, 1999, 214.
20   Ibid., 212.

What ultimately transpired was nightmarish. Agricultural production plummeted, local reporting of crop yields was widely falsified, drought took hold, and food became scarce. Backyard furnaces melted woks and cooking implements without producing anything usable. Labor was siphoned off to build huge dams and other infrastructure that, however much they were needed, became net drains on human resources at the time. Was the GLF a deliberate attempt by Mao to kill off huge numbers of people, undertaken because he was a heartless tyrant?[21] Was the GLF doomed to failure by its very design? Or was its spectacular failure an outcome of a series of contingent political, social, and environmental circumstances?[22] The arguments rage in polarized ideological and disputed empirical detail. What is clear is that many millions of mostly peasants died of starvation due to a profound famine (the numbers are in great dispute); many millions of others, urban and rural, suffered stunted physical and intellectual growth because of malnourishment; and, along with the huge human toll, the political-social cost was also enormous. Mao alienated his most trusted comrades, including the redoubtable General Peng Dehuai, who tried to warn him in 1959 that the movement was far from achieving its utopian goals and who thereupon was accused of petty-bourgeois fanaticism and purged. The country's economy all but collapsed, and food had to be imported from Australia at huge debt-financed expenditure. Tensions with the Soviet Union came to a head over the meaning and process of achieving socialism and communism, with Mao proclaiming that China had entered communism and Soviet CP secretary Nikita Krushchev mocking him for the claim. Soviet loans were called in for repayment, stretching China's meager finances to the limit; Soviet advisors were withdrawn; aid was halted; a border war was threatened and eventually fought. The Sino-Soviet split was complete. Tibet was invaded

---

21   See Frank Dikkötter, *Mao's Great Famine: The History of China's Most Devastating Catastrophe, 1958–62*, London: Walker & Company, 2010; Yang Jisheng, *Tombstone: The Great Chinese Famine, 1958–1962*, New York: Farrar, Strauss, & Giroux, 2013.

22   Carl Riskin. "Seven Questions about the Chinese Famine of 1959–61," *China Economic Review* 9:2, 1998.

and occupied and the Dalai Lama forced to flee; India objected and in 1962 fought a losing border battle with the PRC. The island of Quemoy (*Jinmen* / 金门), heavily militarized by the GMD on Taiwan, became a flash point, and the United States Navy seemed poised to contribute to the outbreak of full hostilities. That eventuality was avoided, but all of Taiwan, the strait, and the Fujian coast became a tense military zone of frequent small-scale clashes and daily dueling propaganda wars. The GMD's noose around Taiwanese society tightened; the CCP's paranoia about spies and counterrevolutionary infiltrations escalated. The US covert war in Vietnam was now in full swing, and while it was kept secret from US citizens, it was no secret to the Chinese, who offered to help train the Viet Minh and host Ho Chi Minh.

A politically weary and economically devastated populace—unaware for the most part of the dimensions of the GLF disaster, which were carefully hidden from view—was grateful to resume life along a less exacting and more predictable political and economic track after 1961. In what one historian has called the "Thermidorian reaction" (1962–1965),[23] bureaucratic rule and prerogatives were resumed as the norm of socialist life in post-GLF China. Old-style party technocrats such as Deng Xiaoping and Liu Shaoqi re-established the commanding heights of the state in directing the economy, and yet certain features of the GLF such as rural communes and urban work units were retained as administrative conveniences, although the bases of their productive and social activities were regathered under the aegis of the centralized state, and any autonomy of decision making was curtailed. Vestiges of the industrialization of the countryside, including small factories that soaked up seasonal labor, remained, although their profits and products were less integrated into the communes and rather were appropriated into the centralized economy. The collective canteens, intended during

---

23 Meisner, *Mao's China and After*, part 4. For further contextualization, see Rebecca E. Karl, "China," in Andrew Pendakis, Jeff Diamanti, and Imre Szeman, eds., *Bloomsbury Companion to Marx*, London: Bloomsbury Press, 2018.

the GLF to alleviate women's cooking and household burdens and to "free" their labor for public production, were abolished (they never worked very well, in any case), although collective childcare arrangements continued, having proved to be popular among childbearing women and deputized grannies and grandpas alike. The vast mobilization of labor power into the workforce—male and female—remained a cornerstone of China's post-GLF socialist practice. Female workers able to achieve productive output comparable to their male counterparts were christened "iron women" and celebrated across the nation; some were even sent abroad as exemplary ambassadors of what socialism could do for women. Films featuring such women were produced, the most popular being *Song of the Reservoir* (*Shuiku shang de gesheng* / 水库上的歌声), in which labor heroine Gao Lanxiang extols the GLF virtues of hard work, diligence, and thrift.[24]

Meanwhile, the system of household registration (*hukou*/户口), established during the GLF to lock peasants into their localities and prevent them from flooding into cities as famine refugees, became an unalterable feature of life from then onward. *Hukou* came to manage population mobility of all sorts; it was underpinned at this time by a system of rationing that ensured all urban residents properly employed by work units (*danwei*/单位) received a minimum amount of staple foods and goods, to allow for the relatively smooth reproduction of proletarian and bureaucratic labor power. As these goods were not available on the market, those without proper *hukou* rationing had no access to necessities. The state guaranteed a certain price for peasant output through the ration system, but because of *hukou* peasants were now peasants for life. Nationwide, a huge baby boom got under way, and because of better midwifery a larger-than-ever number of women survived childbirth, and many more babies survived infancy.

*   *   *

---

24   *Song of the Reservoir*, Changchun Film Studio, 1958. See Matthew D. Johnson, "Cinema and Propaganda during the Great Leap Forward," in J. A. Cook et al., eds., *Visualizing Modern China*, New York: Rowman & Littlefield, 2014.

The first seventeen years of socialism fundamentally transformed the social relations of production and the material realities of social life in China. It is particularly important, then, to recall that China's 1949 Revolution was never purely a nationalist endeavor. It was of course based in and on the given premises of China's historical-territorial circumstances in the mid twentieth century. Yet, the 1949 Chinese revolution aspired to socialism, an internationalist movement and ideology that is local, national, regional, and global in its commitments to the vanquishing of the dominance of capitalism as a differentially lived economic, cultural, political, and social form the world over. In this sense, China's socialism of the 1949–1965 era was profoundly local, as it had to incorporate and transform specific peasant lifeworlds, habits, cultures, and customs into the foundations of a very partially industrialized and very uneven petty-bourgeois urban sphere. It was also fundamentally global, as it opposed capitalism and was embedded in the unfavorable conditions of the world at that time, cut in two between a fractious Communist movement and a divided but powerful capitalist global system. It is the incommensurability among these levels that constituted the historical space in which China's socialism strove to come into being.

The "mobilization structure" of China's socialist transformation required the active participation of all the elements of society.[25] This presented an opportunity to shape lifeworlds as well as an endless demand on people's time and energy; it was an ethical hope and an imposed responsibility. At its foundations stood local social practices and economic arrangements that could not simply be steamrolled into a new form without losing the confidence and support of local people; instead, the given local situations needed to be shaped and reshaped through active and careful political, cultural, and economic work. There was intentionality, as the ideological commitments to socialism were serious; and there was contingency, as local circumstances rarely conformed neatly to centrally devised plans. The sought transformations were as quotidian as they were abstract, and they

---

25   Cai Xiang, *Revolution and its Narratives.*

created new obstacles and problems, new material realities on the ground. Cultural workers became preoccupied with the presentation of these different levels in narrative form. In their writings, dramas, and cinematic efforts, social tensions were maintained in the service of plot, but they increasingly refrained from making politically regressive social types complex by representing such figures as absolutely evil. It was this fine narrative line—Who is evil and who is good? How to tell that story in a historically acceptable fashion?—that became the trip wire for the next large revolutionary movement, the Great Proletarian Cultural Revolution of 1966–1976.

Interlude: The Invasion of Tibet (1959)

> Chinese should go back to China;
> Tibetans are the rightful owners of Tibet;
> Tibetans are capable of taking care of all their affairs;
> China has no right whatsoever inside Tibet;
> Tibetan women will continue with their struggle
> until the Chinese stop interfering in Tibetan affairs.
>
> —Tibetan women's group (March 1959)[1]

On March 12, 1959, thousands of Tibetan women surrounded the Dalai Lama's palace in Lhasa to protest Chinese rule and protect their spiritual leader. Within days, armed conflict was engaged between Tibetan rebels and the People's Liberation Army (PLA). On March 17, the Dalai Lama escaped. Traveling across some of the harshest landscapes on earth, pursued the whole way by Chinese troops, the twenty-three-year-old Dalai Lama and a small entourage reached safety in India, where they soon established a government in exile. Indians, angered by the repression in Tibet, rallied in their thousands to protest in New Delhi. Monks in the Tibetan plateaus and mountains armed themselves against the PLA invasion; they were forced by mid April to surrender or be massacred. Large numbers of refugees streamed into India to join their leader in exile, thus aggravating already-outstanding border tensions between India and China. By May 1959, remaining Tibetan rebels, who had been under siege for two months in the Potala Palace in Lhasa, surrendered to PLA troops. The number of Tibetans who died in these events is hotly disputed: numbers in the 85,000 range are cited by some, although judicious historians cannot find corroboration. However many died, it is

---

1 "The Genesis of the Tibetan Women's Struggle for Independence," Tibetan Women's Association official website, tibetanwomen.org.

indisputable that in 1959 Tibet was violently "liberated," pacified, and occupied by the PLA. In the ensuing decades, there have been a number of mass anti-Chinese uprisings in Tibet, most recently in 1987 and 2008. All were savagely suppressed.

The 1959 events did not emerge from nowhere. Well before 1950–1951, when the PLA occupied Tibet as part of the national territorial unification of China under the PRC government, the status of Tibetan sovereignty was already at issue. The Republic under Chiang Kaishek had always laid weak claim to Tibet as an inalienable part of territorial "China," a legacy of Sun Yatsen's and other Republican leaders' convictions that the Qing Empire's loose boundaries should become the hard territorial borders of the new Chinese nation-state. Yet because Chiang's government could not enforce the claim, Tibetan leaders had never turned their de facto independence into anything diplomatically solid. From nearby India, the British colonial government had decided that Tibet was geographically strategic, culturally exotic, and economically useless; meanwhile, the United States began to eye Tibet as a conduit into China, but only after the CCP's seizure of power in the mainland. In culturally ethnic Tibetan communities outside the plateau, in Kham (western Sichuan Province) and Amdo (Gansu and Qinghai Provinces), Chiang's military had cultivated allies, including those who had assisted in the GMD's anti-Communist campaigns of the 1930s and 1940s. The Khampa, often chafing against Lhasa's dominance over questions of culture, religion, land, and lordship, also were episodically enlisted to contest the Dalai Lama's hegemony.

With the CCP's post-1949 consolidation of control over the territory of China (minus Hong Kong, Macau, and Taiwan), Kham and Amdo were subjected to the same land reforms and other revolutionary transformative treatments as the rest of China. By contrast, political Tibet (on the plateau) was made to sign a Seventeen-Point Agreement in 1951 acknowledging that Tibet was part of China and that Tibet would not collude with imperialist powers, but also allowing Tibet limited autonomy to preserve its political, cultural, religious, and economic forms. A functioning feudal theocracy of sorts, this gave the Dalai Lama and the monasteries leeway to extract taxes and religious dues as usual; to educate children in Tibetan language, culture, and religion; and to continue the forms of land tenure that tied Tibetans to place. PLA troops garrisoned in Lhasa and elsewhere soon came into conflict with residents, monks, and monasteries, with tensions emerging from Communist ideological commitments to oust feudalism and feudal social relations, as well from the Han chauvinist racism toward Tibetans, whom the PLA—and CCP leaders in Beijing—regarded as an uncivilized people. In Chinese eyes, Tibetans' refusal to accept their own backwardness and their reluctance to transform their serf-like enslavements and loyalty to religious leaders were frustrating and proved Tibetans unfit for self-rule.

The general radicalization of the late 1950s all over China led to policies that contravened Tibetan autonomy and the Seventeen-Point Agreement. Existing tensions were aggravated. When the Dalai Lama visited India in 1956 to celebrate the 2,500 year anniversary of the Buddha's birth, the PLA tightened its grip on Tibetan life. Premier Zhou Enlai was tasked with enticing the Dalai Lama to return to Tibet, which he did. However, at the same time, in Kham and Amdo, rebellious factions were organizing under the aegis of the CIA, part of the US Cold War destabilization of China; they were assisted by GMD agents, smuggled into China by US forces encamped in Indochina. When these CIA-backed rebellions were quashed by the PLA, remaining armed Tibetans fled to Lhasa, where they linked up with those elements of the Tibetan political leadership who had never been happy about any aspect of the Seventeen-Point Agreement.[2] The GLF, whose radicalism was imposed without regard for the Seventeen Points, crashed into Tibet as a package of "democratic reforms," purportedly to free Tibetan serfs from feudal servitude. It was unilaterally rejected by Tibetan political and religious leaders and by most civilians as well.

---

2   Chen Jian, "The Tibetan Rebellion of 1959 and China's Changing Relations with India and the Soviet Union," *Journal of Cold War Studies* 8:3, 2006, 54–101; Tsering Shakya, *The Dragon in the Land of Snows*, New York: Penguin, 2000; A. Tom Grunfeld, *The Making of Modern Tibet*, New York: Routledge, 1996.

By March 1959 rumors began to fly that the Dalai Lama was to be kidnapped by the PLA and spirited to Beijing, where he would be held incommunicado. Whatever the truth-value of these rumors, Tibetans gathered at the palace to protect their spiritual and political leader from such an ignoble fate. The PLA took this as a provocation. Shots were fired, the rebellion turned bloody, and PLA troops flooded the region. No longer willing to wait for Tibetans to "wake up," the CCP now decided that they would be awakened to the benefits of socialism and the ills of feudalism and religious belief by a complete occupation and re-education.

For sixty years, the so-called Tibet "problem" has persisted. However, it has recently changed aspect. Since 2008, Han Chinese migrants, who receive subsidies from the central government to develop, extract from, and "civilize" Tibet, have overrun the region and, with a train now directly connecting Lhasa to Beijing, travel to the plateau is more convenient than ever. No longer occupied only by an army, the region is densely settled by the Han, whose now-capitalist values and modes of modernization fit as uneasily in Tibet as did the socialist commitments before them. Fruits of development accrue to the Han, while Tibetans are marginalized in their own land. Tensions simmer between the mostly segregated communities, with conflict roiling just beneath the surface. Monasteries are isolated, monks and nuns are persecuted.

At the same time, a so-called "cultural renaissance" has emerged among Tibetans in China; novels, poetry, drama, art, and cinema are flourishing and are widely translated into Chinese, English, and other languages for enthusiastic audiences. Yet, new assimilationist policies aiming to erase the Tibetan language, culture, and religious belief systems on the plateau itself are now a focus of the Xi Jinping regime. And the Dalai Lama is old and still in exile. There is no credible system in place to replace him in the traditional religious mode. What the Tibet "problem" might look like in a generation is thus entirely unclear.

CHAPTER 6

The Cultural Revolution

Marxism comprises many principles, but in the final analysis they can all be brought back to a single sentence: it is right to rebel [*zaofan youli* / 造反有理].

—Mao Zedong (1939)[1]

Debasement is the password of the base,
Nobility the epitaph of the noble.
See how the gilded sky is covered
With the drifting twisted shadows of the dead.

—Bei Dao (1976)[2]

In 1964, Jiang Qing, Mao's wife, convened a meeting to discuss with culture workers how best to dramatize the protagonists and values of Chinese socialism in Peking opera. In her speech she noted, "We stress operas on revolutionary contemporary themes which reflect real life . . . and which create images of contemporary revolutionary heroes on our operatic stage. This is our foremost task . . . Historical operas portraying the life and struggles of the people before our Party came into being are also needed."[3] Jiang particularly extolled *Little Heroic Sisters on the Grassland* by the Peking Opera Troupe of the Inner Mongolian Art Theatre for its unambiguous depiction of "positive characters." Highlighting opera's potential as an ideal cultural container for a new socialist content, Jiang drew upon its exaggerated movements on stage;

---

1   Mao Zedong, "Speech Marking the 60th Birthday of Stalin," December 20, 1939, available at *Marxists Internet Archive*, marxists.org; the phrase became ubiquitous after Mao's "A Letter to the Red Guards of Tsinghua University Middle School," August 1, 1966. In its Cultural Revolutionary life, the phrase "It is right to rebel," was followed by "making revolution is no crime" (*zaofan youli* / *geming wuzui*; 造反有理, 革命無罪).

2   Bei Dao, "The Answer," *The August Sleepwalker*, tr. Bonnie S. McDougall, New York: New Directions, 1990.

3   Jiang Qing, "On the Revolution of Peking Opera," wengewang.org.

its relatively formulaic vocabulary of gestures, costumes, and masks; and its mass appeal to promote it as the creator and conveyor of emerging dictates to delineate good and bad social types, and to offer clear historical summations. Jiang's appeal to opera demonstrates how traditional forms were to be bent to socialist purpose; it also indicates how central the relationship between historical narrative and socialist consciousness was to cultural production at the time. Ultimately, opera could not bear the weight of these expectations; rather, it was the utterly alien and thoroughly bourgeois ballet that made for a more malleable revolutionary cultural form. Nevertheless, Jiang Qing's articulated concern about how to think and narrate the past in the socialist present became incantatory over the ensuing decade. Indeed, as theorist Dai Jinhua has argued, the primary goal of socialist culture and the culture of socialism was to "completely rewrite sensuous cultural thematics" into non-bourgeois idioms. These were meant to create and reflect the necessity for class revolution and the right to rebel against established social and political hierarchies; to establish the legitimacy of class equality and, in the parlance of the day, to enable the socially most base to rise into the most noble positions; to use the methods of historical materialism to center the subjectivity of the revolutionary people in the past and the present.[4] While these themes all had been emphasized in the cultural production of the post-1949 period, the Cultural Revolution (CR) extended them to the limits of expressive possibility.

The field of culture animated the first three years of the CR, 1966–1969. Of course, the CR was also about politics, in the sense that it concerned the future of the Chinese Revolution and which social constituency was going to carry the revolution forward after Mao. In Mao's estimation, the retrenchments following the Great Leap Forward had led to the quashing of popular enthusiasms for social transformation. Revolutionary consciousness—always central to the formation of class and the waging of class struggle in Maoism—was fading, he

---

4 Dai Jinhua, "Culture of Socialism," tr. Rebecca E. Karl, in Christian Sorace, Nicholas Loubere, and Ivan Franceschini, eds., *Afterlives of Chinese Communism: Political Concepts from Mao to Xi*, London and New York: Verso, 2019.

thought, under the dead hand of technocracy. A generation had been raised who had never participated in revolutionary activity: in particular, urban youth had benefited most from the revolution and yet done the least for it. They needed to be mobilized to shake up their comfortable worlds, to experience socialism as a constantly revolutionizing endeavor rather than a routinized bureaucratic slog. Culture was the key arena because it held a transcendent position as ideology, human will, and creative capacity in Mao's thought and practice. As a cultural and political movement, the CR was thus anti-bureaucratic and anti-intellectual because bureaucrats and intellectuals, as premises of their social existence, reproduced themselves and their class prerogatives—a class reproduction located for bureaucrats in the context of the party, and for intellectuals in the context of educational and research institutions. Class privilege and its social reproduction had to be fought so that the renewal and deepening of revolution could stand a chance.

The Great Proletarian Cultural Revolution was a polemic. It was an inherently conflictual endeavor, intended to oust what were considered "class enemies" from positions of power in defense and further pursuit of the socialist revolution. Those labeled enemies fought back. At its end, the CR was labeled by its initial targets the "ten-year catastrophe" (*shinian haojie* / 十年浩劫). Thoroughly repudiated, it was categorized as so many aggregated traumas that could be poetically whispered but not historically explained. Thus, in order to understand something about the CR, we must first visit its ending and how its declared enemies regained the upper hand. The narrative spun at its end shapes to this day how we see its beginning and process.

The end began with the arrest in October 1976, within weeks of Mao's death in September, of Jiang Qing and three of her supporters, then labeled the "Gang of Four."[5] Charged with plotting a coup, perverting socialism, and having poisoned Mao's mind if not his

---

5 The "gang" was comprised of Jiang Qing, Yao Wenyuan, Zhang Chunqiao, and Wang Hongwen. Yao and Zhang were political and literary theorists; Wang was a labor activist. All were from Shanghai.

body, the "gang" quickly became targets of social revulsion and political retribution. Jiang Qing, previously portrayed in propaganda posters as a loyal servant of Mao Zedong Thought, as a standard-bearer of cultural progress and of "women holding up half the sky" (*nvren chengqi banbiantian* / 女人撑起半边天), now was depicted as the personification of the mythical white-boned demon, a snake monster, the depraved woman behind the throne dragging her man down. She became the prime exhibit in an emerging argument claiming that empowered women were bad women, part of a sexist and chauvinist backlash that has not abated to this day.

By 1980–1981, Jiang and her collaborators were put on televised public trial, held accountable for the whole of the CR, in an attempt to neatly package the period in preordained judicial findings. The trial staged a masterful performance by the post-Mao state of a hastily summoned new rule of law, and by the accused, who tried to make clear how arbitrary it was to hold four people responsible for the ten years and tens of millions of participants. In her own defense, Jiang Qing shifted blame to her still-revered husband: "Everything I did, Mao told me to do. I was his dog; what he said to bite, I bit." And she reminded the judges that they, too, had persecuted victims of the CR-era purges as fervently as had she: "If I am guilty, how about you all?"[6] Predictably yet cathartically, each of the "gang" was sentenced to death, commuted later to life imprisonment. Jiang Qing committed suicide in 1991, while the others lived on into the 2000s. Unrepentant to the end, Jiang's suicide note read, in part: "Today the revolution has been stolen by the revisionist clique of Deng [Xiaoping] . . . Chairman Mao exterminated Liu Shaoqi, but not Deng, and the result of this omission is that unending evils have been unleashed on the Chinese people and nation. Chairman, your student and fighter is coming to see you!"[7]

The tidy ending belies the messiness of the revolutionary attempt.

*   *   *

6   Alexander Cook, *The Cultural Revolution on Trial: Mao and the Gang of Four*, Cambridge, UK: Cambridge University Press, 2016.

7   Ross Terrill, *The White-Boned Demon: A Biography of Madame Mao Zedong*, New York: Morrow, 1984.

Before it could end, the CR had to begin. And while a chronology of events is hardly adequate to historical explanation, it is necessary to ground the movement in the concrete practices that unfolded in and through time.

Conventionally, the beginning of the CR is said to reside not in Jiang Qing's 1964 extolling of opera, but rather in the 1965 critique launched in a Shanghai literary journal against the new-style opera *Hai Rui Dismissed from Office* (*Hai Rui baguan* / 海瑞罢官). Wherever one begins, at the heart of the CR was the problematized relationship between the past as history and its narrativization in the socialist present. This was the issue Jiang Qing had raised with regard to opera in general, and it was the issue raised by the *Hai Rui* script. Written by the Ming historian and Beijing municipal official Wu Han, the opera had been performed in Beijing several years earlier to some acclaim but little fanfare. The 1965 critique, entitled "On the New Historical Play 'Hai Rui Dismissed from Office,'" was signed by Yao Wenyuan, a literary critic in Shanghai accustomed to attacking his peers for their lack of socialist purity. Originally ignored, Yao's essay was reprinted within the month by the *People's Daily*, mouthpiece of the Chinese Communist Party and a newspaper read habitually by most literate people in China at the time. With that kind of exposure, the critique had to be acknowledged as an important political intervention. Peng Zhen, mayor of Beijing, was put in charge of coordinating the effort to make sense of the cultural-political problems posed by the script.

The crux of Yao's critique revolved around a discussion of how to write the past in the idioms and spirit of the socialist present. Hai Rui had been a Ming dynasty official who sided with peasants residing in his jurisdiction during a land dispute with one of the gentry-landlords of the area; he had been dismissed from office by the emperor as a consequence. The script took up this historical vignette. Yao asked: Should Hai Rui, an upright servant of feudalism, be presented as a hero, a class traitor, or a model? He accused Wu Han of treating him as a hero, raising the question of how the past should be narrativized historically as a classed process? He charged Wu with ignoring class altogether. These accusations were not answerable through compilations of empirical detail, but rather only through a methodological exploration of social relations in a historical materialist vein. As Yao wrote, "We do not expect a new historical play to agree with history in every detail, but we do expect that the class stand and class relationship of the characters portrayed therein should agree with historical facts." That is, historical details can be manipulated for aesthetic reasons, but the spirit of history—its class struggle—cannot be confused. Yao further noted: "The course of class struggle tells us that there was no way for Hai Rui or other feudal officials after him to restore vitality to the rotten and degenerated Ming Dynasty . . . After Hai Rui, the peasants of Songjiang were ruthlessly oppressed and exploited as usual . . . the class contradiction went on to grow more acute."[8]

The problems of approach and ideology, of the relationship of the past to an always-changing present, were hugely important.[9] It was these issues that motivated Yao's critique. However, initially, in the ensuing discussion, these problems of historical narration were distilled into a purely political mode. In this political vein, it was not clear why *this* play was being criticized at *this* time, several years after it had already appeared on stage. It was suggested, obliquely by Yao and more directly by others, that Hai Rui was raised as a veiled defense of Peng Dehuai, dismissed from office in 1959 for having criticized Mao during the Great Leap Forward. In this scenario, Peng was Hai Rui and Mao was the Ming emperor. Wu Han vigorously denied this point, although he was induced to write self-criticisms admitting he had not paid enough attention to class struggle. Those following the story thought it would end there. It did not.

The story gathered momentum, and speculation raged about who was behind it and who was its real target. Famous cultural figures

---

8   Yao Wenyuan, "On the New Historical Play 'Hai Rui Dismissed from Office,'" available at *Marxists Internet Archive*, marxists.org.

9   Alessandro Russo's forthcoming book contains detailed chapters on this episode.

were encouraged to pile on, to critique Wu Han. The results of this forced discussion were desultory, as few were enthusiastic about the task. But, Wu Han was dismissed from his post in the Beijing government even though the hand behind the scheme was not yet revealed. It turned out to be Mao via Jiang Qing. Yet, clearly, lowly Wu Han could not be the end point, and soon the real target came into view: it was Peng Zhen. Peng was a longtime party member, Long March survivor, and close associate of then-president of the PRC Liu Shaoqi, himself a staunch comrade of Mao's for almost the entirety of the Communist Party's existence. But Peng, as mayor of Beijing, had long since rejected the implication that culture had to be produced in lockstep with the party-state and thus, in this instance, he had not vigorously pursued Wu Han's alleged historical wrongdoing. He was accused of harboring petty-bourgeois thinking, of having hidden in the bosom of the party for thirty years.[10] By May 1966, he was deposed; several high-level long-term party members were ousted along with him.[11]

The May 16, 1966, circular issued by the Central Committee of the Communist Party of China on the Great Proletarian Cultural Revolution confirmed Peng's traitorous tepidness, and it announced the reorientation of cultural work around new mandates. While the problem of historical narration for socialist purposes was highlighted, nevertheless and curiously, the circular ended with the following mystery:

> Those representatives of the bourgeoisie who have sneaked into the party, the government, the army, and various cultural circles are a bunch of counter-revolutionary revisionists. Once conditions are ripe, they will seize political power and turn the dictatorship of the proletariat into a dictatorship of the bourgeoisie. Some of them we have already seen through, others we have not. Some are still trusted

---

10 Mao Zedong, "Criticize P'eng Chen [Peng Zhen]," April 28, 1966.
11 Wu Han died in jail in 1969 (maybe of tuberculosis, maybe of suicide); Peng Zhen survived the events and was rehabilitated under Deng Xiaoping in the early 1980s.

by us and are being trained as our successors, persons like Khrushchev, for example, who are still nestling beside us.[12]

That the bourgeoisie had infiltrated the party; that the party harbored hidden "Krushchevs"—traitors to socialism—who "nestled" close; that the party was fallible and was unreliable; these were serious charges. Peng Zhen and the Beijing party apparatus seemed not to be the final target, after all. Remarkably, according to this circular, it appeared it was the more general party organization itself, or at least the nestling Krushchevs, that apparently was eager to reverse the revolution. But who were these nestlers?

Events snowballed through the summer of 1966. Students in Beijing's middle and high schools took up the call to expose bourgeois ideological tendencies in the party—those ideologies nestling undetected—most notoriously at the middle school attached to Tsinghua University, training ground for party cadres, the most privileged elements of socialist society. They agitated against the rigidities and constraints imposed upon them by strict teachers, inflexible exam regimes, and the ever-narrowing funnel that determined who advanced politically and who did not. Articulated as a struggle against party domination of social life, these agitations came in the form of "large-character posters" (dazibao/大字报), hastily composed denunciations of school authorities and party stalwarts, written with calligraphy brushes in ink on flimsy paper and glued to the very surfaces in central campus locations usually reserved for the circulation of official announcements. These quickly were torn down by the authorities, who then came under fiercer attack for upholding class privilege, protecting class enemies, and dampening revolutionary enthusiasms. New posters were posted. They festooned the campus, hung as streaming banners resembling bandages across now-gaping political wounds. Layer upon layer, accusations flew.

---

12   Central Committee of the Communist Party of China, "May 16 Circular," available at *Marxists Internet Archive*, marxists.org.

Students formed loose organizations, calling themselves "Red Guards" (*hongweibing*/红卫兵). Arrayed against them were teachers, party bureaucrats, experts, and others who strove to maintain social order. On August 1, Mao wrote to the Red Guards praising their initiative: "No matter where they are . . . I will give enthusiastic support to all who take an attitude similar to yours in the Cultural Revolution movement." He also urged the students to find areas of unity, and to remember Marx's words: "The proletariat must emancipate not only itself but all mankind. If it cannot emancipate all mankind, then the proletariat itself will not be able to achieve final emancipation."[13] Here, the major class targets of the CR were announced: party officials, educational authorities, and intellectuals, all of whom were allegedly intent on restoring and reproducing the bourgeoisie, opposing the proletariat, and obstructing the liberation of mankind. On August 5, 1966, Mao doubled down on his conviction that the party was riddled with vipers, and he wrote his own "big-character poster" urging students and others to "bombard the headquarters" (of the party). In Mao's words, "leading comrades" in the party and in the schools had "puffed up the arrogance of the bourgeoisie and deflated the morale of the proletariat. How poisonous!"[14] He called for the "four bigs" (*sida*/四大) to prevail: big release, big outcry, big debates, big-character posters (*daming, dafang, dabianlun, dazibao* / 大鸣大放大辩论大字报); these were to comprise the "big democracy" (*daminzhu*/大民主) of the masses.

Many scholars believe Mao was mad, and that the Cultural Revolution was an expression of this madness. The Chinese categorization of the CR as a "catastrophe" tends to support an interpretation of the movement as irrational and unexplainable. Others have promoted the idea that the CR was a conspiracy hatched by Mao as part of a peevish power struggle in the name of a politics shorn of ideological substance. Mao the naked powermonger becomes the

---

13 Mao Zedong, "A Letter to the Red Guards of Tsinghua University Middle School," available at *Marxists Internet Archive*, marxists.org.

14 Mao Zedong, "Bombard the Headquarters—My First Big-Character Poster," available at *Marxists Internet Archive*, marxists.org.

narrative frame through which the CR story is told. While official Chinese interpretations tend to shy away from pinning blame on Mao exclusively—after all he needs to be retained as titular father of the PRC—popular Chinese and many foreign assessments tend toward this authoritarian-tyrant explanation. However, much new scholarship addresses more complexity and asks better questions.

Why was the problem of narrating the past in the present so compelling? Why did the call to rebel resonate so strongly with students and others? That is, why did so many—in their tens of millions—respond so vigorously when they were summoned to political action? "The Cultural Revolution began for the most part as a revolution from above," historian Yiching Wu writes, "[but] more than a decade and a half after the victory of the Communist-led revolution, popular resentment of bureaucratic privileges and cadre abuses of power was widespread, and many citizens were only too eager to take advantage of the newly proclaimed right to rebel against established authorities."[15] It seems clear that there was a real sense at that time that rebelling would contribute to the making of a new world, and that smashing the old world that had persisted into and was being recreated within the socialist era was a necessary step along that path. Indeed, a Red Guard publication from late August 1966 proclaimed that theirs was a "revolutionary storm" and that "as critics of the old world, we are the builders of the new world," a world that could emerge only once "all the old ideas and habits of the exploiting classes" had been swept away.[16] From this on-the-ground perspective, the CR must be understood as a mass movement that, however mobilized from the top, resonated very widely and took on its own momentum and its own logics as it progressed.

Ideas and habits, customs and culture—the "four olds" (*sijiu*/ 四 旧), whose manifestations could be as quotidian as raising goldfish or caged singing birds (effetely bourgeois), or as huge as Buddhist

---

15   Wu Yiching, *The Cultural Revolution at the Margins*, Cambridge, MA: Harvard University Press, 2014, 51.

16   "Red Guards Destroy the Old and Establish the New," *Peking Review* 36, September 1966, 17.

temples and ancestral worship sites (dangerously feudal)—had to be opposed. From the mundane to the monumental, material things were to be destroyed and ideologies along with them. After all, Mao repeatedly said, "Without destruction there can be no construction."[17] Red Guards roamed the cities looking for the "olds," taking it upon themselves to search, seize, display, and destroy as they deemed necessary. Sartorial attire was important to this endeavor, as students took their "guard" identities seriously and dressed in military garb. Some, whose parents had been early CCP members, borrowed PLA gear from their family closets, cinching their waists with big belt buckles and parading their parents' faded clothes like so much vintage gold; others, whose parents hadn't been so presciently revolutionary, fashioned a semblance of the required uniform out of scrounged surplus military supplies. Girls braided their hair in two plaits, or cut it into short bobs, to better resemble the plain-living Yan'an troops of yore. Ribbons, barrettes, perms, and adornments were labeled bourgeois and banished.

Red Guard factions soon came into conflict with one another over correct interpretations of Mao Zedong Thought, over big philosophical and petty turf matters, and over large and small issues that loomed as major problems. As social order broke down, few dared intervene. Even Mao was taken aback by the expansive social response and the vehemence of the mass activity he had summoned. Yet on August 8, the Central Committee issued a document known as the Sixteen Point Decision that thoroughly affirmed the direction of the CR. The first line of the document is often cited: "The Great Proletarian Cultural Revolution now unfolding is a great revolution that touches people to their very souls and constitutes a new stage in the development of the socialist revolution in our country, a stage which is both broader and deeper."[18] Souls were touched; enthusiasms soared. Mao "received" wave upon wave of Red Guards on Tian'anmen Square

---

17   Sixteen-Point Decision, August 8, 1966, available at wenwang.org.

18   Decision of the Central Committee of the Chinese Communist Party concerning the Great Proletarian Cultural Revolution," *Peking Review* 9:33, August 12, 1966, available at wenwang.org.

from the rostrum of the Forbidden City gate, as young people gathered in their hundreds of thousands from around the country through a big "linking up" (*dachuanlian*/大串连) with like-minded others to trade experiences and make revolution.[19] The "Little Red Book," containing quotable nuggets of Mao Zedong Thought, was printed by the PLA presses, adorned with a preface by General Lin Biao, PLA chief and Mao's closest comrade in arms. Second only to the Bible in the number of volumes printed, each student carried a mini-sized, laminated Little Red Book close to their bosom, to read, memorize, recite, and brandish during mass meetings. Metal badges were produced in the millions, depicting Mao in every conceivable revolutionary pose and causing tin to run scarce. Pinned on uniforms as trophies, they became a form of revolutionary currency.

Schools were closed, while teachers and authorities were dealt with harshly by Red Guards, who forced them to admit to bourgeois thinking, class crimes, and other infractions. Locked up to write endless self-criticisms or paraded in dunce caps and made to stand on stages in painful positions for hours at a time, they were berated by irate students enjoying the reversal of power roles. Dragooned into manual labor as a form of reeducation from their privileged mental labor positions, many educators and intellectuals were hounded to death or despair, their lives and health ruined, their families broken. Freed from school and parental strictures, students relied on one another and upon the revolutionary kindness of local people to travel for the first time around their country. Trains and buses transported students at no cost, and young Red Guards set out in groups to retrace the steps of the Long March, of the establishment and growth of the Communist Party, to reenact and re-narrativize the revolution as personal experience. In their travels, they witnessed their country's poverty and richness, its beauty and crudeness. Shocked, often, by the evidence of their own privilege, some students conceived the desire to

---

19   Yan Fan [燕帆], 大串连：一场史无前例的政治旅游 [*Da chuanlian: Yichang shi wuqianliede zhengzhi lüyou*/The great linking-up: A historically unprecedented political travel experience], Beijing: Jing guan jiaoyu chubanshe, 1993.

voluntarily go to the countryside (*xiaxiang shangshan* / 下乡上山) and into the factories to work alongside peasants and proletariat; others responded by working to consolidate their own class advantages.

School dormitories became battlegrounds for militant Red Guards, who parsed and quarreled over every Mao statement. Party committees were in disarray. Workers took up the cause and began to promote factory democracy against the centralized "commandism" that still prevailed in industry; soon the worker movement gained a temporarily unified voice, a plan, and a momentum. In 1967, the Shanghai proletariat unleashed the "January Storm" (*yiyue fengbao* / 一月风暴) and established the Shanghai People's Commune (*Shanghai renmin gongshe* / 上海人民公社), modeled on the Paris Commune of the 1870s. The goal was to seize revolutionary power from party bosses in the factories, but more important, even, from leaders of the Shanghai municipal government. In the factories, the "wind of economism" (economic incentives) was criticized for treating workers not as masters with political subjectivity (*zhurenweng*/主人翁) but as mere producers; for the Shanghai workers, speaking for the national proletariat, political equality and genuine mass democracy, rather than the creation of new economic inequalities through the incentivization of productivity, constituted true socialism. On January 5, 1967, over 1 million people filled Shanghai's People's Square—a vast space in the center of the city, refashioned after 1949 from its previous colonial life as the Shanghai Race Club, where gambling and horse racing had flourished. Summoned there by the workers, the Shanghai leadership was denounced and deposed by mass action. The workers' committee took over, pledging itself in the name of mass democracy against economism, commandism, and dictatorship.

The victories were short-lived, as internal division within the worker movement sank some of the utopian vision, and timidity doomed the radicalism of the rest. By February, spooked by the assertiveness of the proletarian practice of democratic politics and organization, Mao ordered Jiang Qing's associates Zhang Chunqiao and Yao

Wenyuan to unify with Wang Hongwen (a worker who thereafter rocketed to powerful position in the politburo) to transform the unruly commune into a revolutionary committee, a "three-in-one combination" (*san jiehe* / 三结合) of the PLA, workers, and party cadres. This form, according to Mao, was "a provisional organ of power that is revolutionary and representative and has proletarian authority."[20] But, it was clear: proletarian autonomy was to be curtailed by the army and the party.[21]

In tandem with the radicalization of workers, 1967 saw an acceleration of the movement at all levels of society. One impetus for this was the dissemination of Yu Luoke's treatise "On Class Origins." Yu was an apprentice at a machine factory in Beijing, having been denied admission to college because his father had been branded a rightist in 1957. He took aim at what was called the "bloodline theory" (*xuetonglun* / 血统论) of revolution, which held, in its crudest form, that "if the father is a hero, the son is good; if the father is reactionary, the son is rotten" (*laozi yingxiong er haohan, laozi fandong er hundan* / 老子英雄儿好汉，老子反动儿混蛋). Yu refuted this theory, considering it a justification for the perpetuation and reproduction of privilege among a closed group who could trace their revolutionary political lineage to the earliest Communist times. (Of course this was articulated as a patriarchal lineage, moving from father to son/daughter, although perhaps in practice, a mother's revolutionary lineage also sufficed.) Those whose parents had not been revolutionary, or who had been explicitly anti-revolutionary, were locked out of political participation by this theory. Yu argued that this was anti-Maoist, as Mao had always emphasized revolutionary consciousness and activity as a way for anyone to join the leading peasant/proletariat class, no matter what the individual class background. Yu advocated that "all revolutionary young people descending from diverse class origins should be treated equally," and that students be given the chance to

---

20   "On the Revolutionary 'Three-in-One' Combination," Beijing: Foreign Languages Press, 1968, available at wenwang.org.

21   Hongsheng Jiang, "The Paris Commune in Shanghai: The Masses, the State, and Dynamics of 'Continuous Revolution,'" PhD diss., Duke University, 2010.

demonstrate their revolutionary commitments.[22] Here, as Yu argued, the abstract problem of the classed past had become a lived problem of revolutionary life in the present.

Much of the fighting in 1967 was between the Red Guard and worker groups who adhered to versions of one or the other of these theories. At issue was not only who could belong to what, but more important, how an inherited past might structure, bleed into or be overcome in the present, specifically as this pertained to the question of who could claim the revolutionary subjectivity of "the people." By 1968, the bloodline theory had won the day, and class became a matter of origins, of a rigidly understood past hierarchy locking contemporary individuals in its embrace. Yu was arrested and jailed. He was executed as a counterrevolutionary in 1970.

Through these years, the permutations of language were dizzying. Speech could be turned against itself by altering perspective—for example, the ubiquitous slogan "Waving red flags to oppose the red flag" (*huiwuzhe hongqi fandui hongqi* / 挥舞着红旗反对红旗) pointed to those pretending to be socialists but who instead were "Krushchevs." Words used for bad behavior included: "capitalist roader," "revisionist," "traitor," "spy," "monster and demon," "black," "futile," "reactionary," "deviationist," and "stinking ninth" (*chou laojiu* / 臭老九, an epithet for intellectuals), among others. Mao Zedong Thought was said to be "an invincible weapon" and "our lifeblood." It was "a lighthouse," "a compass," "a telescope and microscope," "a spiritual atom bomb," a supernatural, magic weapon called a *fabao* (法宝).[23] Those who worked with language walked a tightrope of usage. Perhaps this is one reason ballet became a preferred cultural form: even with innovative admixtures of revolutionary gestures and martial arts sequences, ballet vocabulary remained relatively rigid and unspoken. Such classics of the revolutionary form as *Red Detachment of Women* and *The White-Haired Girl* were performed

---

22   Yu Luoke, "On Class Origins," cited in Wu Yiching, *Cultural Revolution at the Margins*, 83.

23   Ji Fengyuan, "Language and Politics during the Chinese Cultural Revolution: A Study in Linguistic Engineering," PhD diss., University of Canterbury, 1998, 210–30.

live on stages across the country; as films, they were screened endlessly. They were not overtly open to alternative interpretations.

Meanwhile, painting practices rotated between the hard socialist realism of muscle-bound proletariats with factories and technologies sprouting in the background as subjects of one propaganda poster after the next, to softer folk art forms used to depict peasants, rural settings, and socialist abundance. Music composed in major keys, and big symphonic compositions, with Chinese instrumentation added, became the norm. Huge efforts went into collective cultural productions for every level of society, although final formats of the more prominent pieces were heavily controlled by committee consensus. The ubiquity of the cultural realm subtended the period and gave it literary, linguistic, visual, and representational expressive form.

In late 1967, a shocking announcement transfixed the party and the nation: Liu Shaoqi, president of the PRC and stalwart of the revolution, had been arrested. Relieved of his many official duties, he was revealed to be the big "Krushchev," a "capitalist-roader" hiding in the party, nestling in the bosom of China's socialist revolution. Author of a popular pamphlet written in 1939 entitled *How to Be a Good Communist*, Liu now was exposed as a covert agent of the bourgeoisie. And indeed, he had supported the post–Great Leap Forward retrenchments, even though he had also supported the launching of the Cultural Revolution. His wife, Wang Guangmei, a physicist and English-language interpreter, also was vilified. Most publicly, she was pilloried for having worn a string of pearls on a diplomatic visit in Indonesia. The pearls—replicated in a string of ping-pong balls she was forced to don in public humiliation ceremonies—became a symbol of her irrepressible bourgeois tastes, her indecent betrayal of the proletariat when abroad, and her anti-revolutionary female vanity. As her husband's "crimes" were enumerated and his reputation destroyed, Wang fell with him. After very ill treatment, Liu died in 1969; Wang died in 2006. Liu's fall was surprising and yet still understandable within the parameters of the discourse and politics of the day.

By the end of 1967, the CR was passing its peak. In a final gasp of mass radicalism, an alliance of rebel groups from Hunan, called Shengwulian (省无联), attempted to oppose the restoration of bureaucratic power to the party and the army. Their signature manifesto, "Whither China?," written by Yang Xiguang, a high school student, argued that "the major conflict in China was not between Mao's supporters and the revisionists, nor between the proletariat and the remnant of the propertied classes, but between a collective red capitalist class and the people as a whole."[24] Taking Mao's observation that the party had become an enemy of the people, riddled with vipers and would-be bourgeois restorers, Shengwulian wanted to definitively smash the party apparatus by condemning it as the representative of capitalism in socialist China. Its bureaucratism, in this analysis, would be replaced by the exercise of mass democracy. In 1969, Yang was declared a Trotskyist and arrested, while Shengwulian was disbanded. Yang survived his decade of imprisonment, emigrated, and under the name Xiaokai Yang became a neoliberal economist, with a Princeton PhD and a professorship in Australia.

The CR, having begun with such spontaneity and hope, was now exhausted. Weary of the social and political costs of instability, Mao called in the army in 1969 to put down remaining Red Guard and radical proletariat activity. The PLA was indiscriminate in its crackdown on students and workers, and the vast majority of deaths ascribed to the CR happened at the hands of the army. Cities were emptied of unruly students, now forced to go to the countryside and factories in wave after wave of evictions. Parents waved good-bye to trains, buses, and flatbed trucks loaded with their precious progeny, bedding rolls and thermoses and padded coats and suitcases filled with necessities piled around them. Thousands of educated, effete, hormonal teenagers headed to remote and rough terrains to learn where their food came from, and by whom and how it was grown; to build infrastructure and engage in manual labor; and, as an unforeseen bonus, to learn about sex and their bodies far from prudish

24   Wu Yiching, *Cultural Revolution at the Margins*, 170.

parents and ascetic authorities. None expected these sojourns to last for long. Yet, *hukou* (household registration) was transferred with them, thus blocking return to their homes and locking them into their new locations, where often they were treated as burdens on productive resources by peasants, themselves just scraping by. As students perceived the enduring dimensions of their new situation, their enthusiasms waned. Those with political connections intact found ways back to the cities, *hukou* included; those without connections or who married locally were stuck.

In the meantime, these "sent-down youth" had to learn to work. They had to produce food for their own consumption and to support the units—commune or factory—to which they were attached. Many learned new skills and perspectives on life—most famously, today's leader, Xi Jinping, was a sent-down youth and his memoir of his time in the countryside is a bestseller in China today—and some even became sympathetic to the peasants and proletariat among whom they lived. They helped raise the level of schooling for rural children and attempted to pass along their knowledge in ways that were practically useful for their locales. A number of rural girls, living under stiff patriarchal family conditions, experienced their interactions with female former Red Guards as revelatory. Many sent-down youth also fought to continue their educations, if only through random assortments of books obtained and passed by hand from district and provincial libraries. Exposures to literature, music, poetry, and science were pursued in the interstices of manual labor. The teenagers grew up, and without much adult supervision, sexual exploration was undertaken in a wide variety of combinations. As elsewhere, girls paid a higher price for their heterosexual experiments than did boys. While pregnancies were terminated, if possible, a girl's reputation was permanently stained. Same-sex liaisons flourished. Sexual assaults also were common. Tensions between experimenting students and conservative peasants rose.

By the early 1970s, May Seventh Cadre Schools—so called after Mao's May 7, 1966, directive prevailing upon mental workers ("experts") to become more revolutionary ("red") through manual labor—were filled with party cadres, intellectuals, and other urban elites deemed re-educable. Labeled one of the "new-born things" (*xinsheng shiwu* / 新生事物) brought forth by the CR, these schools were essentially labor camps, although their residents continued to draw regular salaries while learning to work alongside the masses. Often located in difficult environments, the camps were modeled on idealized Yan'an forms of plain living, frugality, hard struggle, and self-reliance; they were intended to remold those who worked with their brains so they could acquire correct class perspective and a proper socialist outlook. As the relevant document put it, "The object of students taking part in industrial or agricultural productive labor is not only to create material wealth for the country but mainly to better their ideology and to transform their subjective world as they transform the objective world."[25] "Red and expert" (*hong yu zhuan* / 红与专) became the ideal.

As red experts, scientists were charged with finding solutions to practical, everyday problems faced by the masses—for example, biogas experiments in Anhui and Sichuan yielded low-cost and easily obtained energy for rural communes produced out of human and animal waste; agronomists were asked to find and cultivate better rice strains, through a combination of local (*tu*/土) and foreign (*yang*/洋) knowledge, that could provide more nutritious grain with higher yields;[26] engineers were tasked with devising and building mechanisms that could be sustained in harsh environments. An exemplary protagonist of the latter endeavor was Wang Jingxi, "Iron Man Wang," a laborer with self-taught engineering skills who helped develop the drills and procedures used to open the Daqing oil fields. Experiments in agricultural organization and crop rotations were the product of collaborations between red experts and local peasants, and such communes as Dazhai in Shanxi Province—"learn from Dazhai" (*xiang Dazhai xuexi* / 向大寨学习)—became national

---

25   "The 'May 7' Cadre School," *Peking Review* 19, May 12, 1972, 5–7.

26   Sigrid Schmalzer, *Red Revolution, Green Revolution: Scientific Farming in Socialist China*, Chicago, IL: University of Chicago Press, 2016.

models of how to turn a poor environment into a productive one. Throughout these years, the elite nuclear program remained intact, allowing China to attain weaponized nuclear capacity without Soviet assistance.

Rural areas were in part remade through the CR, although the gap between rural and urban remained insurmountable. As historian Han Dongpin has documented, rural schools and curricula geared to local needs increased hugely, allowing peasant children a real chance at education.[27] "Barefoot doctors"—rudimentary medical personnel trained to treat common symptoms and diseases—offered peasants basic medical care on site. Life expectancy soared. In the early 1970s, when city schools were reopened, peasant children were sent to study in urban universities and institutes as a way to try to even out the class privileges of urban-born youth. Their educational levels often were inadequate for elite courses, but their very presence forced institutions to adapt education to different needs. Many such students were trained in agronomy, useful for when they would return to their villages and communes. And return they did: peasants were not permitted to stay in the cities; they were expected to bring their training back to benefit their native places.

When Martin Luther King Jr. was assassinated in 1968, Mao called for a "new storm against imperialism," with US racist capitalist domination the target of that storm. Already in 1964, as the situation in the Congo had deteriorated, US imperialism was declared the common world enemy: "It is engaged in aggression against South Vietnam, it is intervening in Laos, menacing Cambodia . . . It is trying everything to strangle the Cuban revolution . . . It ganged up with England in creating so-called Malaysia to menace Indonesia and other-southeast Asian countries. It is occupying South Korea and China's Taiwan province. It is dominating all Latin America." Mao called for the people of the world to "unite and defeat the U.S. aggressors and all

---

27   Han Dongping, *The Unknown Cultural Revolution: Life and Change in a Chinese Village*, New York: Monthly Review, 2009

their running dogs!"[28] Fashioned as a "global people's war," the historic wrongs of capitalist imperialism were to be redressed with PRC material and ideological assistance. Arms and food were shipped to North Vietnam to aid in the struggle against the United States, and help building a railway in Tanzania and Zambia was supplied as a form of socialist fraternity and anti-imperialist solidarity.[29] China practiced revolutionary internationalism as a direct extension of its domestic revolutionary agenda. Meanwhile, Maoism reverberated through the world. Black Panthers sold the Little Red Book on the corners of Oakland streets to fund their social programs and revolutionary actions,[30] and French radicals raised high the banner of Maoism during the events of Paris in May 1968.[31] The appeal of Maoism to radicals worldwide was not based in expert knowledge of China; rather, it was founded in the crisis of the Soviet-led international Communist movement, which, particularly after Hungary in 1956 and Prague in 1968, proved to be part of the global problem, not the solution. The appeal of Maoism also was founded in widespread opposition to the socially reproduced elite, militarized, racist, and gendered dominations that shaped life in most places at that time. These dominations took different form in different locations, but Maoist rhetoric and action against technocratic bureaucracy and in favor of overturning entrenched privilege and reversing the power of "the West" over "the rest" were deeply attractive. In these adoptions, Maoism named an aspiration for collective liberation from capitalist and socially dominating constraints at the individual, national, and global levels.

*   *   *

28   Mao Zedong, "American Imperialism Is Closely Surrounded by the Peoples of the World," November 28, 1964, available at *Marxists Internet Archive*, marxists.org.

29   Jamie Monson, *Africa's Freedom Railway: How a Chinese Development Project Changed Lives and Livelihoods in Tanzania*, Bloomington, IN: Indiana University Press, 2009.

30   Robin D. G. Kelley and Betsy Esch, "Black like Mao: Red China and Black Revolution," *Souls* 1:4, 1999, 6–41.

31   Alexander Cook, *Mao's Little Red Book: A Global History*, Cambridge, UK: Cambridge University Press, 2014.

In late 1971, Lin Biao—commander of the PLA and revered general, credited with crucial victories against the Japanese and the Guomindang, closest comrade to Mao—secretly fled China in a plane headed to the Soviet Union. His plane was shot down over Mongolia (by whom is not clear). Shrouded in mystery, the Lin Biao incident became public a year later. In the official narrative, it was said that Lin, along with his perfidious wife, Ye Qun—a politburo member at the upper echelons of power—and his scheming son Lin Liguo—a senior air force officer—had plotted a coup against Mao. When discovered, they had attempted to flee. Yet, how could someone so completely tied to Mao and a history of revolutionary comradeship have done such a thing? A purge of military personnel close to Lin ensued. Whatever the real story—all documents related to the episode were destroyed deliberately in the late 1970s, leaving only fevered speculation and partial historical reconstructions—the fact of Lin Biao's apparent betrayal amplified public suspicions that whatever utopian hopes of socialism the CR had been launched to realize, it was no longer sustainable as a political, ideological, or social movement.

The final act of the CR in 1973–1974 re-engaged explicitly the narrative problem of the past in the present, the historical-cultural issue that had inaugurated the movement to begin with. It revolved centrally around the vilification of Lin Biao, which proceeded in a characteristically political-cultural mode. Overseen by Jiang Qing, the campaign enlisted some of China's most famous historians, who were plucked off farms and out of factories to gather in Beijing for the effort. Despite its risible and improbable title, "Criticize Lin, Criticize Confucius" (*pi Lin pi Kong* / 批林批孔), the campaign presented a complex argument about how to reconnect the autonomy of Chinese history to world history through Marxist historiography.[32] The problem was to square a circle: historical materialism in an orthodox

---

32 Wang Gungwu, "Juxtaposing Past and Present in China Today," *China Quarterly* 61, 1975, 1–24; S. Weigelin-Schwiedrzik, "The Campaign to Criticize Lin Biao and Confucius (批林批孔/pi Lin pi Kong) and the Problem of 'Restoration' in Chinese Marxist Historiography," in Viren Murthy and Axel Schneider, eds., *The Challenge of Linear Time*, Amsterdam: Brill, 2014.

Marxist sense holds that history progresses through stages in a linear march of time; yet, in practice, that history also is reversible—peoples could and did "restore" (fubi/复辟) the past. Indeed, the drag of China's past on its present represented the constant danger of "changing color" (bianyanse/变颜色): from revolutionary red to counter-revolutionary white or black. The linear historical time posited by the Marxist march of historicist stages was at risk of being disproved by the particularity and historical weight of the Chinese past. This was a practical revolutionary problem, not merely an abstract one. It was only resolvable if revolutionaries remained continuously vigilant against restoration.

The problem was explicated through a tendentious relation established between Lin Biao and Confucius. Lin was said to have upheld Confucianism against Legalism, a historically opposed school of thought with a different temporal orientation. Confucianists, it was said, were backward looking and Legalists were forward facing; Confucianists wished to restore the past, and Legalists hoped to move into a future; Confucianists were reactionaries, and reactionaries were closet Confucianists, while Legalists were progressive and revolutionaries tended toward Legalism. By forcing Lin Biao to inhabit the same time-space of historical analysis as Confucius, both were condemned and tarnished. Meanwhile, revolutionary historicism could be secured through a rereading of the Chinese past: Legalism participated in the revolutionary wave of the global future, while Confucianism was to be consigned to the historical dustbin.

The campaign largely was seen as the last gasp of a regime on the verge of collapse. In the event, Zhou Enlai was almost taken down, and it was only his terminal cancer that "saved" him; Deng Xiaoping, restored to power briefly in 1973, was sent back to the countryside to repair tractors; and no one was convinced that Lin Biao had anything to do with Confucius. The warnings about "restoration," however, proved to be quite accurate and true.

In 1971, on the strength of support from recently independent Third World nations, the PRC was voted into the China seat at the United

Nations, occupied by the GMD since 1949. Mao's China took its place as a permanent member of the UN Security Council. A vindication of PRC Third Worldist foreign policy, this was a triumph of Zhou Enlai's patient diplomacy since 1949. Brewing alongside this Third World victory was a fundamental betrayal of all things revolutionary. In 1971–1972, Henry Kissinger secretly visited China to arrange for the US president, Richard Nixon, to travel to and effect a rapprochement with the PRC. Having led hostile global relations toward Mao's China since 1949, and still enmeshed in a vicious war against the Vietnamese, Cambodian, and Laotian people on China's southern border, Nixon and Kissinger wanted to "play the China card" against the threat of the Soviet Union—and deflect attention away from the growing Watergate scandal in Washington DC. Secret negotiations for a visit to Beijing, including a sudden invitation to the US national ping pong team to engage in friendly competition with China (they lost every match they played), resulted in a magnificent reception in 1972 for Nixon, his wife Pat, and their entourage. Presented to a puzzled Chinese people and a quizzical American public, the dawn of a friendly relationship between the two enemies could be seen as the conclusion to the radical possibilities of the CR and the end to Maoist revolutionism. Meanwhile, the United States betrayal of its GMD allies on Taiwan became a rallying cry of the China lobby in Washington, DC, whose political strength would block the normalization of relations until the Carter presidency in 1979. As theorist Dai Jinhua confirms, "In China, we actually began our post–Cold War era before the rest of the world. The starting point can be dated back to . . . 1973—in my view, it can be said that the 'Cultural Revolution' ended in 1973."[33]

Chiang Kaishek died in 1975. Mao exulted that he had outlived his nemesis. Zhou Enlai died in January 1976. Considered a man of urbane intelligence and cosmopolitan integrity, Zhou's death was widely mourned. Jiang Qing and military personnel prohibited public

33   Wu Qi and Yun Zhu, "Living in the End Times? An Interview with Dai Jinhua," *Chinese Literature Today* 7:2, 2018, 82–91.

demonstrations during the state funeral, but they were defied in April on the occasion of the traditional "tomb-sweeping festival," when hundreds of thousands of mourners, carrying wreaths and banners to commemorate the dead statesman, lay tributes at the base of the Monument to the People's Heroes in Tian'anmen Square. When the city of Tangshan, in Hebei Province, was flattened by an earthquake of unprecedented strength in July 1976, it was taken as an augury of end-times. When Mao died in September that year, people held their breath.

Memoirs and poetry became central to the retrospective depiction of the CR: personal and subjective, these texts create compelling individual "truths" and settle personal scores. "Misty" poetry and "Scar" literature were written immediately on site by young intellectuals—such as Bei Dao, the original bard of the genre—whose lives had been altered by their participation in the events.[34] These pieces circulated widely in China by the early 1980s. Memoirs were written, at least originally, from outside China and often in English, by those who had managed to leave. These circulated abroad and confirmed to Euro-American audiences that Mao had been crazy and that socialism was bankrupt. Combined, these narratives became very important to how China's immediate past could be disavowed in the service of an entirely different present. By 1979, that disavowal was well under way.

34 Michelle Yeh, "The 'Cult of Poetry' in Contemporary China," *Journal of Asian Studies* 55:1, January 1996.

Interlude: Assessing Mao, 1979–1989

> Comrade Mao Zedong said that he too had made mistakes . . . He
> said that . . . he himself would be very happy and satisfied if future
> generations could give him [a] "70-30" rating after his death.
>
> —Deng Xiaoping (1977)[1]

Mao's death and the arrest of the "Gang of Four" drew China's socialist revolutionary era to a close. The official assessments discursively
reconnected China's present to a differently read past that sanctioned
an entirely different approach to life in China and the world. At the
same time as the cultural sphere saw the emergence of "Misty" poetry
and "Scar" literature articulating the traumas of a student generation
grasping the contours of its plight, the economy and social life were
being transformed, and political power was reconsolidated in the
centralized party structure. On his deathbed, Mao reportedly had told
his handpicked successor, Hua Guofeng, "With you in charge, I am at
ease" (*Ni banshi, wo fangxin* / 你办事我放心)—a phrase now refer-
enced only in a highly sarcastic mode—but Hua failed to garner an
independent power base in the party or military and soon was sidelined. His mushy early-1977 policy, the "Two Whatevers" (*liangge
fanshi* / 两个凡是)—"We will resolutely uphold whatever policy decision Chairman Mao made, and unswervingly follow whatever
instructions Chairman Mao gave"[2]—proved he had neither the
vision nor the luster to steer China in a new direction. Instead, Deng
Xiaoping's titanic stature, despite his diminutive size, among party
and army secured for him the position of party leader by December
1978.

---

1 Deng Xiaoping, "The 'Two Whatevers' Do Not Accord with Marxism," May 24,
1977, available at dengxiaopingworks.wordpress.com.

2 "Study the Documents Well and Grasp the Key Link," *People's Daily*, February 7,
1977.

If it had been the goal of the Cultural Revolution—as a bid for the permanence of revolution in China—to dismantle the bureaucratism and privilege of the party and to empower a new generation of revolutionary leaders, the movement must be judged a total failure in those terms alone. If it had been the goal of the CR to re-narrate Chinese and global history in the idiom of a non-historicist Third World Marxism—to demonstrate that formerly colonized or semicolonized countries could leap into socialism without the rapaciousness of capitalism—that, too, was a failure. After Mao's death, the party technocracy returned to political centrality, strengthened in organization and purpose from the years of attack and grassroots rebuilding. Indeed, through the early 1980s, the grassroots was uprooted, as those who had fueled CR passions from the ground up now were deemed to be too radical, too rural, too peasantized, in a word, too "feudal." In repositioning the historical peasant-centeredness of the party as a "feudal" remnant rather than a harbinger of class progress, the meaning of China's socialist revolution, as well as the locus of social and political life, was shifted. Urban life was revalidated, intellectuals rehabilitated, expert knowledge and know-how re-legitimated. Peasants and proletariat were demoted from being "masters" of society, with affirmed revolutionary political subjectivity, to being mere producers and "backward" sociological fractions of a reimagined social whole whose main values now lay elsewhere. To the degree, then, that Maoism forged the foundations for an independent and modernizing nation-state, it also forged the conditions for its own ideological obsolescence: the party-state form survived Mao, while Maoism—the practice of mass politics combined with noncapitalist development—was judged mistaken and rendered irrelevant.

In 1978, Vietnam invaded Cambodia to depose Pol Pot, whose political fanaticism not only had devastated Cambodia—millions dead and millions more lives destroyed—but also had spilled into Vietnam, threatening their newly won peace. Battle-hardened through years of war with the United States, the Vietnamese army easily evicted the

Khmer Rouge from Cambodia, but they then had to deal with their erstwhile fraternal socialist ally, China, coming to Cambodia's aid. In February 1979, the People's Liberation Army invaded Vietnam; in a few weeks of incredibly bloody engagements, the Chinese were decisively defeated and chased back across the border. The humiliation was not publicly acknowledged; indeed, unlike those sacrificed in Korea in the early 1950s, the 7,000 or more war dead in Vietnam are not treated as heroes but are ignored. Yet the PLA's weakness and defeat in face of a stronger foe were certainly lessons well learned in Beijing.

The policy direction called the "Four Modernizations" (*sige xiandaihua* / 四个现代化)—in agriculture, industry, national defense, science, and technology—was announced. Before it could get properly launched, an urban movement centered in Beijing was mobilized to urge a "fifth modernization": democracy. Wei Jingsheng, one of several leaders of the "Democracy Wall movement," was at the time an electrician at the Beijing Zoo. A former Red Guard, he was convinced that democratic socialism was the only way forward and that Deng Xiaoping would be its champion. Using the Cultural Revolutionary tactics of "big-character posters"—although not to denounce but to remonstrate with power—Democracy Wall activists enjoyed a brief efflorescence while Deng used them to shove aside remaining obstacles in his path to power. Then, they were labeled counterrevolutionaries, arrested, and imprisoned. The year 1979 marked what seemed to be an answer to the question of political democracy in China: not now, not soon, perhaps not ever.

Unlike the Mao-era concept and practice of socialist construction, modernization has its roots in bourgeois economics and Cold War global practice. Emphasizing the national benefits in wealth and power of endless economic growth, it treats accumulation as sufficient measure of national success and validates those social and economic hierarchies and ideologies that deliver such success. Socialist construction, by contrast, had attempted to take into account the social costs of development by remaining concerned about basic livelihoods for laborers (the "iron rice bowl" [*tie fanwan*

/ 铁饭碗]), minimizing inequalities generated in economic practice, and thoroughly revolutionizing the social relations of production by eliminating landlords and capitalists as classes, and thus their material bases of social, economic, and cultural domination. One could say that socialist construction and modernization had been the competing ideological poles of Mao-era party factionalism and socialist practice. Deng Xiaoping unambiguously declared modernization, with a so-called "pragmatic" twist, the new Chinese goal: "It does not matter if the cat is black or white, so long as it catches the mouse," he repeated, indicating that the ends of national wealth justified the means of social inequality. Far from ideologically neutral, pragmatism indicated a direct path to capitalist restoration.[3]

This turn needed ideological sanction, as everything the revolution hitherto had been pledged against was re-emerging: bureaucracy, technocracy, developmentalism, class hierarchies in wealth and power. One of Deng's first tasks, then, was to "evaluate" properly the Mao era so as to reposition it as antecedent to the present and not guide to future. It was impossible simply to denounce Mao, as his revolutionary success historically legitimized one-party rule. However, Maoist policies had to be relegated to the past in order to be dismantled in the present. With the "Gang of Four" trial over, an evaluative document, cumbersomely entitled "Resolution on Certain Questions in the History of Our Party since the Founding of the People's Republic of China," was issued in 1981 after numerous revisions. The verdict: Mao was 70 percent correct and 30 percent wrong. Specifically, Mao's revolutionary leadership from 1927 to the late 1950s was entirely affirmed; the Great Leap Forward was not fully denounced, although its "setbacks" were questioned; and the Cultural Revolution demonstrated Mao's mistakes could no longer be denied: "Chief responsibility for the grave 'Left' error . . . does indeed lie with

_____

3   Biographies of Deng Xiaoping, e.g., Ezra Vogel's, and A. Pantsov and S. Levine's, treat "pragmatism" as ideologically neutral. For a critique, see Rebecca Karl, "Little Big Man," *New Left Review* 97, 2016, newleftreview.org.

Comrade Mao Zedong. But after all it was the error of a great proletarian revolutionary."[4]

More important was the reinterpretation of what socialism was
for: now, it was not in service of class struggle or the transformation
of the relations of production in pursuit of social equality, but rather
in service of modernization and building the forces of production
leading to the accumulation of national, as well as individual, wealth
and power. By the same token, politics would no longer be a realm for
mass participation but would be re-contained to the party-state, even
while wrong thinking was not to be indulged. Indeed, alongside the
Four Modernizations were the Four Basic Principles (*si xiang jiben
yuanze* / 四项基本原则): upholding the socialist road, the people's
democratic dictatorship, party leadership, and the guidance of Mao
Zedong Thought and Marxism-Leninism. These principles came with
a stern warning: "Any word or deed which deviates from these four
principles is wrong. Any word or deed which denies or undermines
these four principles cannot be tolerated."[5]

Initial beneficiaries of the emphasis on modernization were local power
holders in the countryside. The agricultural economy was the first to
experience de-Maoification, and after 1979, when the mandate to
disband rural communes became mandatory, cadres, village elders, and
their adult male progeny grabbed the lion's share of communal property. This conversion of collective possession into private property was
legalized some time later. Yet the scale of the privatization of public
rural wealth was not yet recognized, in part because many peasants saw
the communes as having facilitated administrative corruption, and
they were pleased to move away from communes into a system of
family plots of land and guaranteed state prices for grain. The new
economic form was called the "household responsibility system" (*jiat-
ing lianchan chengbao zirenzhi* / 家庭联产承包责任制); it worked on

---

4   "Resolution on certain questions in the history of our party since the founding of
the People's Republic of China," 41, available at marxists.org.

5   Ibid., 74.

the principle of maximizing productivity through economic incentives: whatever was produced beyond that contracted with the state could be sold in newly constituted commodity markets, with profits retained privately. The economic unit of rural social life was returned to the family, where labor and assets were now to be concentrated. The old and infirm, the ill, and girls who would marry into someone else's family: all now became burdens. For the dismantling of communes meant the dismantling of medical, educational, and other social facilities hitherto funded through the collective mechanism. Social reproduction was re-embedded in the privatized family, facilitating the powerful reassertion of the socioeconomic logic of patriarchy. Female infanticide followed soon thereafter.

These were the years when the "one-child policy" became a key goal. There was a scientific reason: the baby boomers of the post-GLF period now had matured into a huge cohort entering their peak years of marriage and fertility. A demographic bulge loomed. Deeming biological reproduction a women's problem, the state, through the Women's Federation, reached into female bodies to control fertility with strict birth allocations, abortions, sterilizations, and other intrusive methods. At the same time, the household responsibility system put pressure on women to have more children—specifically more boys, whose labor would stay in the birth family. Pressured by the state in one way, and in another by marital families, whose claims on women's birthing bodies were underpinned by new license given to patriarchal "traditional cultural practices," the social position of rural women deteriorated dramatically. And girl babies died. The later advent of portable sonogram technology made the aborting of girl fetuses more efficient; the result, now, is a huge male/female demographic imbalance. Meanwhile, urban families took up the one-child injunction less reluctantly, in part because urban labor is differently deployed, and the cost of socially reproducing children in the cities soon soared. Population growth *was* controlled, with women's bodies and minds bearing the brunt of the effort. Today, an aging population threatens China's productive future, and women are being encouraged, and often coerced, into having more babies. Again, women's birthing bodies are a major target of state policy.

The rural reforms, which saw an initial leap in productivity, stagnated after 1984. This was when the urban reforms in factory and industrial policy got under way, re-subordinating the rural economy to the urban with dual-track commodity prices and other mechanisms privileging cities over the countryside. Through the 1980s, the rationing economy was curtailed as more goods and services moved onto the market. Industrial wages rose. At first, reform was embraced, as it led to more money in people's pockets; but as rents, utilities, education, medicine, and everything else that hitherto had been state-subsidized now floated on the market, life became more expensive. Industrial production was now geared more toward profit making than supplying domestic requirements; factory managers and party bosses became less willing to cover the livelihood needs of their socialist-era workforces. State-owned enterprises—weighed down with historical socialist obligations toward workers—scrambled to retool, reorganize, and shed labor power, with the old and the women the first to be dismissed, so as to compete better in the new environment. Opening trade doors to the capitalist world only added to the pressures, forcing factories to become more efficient. The logic of whom and what the economy served changed: rather than the provision of conditions for at least minimum levels of livelihood for a maximum number of people, now competitive profitability through efficient management was to be the measure of success.

Urban unemployment—euphemistically termed "youth waiting for jobs"—skyrocketed. Rural inequality rose, and migration into the cities, which began as a trickle, soon grew. Competition among urban elite children for slots at good schools and universities became fiercer as the educational funnel, always drastic, seemed to be closing into an ever-narrower channel. And job allocations were becoming less attractive: in return for the state's support for their education, graduates had to accept jobs wherever the state sent them. Those with "back doors" (houmen/后门) or connections (guanxi/关系) secured scarce desirable posts in good cities; those without saw their life chances dissipate, as they and their *hukou* got transferred to remote assignments. Social inequality became an endemic feature of life as economic and political spheres consolidated into a new, savage classed structure.

Several urban movements arose in protest of various aspects of these conditions; they quickly were suppressed. By the spring of 1989, grievances could no longer be contained.[6]

---

6   Wang Hui, "The 1989 Social Movement and the Historical Roots of Neoliberalism in China," tr. Rebecca E. Karl, *positions* 12:1, Spring 2004, 7–69.

CHAPTER 7

1989 and Its Aftermath

The nature of this turmoil is extremely clear: its bottom line is death to our Party and state.

—Li Xiannian (June 1, 1989)[1]

Stability must take precedence over everything.

—Deng Xiaoping (June 1, 1989)[2]

The events of 1989 are a taboo topic in China to this day. A mark of how thoroughly threatened the CCP was by the social movement of that year, any mention of it outside official denunciation is scrubbed from print, thought, and memory. At each anniversary, the state militarizes places of potential public gathering to prevent visible signs of coordinated dissent while also clamping down on possible sources of information. Hong Kong still holds yearly mass commemorations, although the encroaching PRC presence there dampened participation for a time. The mothers of the dead have attempted to emulate the Argentinian Madres de Plaza de Mayo[3] to force the state to account for their children; but the Chinese mothers' voices are uniformly suppressed. Beyond the tragic individual stories, the year 1989 also represents a historical divide. As theorist Dai Jinhua puts it, "The violent conclusion of the Tiananmen protests totally destroyed and purged socialism's spiritual legacy and mobilization potential . . .

---

1 Li Xiannian was a former president of the PRC. This was reportedly said in a meeting with nine party elders, including Deng Xiaoping, as they decided how to deal with the social movement they called "turmoil" (luan/乱).

2 Speech at the meeting referred to in note 1.

3 The "Mothers of the Plaza de Mayo" kept the memory of the state terrorism and the military dictatorship in Argentina from 1976 to 1983 alive and visible in the heart of Buenos Aires.

The Chinese regime began pushing for capitalism with unprecedented energy."[4]

The 1989 protests were not initially about party legitimacy. Rather, the increasingly brazen privatizations of urban social property through the 1980s spawned a demand by students, intellectuals, professionals, workers, and other urban denizens for procedural transparency and freedom to critique and investigate the economic practices of party officials. During the seven weeks of the movement, this evolved to include a more capacious demand for political democracy, but not a call for the overthrow of the CCP. Indeed, as the movement itself was criminalized—especially after an editorial published on April 26 in the *People's Daily* that officially labeled protesters "counter-revolutionaries"—demonstrators demanded they be declared "patriotic" (thus legal), not "counterrevolutionary" (thus illegal). This was important for their own self-recognition as well as for the aftermath: if they were considered "patriotic," leniency could be expected. In the event, the movement was condemned as counter-revolutionary turmoil, and participants were dealt with harshly.

The movement unfolded as a series of accidental mobilizations. Beginning in mid April 1989, students in Beijing gathered to mourn the death of erstwhile CCP leader Hu Yaobang, briefly heir apparent to Deng Xiaoping before being deposed for his alleged sympathy for intellectuals' desires for political democracy. After a week of publicly petitioning the party for transparency, students occupied Tian'anmen Square—the ritual and political center of Beijing and the nation—in a deliberate echo of the 1976 mourning for Zhou Enlai and the 1919 May Fourth Movement. Police attempted to disperse the occupiers, but as more students marched to the square in solidarity, crowds grew. Students in other cities soon mobilized, with Shanghai, Changsha, and Xi'an major hubs. Within a week, the movement in Beijing had grown from 2,000 to over 100,000 participants; in another few days, classes were being boycotted. Journalists wrote about the events

---

4   Dai Jinhua, "Introduction," tr. Jie Li, in Lisa Rofel, ed., *After the Post-Cold War*, Durham, NC: Duke University Press, 2018, 5.

sympathetically, and TV anchors broadcast relatively objective accounts for the usually tightly controlled nightly news. On May 4, over 100,000 people occupied the square to commemorate the seventieth anniversary of the May Fourth Movement, and as class boycotts continued nationwide, Communist Party Chief Zhao Ziyang argued for dialogue with students. Zhao soon was sidelined, and then, after he appeared on the square in sympathy with students, he was ousted.

The movement grew, albeit without centralized leadership. The entry of worker groups onto the square, in solidarity with and yet autonomous from the students, highlighted demands for economic equality rather than only political democracy. This strained the party's thinning tolerance: the specter of a cross-class urban alliance prompted many in the Politburo to harden their resolve against concessions; the ghost of the Cultural Revolution now stalked the events. In mid May, Mikhail Gorbachev arrived for a state visit, the first to China of a Soviet leader since the Sino-Soviet split of the early 1960s. It proved diplomatically embarrassing when access to the square was blocked. Upping the ante, 2,000 students began a hunger strike—soon joined by another 1,000—in an attempt to force party leaders to talk. Images of wilting young people swathed in white headbands, exhibiting willingness to starve for social principles, gained the sympathy of the urban masses; wave upon wave of ordinary people proceeded to the square, to help with sanitation and demonstrate unity. As crowds swelled in other cities, domestic transport into Beijing was blockaded to prevent the formation of national alliances.

Global media was riveted by the events. Its coverage amplified them, as students began to perform their abjection for an international audience. Students from the Central Art Academy quickly sculpted a "Goddess of Democracy," resembling the Statue of Liberty; she was positioned beneath the portrait of Mao Zedong that dominates one end of the square. Western media was delighted. Manifestos about freedom and democracy, quoting non-Marxist Western philosophers, were penned and read aloud. Western media swooned. Music was composed by rock stars, to entertain and provide relief: Cui Jian's ballad, "Nothing to My Name," (*Yiwu suoyou* / 一无所有) became the movement song, and then an international sensation. It subsequently was banned.

The hunger strike continued. Doctors gathered to provide medical care and IVs; journalists marched behind banners identifying their places of employ, defying orders to stand down and shut up; professors, teachers, and big-name intellectuals tended to the students; newly wealthy entrepreneurs showed up to distribute food and water. Cities all over the country were overwhelmed with crowds, although rural areas remained uninvolved. Party leaders, in an attempt to claw back control of the narrative, published editorials denouncing the students, accusing murky foreign "black hands" for conspiring and manipulating events, warning workers that they would pay a heavy price if they joined the protests, and condemning supportive intellectuals. On May 18, a delegation of wan hunger strikers attached to IVs was televised in a dramatic encounter with party leaders at the Great Hall of the People; the dialogue went nowhere. Over 1 million people gathered on or near the square. Two days later, martial law was declared. Crowds teemed in direct defiance.

Over the next days, the military mustered, and ordinary people flooded the streets to try to persuade young soldiers not to attack their fellow citizens. To no avail; the iconic photo of "tank man" illustrates the bravery and futility of their efforts. In other cities, authorities mostly avoided bloodshed in dispersing crowds. By contrast, in Beijing, around midnight on June 3–4, the square and adjacent areas were violently cleared: some occupiers were crushed by tanks; others were shot. Taxis and wheelbarrows were pressed into service to transport the dead and injured from where they lay. The process of identifying casualties was hampered for days by a total news blackout and a refusal by hospital authorities to acknowledge they had bodies on hand. Students still standing began to flee; as dragnets closed in around them, escape routes sprang up to funnel them into Hong Kong, Burma, Vietnam, or other border areas. Many soon emigrated to and received expedited political asylum in the United States, Australia, Taiwan, and the United Kingdom. Workers, with fewer social contacts, were savagely suppressed; if not executed, they were imprisoned for long sentences. A whole new roster of TV anchors occupied the airwaves. Other than the shriek of a propaganda machine at full throttle, silence fell on China.

On one level, the upshot of the movement constituted a final answer to the question of political democracy in China: never on the CCP's watch. Equally consequentially, the very direction of reforms was about to change, rendering politics irrelevant for many. In the words of historian Wang Hui: "That which is today called neoliberal ideology . . . began to sprout here." This was an ideology that "promoted . . . all aspects of privatization" and shut politics off from mass supervision.[5] In this process of social depoliticization, the party-state validated an all-out pursuit of wealth by any who could grab it—"To get rich is glorious" is the fictionalized expression of a real sentiment Deng Xiaoping promoted.[6] The consequent economic scramble left demands for political openness in the dust. Within a short few years, the legalized "plundering and hoarding [of] what used to be collective wealth"[7] became a defining feature of China's socio-politics, through which the merging of wealth and power congealed into a heritable stratum of the super-wealthy and super-powerful—a bloodline class of "princelings" (*fuerdai*/富二代)—who count among the richest of the mega-rich global elite. Or, as Dai Jinhua has put it for China and the world, "We have re-entered the age of 'hereditary capitalism,'" a more vivid Chinese phrase for which is "compare daddy capitalism" (*pindiexing zibenzhuyi* / 拼爹型资本主义).[8]

In 1992, after three years of international condemnation and a hiatus in investing; after the realignment between the party and the

---

5   Wang Hui, "The 1989 Social Movement," 20.

6   The phrase was popularized by the American journalist, Orville Schell; Deng never said it. However, Deng did promote "*Rang yi bu fen ren xian fu qi lai* (让一部分人先副起来)"—"Let some people get rich first."

7   Dai Jinhua, "Introduction," 6.

8   Dai Jinhua, "The Dimensions of the Future," tr. Zhou Shuchen, *Chinese Literature Today* 7:2, 2019, 100.

socioeconomic bases of the transforming Chinese economy; after nascent capitalists were encouraged to accumulate wealth and drop politics; and after the disciplining of students and intellectuals, who were forced into military-run political education programs to instill obedience, Deng Xiaoping went south. There, he surveyed the results of unfettered capitalist development in the Shenzhen Special Economic Zone (SEZ) on the Guangzhou–Hong Kong border, and he pronounced it "good." Deng's southern tour (*nanxun*/南巡) unleashed waves of frenzied economic activity, as China's economy opened and "joined tracks with the world" (*yu shijie jiegui* / 与世界接轨). The "world" here referred to the capitalist world of Euro-America, Japan, and Taiwan, since in the interval from 1989 to 1992, the Soviet Union had fallen and was breaking up into national fractions, and the Eastern bloc was entering its final dissolution. The Third World, hitherto a world of revolutionary support and practice, for the time being no longer mattered. Discordantly ruled under the iron grip of one of the last major Communist parties standing, China was propelled into a mutually dependent transformation of the capitalist world. In the resultant global scale of dispossession and accumulation, China was instrumental in the turn to neoliberalism—as both economic and ideological structure—led by the Chinese state and in part by state-owned capital. The resultant symbiotic relation of power and money between the party and multinational capital has become a global phenomenon, sucking individuals, corporations, and whole continents into its rapacious and capacious ambit.

Domestically, the CCP's guarantee of social stability ensured the predictability capitalists desired for large-scale investment. China quickly was inserted into an international division of labor, in which capital investment, tractability of labor, and sexual difference are deeply intertwined structures of organization. Indeed, the huge private and national wealth accumulations of the 1990s and beyond could not have happened without the material dispossessions upon which vast mobilizations of labor depended. Unlike under the socialist regime, when labor had been tightly harnessed to place-based rural and industrial economies, now labor power was "freed" to float on the market for deployment in sweatshops and other manufactures being established in the Shenzhen SEZ, where labor laws were lax, tax laws were relaxed, and environmental regulation was nonexistent. Capital rushed over the Hong Kong border to take advantage of the business-friendliness; it leapt across the Taiwan Strait and over fifty years of political polarization; it surmounted the Euro-American bourgeois distaste for dealing with historically anti-capitalist Communists. Breaching all hitherto-existing barriers and constraints, factories sprouted, and a massive city came into being in less than a decade. Provincial leaders around China clamored to follow with their own SEZs, to avoid the remnants of socialist-era regulations on labor, governance, and compensation and to capitalize on global capital mobility and domestic labor abundance.

The 1990s saw the partial dismantling of state-owned enterprises (SOE) and the transformation of the township and village enterprises (TVE) that had survived from the late 1950s, releasing labor onto the market as ever-larger numbers of bodies were rendered "surplus" to the existing economy. A seemingly endless stream of young women and men from the countryside and smaller cities, where economies and livelihoods were now precarious because of the withdrawal of state support, traveled to the South, eager to find a way to become part of the waged and consuming masses, to enjoy the promise of new life opportunities. They arrived at the gates of factories and assembly plants, introduced by brokers who vouched for their characters, willing to sell their labor at fire-sale prices and to endure hardship in order to earn more here than they could in their places of origin.[9] Enthusiastic rural-born women became "working girls" (*dagong mei* / 打工妹), cornerstones of a new economic model and social ideology. As sociologist Pun Ngai puts it: "To construct new industrial subjects in the workplace, old socialist and rural beings are constantly devalued, downgraded, and forsaken"; rural bodies are "contrasted with the sharpness and dexterousness of industrial bodies who are often

---

9   For an account of the early part of this process (1990s), see C. K. Lee, *Gender and the South China Miracle*, Berkeley, CA: University of California Press, 1998.

said to be young, female, single, and particularly suited to the new international division of labor."[10]

Conditioned by capitalism, these rural bodies were transformed into consumers at the lower levels of the marketplace; and after some years of toil and being physically worn down, they were spit back out of the factory gates. Because *hukou* never moved with the working girls, when factory work ceased they immediately were rendered redundantly out of place in the urban environment. Patriarchal cultural expectations, seamlessly integrated with the economic disciplining of the state and the market, offered the "half-peasant and half-proletariat" women a new yet simultaneously familiar place:[11] as married and reproductive bodies serving their husband's families in the struggling villages of rural China. With their wages and independence, many women commanded some power over their choice of partner, although many also were expected to help support brothers and male cousins from their natal families, who were allowed to remain in school or were funded to start small-scale businesses. While in the beginning of the era, girls' wages were perhaps not part of a family economic strategy, by the late 1990s the wages girls earned were incorporated into family calculations for how male members could proceed. Thus, in social reproductive terms, women were often doubly subordinated by being embedded as earners and as reproducers in marital and natal families, either simultaneously or serially. Despite all, girls and women often experienced their earned economic independence as a form of at least temporary freedom.

Meanwhile, men who worked in factories, construction, or other urban waged positions were often able to turn their earnings into capital for investment on their own account. While also super-exploited in any number of ways—for instance, working for deferred pay, and then not getting paid when subcontractors absconded with the sums of their salaries—men nevertheless tapped into and

---

10   Pun Ngai, *Made in China: Women Factory Workers in a Global Workplace*, Durham, NC: Duke University Press, 2005, 14.

11   Ibid., 193.

promoted the resurgence of patriarchy in the rural and urban areas alike. In this resurgence, they were empowered to command not only their own wages and bodies, but also the wages and bodies of sisters, wives, daughters, and mothers.

Women and men did not—and do not—go docilely to their fates as factory factotums or underpaid workers. In 1994 and thereafter, movements of resistance—in the form of factory strikes or production line slowdowns, among many others—have provided huge pushback, leading to the first of a number of labor laws promulgated ostensibly to protect workers from the rapaciousness and arbitrariness of employers. And yet, as taxes and profits are dependent upon the success of the enterprises in their jurisdictions, local judges rarely render verdicts against owners; at most, arbitration is offered to calm an immediately critical situation.[12] In the absence of strict enforcement, the labor laws—even the strengthened labor law of 2008—are more a paper commitment than a practical one. Labor unrest remains endemic, although it generally gets contained to single factories in local districts as any hint of class-conscious alliance is crushed mercilessly.

One of the major mitigators against the formation of a stable working class—a new proletariat—has been the fragmentation of labor built into the rural-urban migration structure, the geographical differences between types of labor, and the gendered disparities in rural and urban reproduction of labor power. Until very recently the countryside was the place where the reproduction of labor power happened. In other words, while urban *hukou* families reproduce in and through the urban wage economy—they purchase housing, education, medical care, and so on, with wages earned from their workplaces, which must be minimally sufficient to cover such expenses—the economy based on migrant labor has relied on the reproduction of labor power through the deportation of women from the cities back to their village *hukou* locations

---

12   Kinglun Ngok, "The Changes of Chinese Labor Policy and Labor Legislation in the Context of Market Transition," *International Labor and Working Class History* 73:1, Spring 2008, 45–64.

during their major years of fertility. This has alleviated the burden on industry to pay a living wage to women, while displacing the costs of labor reproduction to the villages, which are already impoverished through reductions in state support and the overextraction of taxes and fees by venal party administrators from the districts up through the provincial levels.

Within the urban workplace, localistic ties (*laoxiang*/老乡) help "support the reproduction of labor power . . . the systemic need for workers to be adequately fed, trained, sheltered, and transported,"[13] because as broker and guarantor of individuals' good behavior, localism ensures discipline. This same localism also functions as a barrier against lasting labor solidarity. When workers are dismissed or finish their terms of employ, they either move to another place of employment or return to their *hukou* villages; any form of collective activism in any given factory, worksite, or any other unit of potential proletarian activity—such as the courthouse—is thus short-circuited. Entirely unlike the socialist-era rhetorical construction of the proletariat as "masters" of society, whose class and political interests were supposed to transcend all differences, the contemporary reliance on localism as a mode of labor control and fragmentation is new. It may appear as a throwback to a different era (the 1930s), yet, as is the case with the resurgence of patriarchal power in its most atavistic ideological and social forms, localism works hand in glove with today's capitalist economy. Far from anachronistic, these resurgent vestiges of the "traditional" past are fully embedded in and crucial to the functioning of the domestic and global capitalist economies of the present.

Meanwhile, toward the end of the 1990s the urban service economy also roared into action. Rural teenage girls migrated in ever-larger numbers to become the nannies, cooks, cleaners, and eldercare companions for many city families now barging their way into a new middle-class existence. Rural twenty-something men migrated into construction, ragpicking, and recycling and trash collection, among other urban jobs. These rural migrants were branded by urban people

---

13   Lee, *Gender and the South China Miracle*, 84.

as "low-quality" individuals (*suzhi di* / 素质底), often mistreated and overworked, with the justification that they were being taught discipline and elevated cultural habits. Men lived in hastily organized collective rooming situations, clustered around their workplaces; girls worked as live-in help, often making due for accommodation with a corner of an outdoor patio space or under a staircase. More than the men, girls did become partially citified, largely resisting re-rustication when their terms of employment were at an end. With cultural desires and curiosities different from their stay-in-the-village sisters or sweatshop equivalents, and with consumption habits informed by their fancier environments, this population became not only *dis*-placed but actually *mis*-placed: neither at home in the cities (having no *hukou*; considered "low quality"), and yet no longer comfortable in the countryside. Rejecting marriages with local boys, whose domineering behavior is no longer acceptable to them, they live their lives in between, constituting a new type of floating population with loyalty to no one but themselves. Many have made livelihoods on the margins of society, some managing to manipulate the interstices into social position and wealth, and others falling into various degrees of destitution, precarity, and even disposability.

Meanwhile, the remnant economy in what sociologist C. K. Lee has called the "rustbelt"—the Northeastern industrial corridor—has faltered in the face of the new realities of competition and efficiency.[14] These bastions of the old socialist "iron rice bowl" are now gutted, with valuable assets privatized by party bosses or factory managers and former workers left to fend for themselves. The deindustrialized North houses a now-vestigial socialist proletariat, which has had a tough time reorienting to new economic expectations and often subsists on traces of socialist-era state support and whatever can be scraped together from children and families. Some of these workers successfully "leapt into the sea" (*xiahai*/下海)—went into private business—in the 1990s, and those self-made fortunes provide plenty

---

14   C. K. Lee, *Against the Law: Labor Protests in China's Rustbelt and Sunbelt*, Berkeley, CA: University of California Press, 2007.

of happy stories to float hopes of rags-to-riches trajectories among many. As a proportion of the population, they are few and far between. By the same token, the "sunbelt" workers—women in the Southern sweatshops—have very little in common with these rustbelt vestiges. The gendered, generational, and general disparities thus militate against proletarian class formation of any real substance.

From the 1990s into the 2000s, many regulatory fetters on private business were lifted, and that sector of the economy soon took off, absorbing large amounts of labor into smaller workplaces. From small-scale coal mines to clothing stalls to mom-and-pop transport services or noodle stands, and countless other types of endeavors, private businesses sprouted throughout the country. Some became behemoths, cornerstones of a new private economy; many failed or barely scrape by. Those SOEs and TVEs that had not been dismantled, meanwhile, moved into profit-making mode, and while they still provide a livelihood for party members and others whose loyalty is required, they also are expected to operate along market principles of competitiveness and efficiency. Often the first in line for state-backed loans and debt financing, SOEs and former TVEs are a major and favored part of the capitalist economy. Indeed, they and their many subsidiaries operate globally, ostensibly as private capital but with state support not far behind.

Intellectuals and professionals traded erstwhile state subsidies for real salaries—indeed, their loyalty to the state was bought through higher compensation, better housing, and enhanced professional opportunities, including trips abroad for research and school advantages for their one child. Elite universities as well as elite elementary and high schools have been lavished with resources, with both STEM and humanities garnering huge state support with the object of propelling a few named Chinese educational institutions into the global stratum of rankings. Whole new campuses on land appropriated from the rural outskirts of cities are constructed as educational satellites, intended to provide security and safe learning conditions to students, as well as a buffer between potential student unrest and urban centers of business and tourism. Alternate schools are allowed to establish themselves with private funding and the intellectual labor of those who cannot gain positions in the favored state sector. Rural schools have fallen further than ever behind their urban counterparts; with diminished state resources and inadequate instructors and facilities, such schools and their students do not stand much of a chance in the hyper-competitive global educational sweepstakes.

Cultural figures, released from the necessity to produce for socialism, now create for vibrant markets, domestic and global. Contemporary Chinese artists broke into the global art market relatively early, with their parodic takes on Maoism and Chinese political visual culture. Zhang Hongtu's play on Mao images, Zhao Bandi's panda photos, Xu Bing's manipulation of Chinese writing, and Ai Weiwei's performance pieces are among some of the more famous examples of globally circulating contemporary Chinese art. Filmmakers and documentarians work now in an environment that far more resembles the European scene than the previous Mao-era studio system; thus, while state-backed films are still churned out at a rapid pace and while state censorship of content remains a huge and growing obstacle, independent filmmakers fund their projects domestically and internationally, circulate them on the world festival scene, and also market them in cinemas at home and abroad. Zhang Yimou and Chen Kaige are two of the original pioneers of the filmmaking model that combined official and unofficial sources of support, and whose aesthetics and storytelling became iconic as a globally marketable category of "fifth generation" artist. Cashing in on the possibilities of television, many scriptwriters and directors began working for multi-episode TV series—long before streaming services made such series writing prestigious in the Western world of cultural production. Creating dramas revolving around romantic and power-soaked themes from ancient dynastic times as well as those centered on more contemporary revolutionary wars, many of these TV series have become wildly popular and have helped shape the historical imaginaries of whole generations. Novelists, poets, and nonfiction writers compete in a vigorous cultural commodity market for notice, access, and consumer power. When novelist Mo Yan won the Nobel Prize in

Literature in 2012, national pride went into overdrive, even though he was criticized from abroad for being a mouthpiece for the Chinese state.

As an ideological promise, the socialist legacy is gone. As a structural matter, certain vestiges remain to be reworked by the capitalist transformation of the Chinese economy. One notable persistence is the *hukou* system, which legally maintains the difference between rural and urban citizens and spaces, forcing them to meet on profoundly unequal terms of engagement. Its longevity can be explained by its regulatory utility. From its beginning in the late 1950s, it was promoted as a barrier to the ghettoization of cities by potential famine migrants; over the years, it has functioned to discipline certain parts of the population for different purposes. Today, more controversial than ever and perhaps soon having outlived its utility, *hukou* nevertheless remains a state tool of population and social control. On the one hand, *hukou* guarantees plots of land in natal or marital villages to those classified as residents of those villages; these plots—taxed and attached with local fees and not treated as privately alienable property, and thus not lucrative as such—can function as a very minimum-level economic guarantee against starvation. They are the site of ancestral and family dwelling, where the young and the old live while those in the middle roam out to earn money. As a measure of control, *hukou* means that those designated migrants in the cities can be deported *to* a place: to the villages where they ostensibly "belong." In 1997 and 2009 and 2015, with economic downturns consequent upon global financial crises, so-called "surplus labor" in the cities was rounded up and shipped out in order to prevent supposed criminality or postulated unrest. Precarious cities-within-the-city—migrant encampments—could be demolished and their denizens moved at the flick of a bureaucratic switch. During the cleanup of Beijing preparatory to the Olympic Games in 2008, for example, migrants—some of whom had lived in Beijing for decades already—were forcibly moved back to their *hukou* villages; most recently, those labeled "inferior humans" (*diduan renkou* / 低端人口) were cleared from a densely settled area in Beijing in 2017 and shipped "home." Living as second-class citizens in urban spaces without access to the amenities urban-ites have, such as public schools and medical care, peasant *hukou* holders are structurally disadvantaged and treated unequally as a matter of systemic logic.

Hukou, however, also has been the barrier to the full capitalist transformation of the countryside; its guarantee of land to village resi-dents has become a legal obstacle to such complete and naked privati-zation. Neoliberal ideologues in China and abroad decry this last socialist vestige, believing that only full privatization can properly stimulate the economy; and many others have argued that the only possible release of peasants from second-class citizenship is through their ability to completely "depeasantize"—that is, by allowing them to rid themselves of their biggest asset, their land, to the highest bidder. Speculators hover, salivating over the prospect of land released from regulation to the market. Meanwhile, the difficulties of rural China, to which the land/*hukou* problem speaks, are real. Through the 1990s and certainly after China joined the WTO in 2001—which, for example, pitted the huge output of US agribusiness against China's household economies—the productivity of China's agricultural sector has not kept pace with population growth or with changing urban consumption desires (more meat, more dairy, more fat). When the state decided to forsake the idea of self-sufficiency in food—a pillar of Maoist policy—the role of the rural sector in the Chinese economy fundamentally was altered. The rural now became the site of land grabs, with village chiefs, who control village land, in cahoots with regional and provincial power holders, who dispossess peasants of their livelihoods in the name of the financial benefit of the village. On the former sites of villages, debt-financed cities are built, while fami-lies are forcibly relocated, paid small one-time or fixed-term compen-sations, and then forgotten. An estimated fifty or more ghost cities built on this model of village dispossession exist around China, with perhaps up to 65 million empty apartments. *Hukou* remains an obsta-cle, albeit an increasingly weak one, to the fullest exploitation of this model of state-funded private enrichment.

On the other hand, early in the reform process (in the 1980s and 1990s), peasants who lived near big cities with access to good markets and who diversified their economic practices were able to take advantage of the new opportunities opened by the relaxation of socialist constraints. In the Yangzi delta region around Shanghai and Nanjing, or in the Pearl River region of the South, peasant-entrepreneurs amassed small or big fortunes, invested in new businesses, and built new, lavish lineage homes in their villages to showcase their prowess and success. The limits of this agricultural model have since been reached, and many of the original peasants as well as others now wish for land privatization, which would facilitate agriculturally well-endowed areas to aggregate plots into economies of scale to compete more favorably with foreign imports and agribusiness. *Hukou* is an obstacle to this type of development too.

Countervailing pressures remain, with the rise of advocacies for "re-peasantization"—that is, making it possible for peasants to be more efficient as farmers. Curbing the excessive taxes and fees levied upon village residents; restraining the corrupt practices of village chiefs and party bosses that have hollowed out and polarized social life in the villages; recommitting resources to neglected areas; experimenting with market cooperatives and other collective forms: episodically, each has been experimented with, implemented, or promoted as a way to allow peasants to remain on the land. *Hukou* permits these types of alternatives to be tried.

It now appears, however, that de-peasantization will have won the day: huge numbers of rural families are being forcibly relocated to second- and third-tier cities, their village *hukou* canceled and exchanged for *hukou* in those cities, so that the land can be confiscated and repurposed. In the new cities, there are few economic opportunities, and existing communities of village social life have been fragmented. Much recent cultural production fictionally and viscerally exposes the chaotic creativity and sometimes criminal activity of individuals at the lower levels of society who are striving to cope with an environment in such constant flux.

*   *   *

There is no doubt that years of exponential economic growth helped huge numbers of people—in absolute terms and as a percentage of the population—move out of the kinds of poverty their predecessors had endured. This has happened at a globally unprecedented pace. Even with nothing but precarity for most and disposability for many, China has tipped over into an economy of abundance rather than the economy of scarcity that dominated the Maoist years. In large part, this is a consequence of the ways in which wealth has been generated from the baseline of a very low level of individual consumption and from the dissolution of the state command economy during which collective wealth was privatized. The state still holds a large sector of the economy, a fact that often needlessly confuses efforts to interpret China's new era as a neoliberal one. On the one hand, the consequences of the past four decades of socioeconomic transformation have been nothing short of dramatic: large numbers in a huge Chinese population now see themselves as part of a middle class whose values and mores are similar to those of their counterparts the world over. They spend, they travel, they consume, they strive: visible as never before, Chinese with money to spare are major drivers of the luxury tourist and commodity economy globally, even as they aim to get their children educated and properly networked in the elite universities of China and the world. And yet, on the other hand, from one of the most economically equal societies in the world, with disparities during the Maoist years measured in political power rather than private wealth, the decades of rocketing growth since the early 1990s have produced one of the most unequal societies on the planet. The inequality can be measured in terms of the Gini coefficient, the vast gulf that separates globe-trotting Chinese billionaires from locally destitute peasants, or in the gendered terms of the massive transfer of urban real estate wealth into the hands of men, as housing bought with funds pooled from marriage is registered in the man's name alone.[15] Far from unique to China, of course, these social and

---

15 This latter phenomenon is meticulously documented by Leta Hong-Fincher, *Leftover Women: The Resurgence of Gender Inequality in China*, London: Zed, 2016.

economic inequalities nevertheless loom large because of China's enormous scale.

In the context of the dual retreat in the 1980s and 1990s from socialism and the narrative straitjacket of the necessary historicist march from feudalism to socialism, serious scholars have made serious efforts to think about how to deal with the problem of universal world-historical narratives in relation to the particularity of Chinese history. These efforts initially followed on the "criticize Confucius and criticize Lin [Biao]" historical revisions promoted at the end of the Cultural Revolution, although in less tortured and less state-directed form. Early in the 1980s, one faction of the scholarly community was politically aligned against the ever-growing prospect of the restoration of capitalism. Thus one trend of the initial rethinkings was intended to provide a historical explanatory foundation for a return to the "new democratic" approach of the early 1950s: a mixed economy under the direction of a class alliance in defense of a strong socialist path. The opposing trend of scholarship was intended to provide a historical foundation for the pursuit of modernization, arguing that without a strong base of the "productive forces"—that is, wealth accumulation— China could never move on from Mao-era poverty. In the latter vein, it was argued that the productive forces were to be developed with little concern for the immediate social costs, and Mao's emphasis on transforming relations of production—the relative strengths of social classes in the economy—was condemned as the utopian egalitarian dream of pre-modern feudal peasants. In both cases of intellectual rethinking, the excesses of Maoism were excoriated, although whether or not one believed that class struggle remained historically necessary and whether socialism was worth fighting for were clear dividing lines between the two factions. The vigorous debates over economic reform of the 1980s were enmeshed in one of these two poles of analysis, even while not hewing exactly to either.[16]

---

16 For the best account of 1980s debates, see Isabella Weber, *Reassessing China's Reform Debate (1978–1988): Price Regulation and Market Creation*, forthcoming.

The fact that Chinese history could never be stuffed into the historicist categories of Marxist materialism—although, truth be told, no history conforms to vulgar Marxist historicism—became the insight through which academic historians claimed autonomy from accepted state historical narrative practices. As the boundaries of what could and could not be critiqued or altered began to change—from the 1990s onward, the professional practice of history has been substantially freed from Maoist strictures—the ways in which China's past has been made to speak to its present and future have changed. By the early 2000s, Marxism—however attenuated it may have always beeen—was no longer a guiding principle of professional historians, and certainly not of popular ones. Rather, China's deep past became a matter of an autonomous and autochthonous trajectory, shaped by what was named and considered an enduring, timeless Chinese culture, with Confucianism at its core. In the idiom of a now-reconstituted Confucianism—the essence of this enduringly timeless China, it is said—the Mao era is now entirely repudiated for *its* renunciation of the Confucian (true Chinese) past. The May Fourth movement, 1911 Revolution, 1898 reforms, and much of the hybridity of the nineteenth century are now labeled too "radical" and un-Chinese to receive approbation in new narratives of the Chinese past.[17] A very conservative and substantial wing of the professional discipline now calls for a return to Confucian norms and ethics, with a strong state, family filiality, and patriarchy defining all aspects of "Chinese-ness" for the present and future. This version of Chinese-ness is exported through branches of the Confucius Institute, established around the world from the 2000s onward, and in China, it has become a pillar of popular and serious education alike.

Meanwhile, at the level of the state, the ideological shift also has been pronounced. The general secretaries of the Chinese Communist Party since Deng Xiaoping's retirement (1992) and death (1997) have

---

17   Exemplary of the trend is Qin Hui, *Zouchu dizhi: Cong Wanqing dao Minguo de lishi huiwang* [Out of the imperial polity: Historical reflections on the late Qing and the republic], Beijing: Qunyan, 2016. See Wang Chaohua's review in *New Left Review* 106, 2017, 125–40.

presented ever more elaborate attempts to square the ideological circle of rapacious capitalism and growing social inequality under CPP governance. For the past four decades, the effort to make the theory of what has been labeled "socialism with Chinese characteristics" (*you zhongguo tese de shehuizhuyi* / 有中国特色的社会主义) fit practices that are at a vast distance from socialism, and to renovate Marxism for a profoundly un-Marxist project, has been a preoccupation of state-funded think tanks such as the Academy of Social Sciences at various levels and of institutes embedded in universities. These encompassing narratives exhibit logical gaps that are ever harder to mask. One of the first of these ideological attempts, in the early 1980s, was to claim that China—after thirty years of Maoist practice—was only now entering the "primary stage of socialism." This fig leaf was soon exposed to be mere placeholder rhetoric, although it continues to carry weight in more recent iterations of state ideology. Thereafter, Jiang Zemin, Deng's immediate successor, was tasked with holding onto social stability in the wake of 1989. He is best known for his articulation of the "Three Represents" (*sange daibiao* / 三个代表): "Our Party must always represent the requirements for developing China's advanced productive forces, the orientation of China's advanced culture and the fundamental interests of the overwhelming majority of the Chinese people. These are the inexorable requirements for maintaining and developing socialism."[18] In practice, this meant opening the Communist Party to capitalist membership, so long as capitalists, as individuals, pledged allegiance to the CCP. This apparently incongruous arrangement passed into policy with little more than a ripple of derision, and now capitalists dominate party posts and membership.

Then came the leadership of Hu Jintao, whose main contribution to state ideology was to promote the growth of a "harmonious society" (*hexie shehui* / 和諧社會) based upon the premise of the "scientific development outlook" (*kexue fazhanguan* / 科学发展观).

---

18   Jiang Zemin, *Selected Works of Jiang Zemin*, vol. 3, Beijing: Foreign Language Press, 2013, 519.

Harmony is an old Confucian value; nothing could be further from class struggle, which pits social divisions toward a historical showdown. Harmony has been dusted off and burnished as a watchword for one of the most class-polarized societies in the world. When Hu pioneered it, the irony was noted, and yet the sentiment—that everyone should just occupy the places they had been allotted and contribute to social order from those stable positions—was and remains highly popular among the striving middle and upper classes, who feel threatened by latent social disorder potentially augured by increased economic and geographic inequality. Meanwhile, the development promoted in the "scientific view" is to be accomplished without Maoist-like political campaigns or social instability. It is just that kind of economic growth achievable through methodical practice. Hu Jintao's era of rhetorical harmony accompanied by increasingly harsh class division paved the way to Xi Jinping, who began to consolidate power in 2012 and became the core of the core, by abolishing leadership term limits, in 2016. Xi came of age during the Cultural Revolution, and was a beneficiary of its policies. His regime is known for the anti-corruption sweeps that have eliminated some of his major party, state, and social rivals; for his "China Dream" (zhongguo meng / 中国梦) that informs the imaginative politics of development domestically and the outward reach of the Chinese state and capital into Africa, Latin America, and Asia; and for his fourteen-point "Xi Jinping Thought," incorporated into the party constitution, that calls for unity and strength above all else.

As the years of savage growth (yeman shengzhang / 野蛮生长) appear to be coming to an end, and with censoring clampdowns on every possibly threatening form of expression and social organization, the Xi Jinping era is shaping up to be at once the most incredibly insular and the most globally oriented of China's modern history.

Interlude: Xinjiang 2009

> Break their lineage, break their roots, break their connections and
> break their origins.
>
> —Maisumujiang Maimuer[1]

On July 5, 2009, in the Xinjiang capital of Urumqi, the accumulated
ethnic and religious anger of thousands of Uyghurs boiled over into
violence. The immediate precipitate was an episode in June when two
Uyghur workers in Guangdong Province were killed by their Han
counterparts. A protest against the police cover-up in Guangdong
was mobilized in Urumqi, and the violent attempt to suppress the
demonstration only further inflamed it. Han and Uyghur attacked
each other, while groups of each prowled the residential enclaves of
the other, smashing property and menacing life. Police restored order
by cracking down on Uyghurs, on whom they pinned the blame for
the loss of life. A swift militarization of the city and surrounding areas
ensued. Shaping the contours of this episode were years of Han migration into the region that marginalized Uyghurs in their homeland;
years of poor and prejudiced treatment in Xinjiang and in the rest of
China of Uyghurs as a people; and years of Uyghurs having their religion, language, and culture constrained and controlled.

As with Tibet, the Xinjiang events had a deep historical derivation. The region came under Qing rule in the eighteenth century, in
the early part of that dynasty's expansion into what is now known as
Central Asia. Situated on a sparsely populated overland trade route
and functioning as a place of exile for those who had fallen out of
favor with the emperor, multiethnic Xinjiang ("new frontier") was
governed as part of the Qing Empire. The republican government of

---

1 *Xinhua News*, October 8, 2018. Cited in Austin Ramzy, "China Targets Prominent
Uighur Intellectuals to Erase an Ethnic Identity," *New York Times*, January 5, 2019.

Chiang Kaishek claimed Xinjiang as part of China's national territory, primarily as a site of resource extraction, although the Guomindang's ability to enforce that claim was relatively weak. Through the Yan'an years, the Chinese Communist Party struck alliances with various Muslim factions to fight the GMD and/or the Japanese, as needed. Some parts of Uyghur society remained hostile to accommodation with the CCP or any Han Chinese party; others were induced to alliances with the promise of eventual autonomy.[2]

In 1955, the CCP proclaimed Xinjiang an "autonomous region," and it was permitted certain forms of cultural, linguistic, and religious self-rule in exchange for loyalty to the CCP and the Chinese state. Part of a more general policy, these dispensations were designed to allow designated ethnicities, called "minorities" (shaoshu minzu / 少数民族), to remain culturally distinct from the Han while being politically integrated into the Chinese national state. Scholars debate if this policy was good, just, or correct—whether it served merely to exoticize and marginalize, by freezing non-Han peoples into place, or rather to assist non-Han peoples in retaining some control over their own lives. However one judges minority policy, periods of relatively smooth implementation have been punctuated by currents of latent and manifest hostility. In Xinjiang in the 1960s, for example, significant tensions surfaced when the PRC decided to use southern parts of the region as nuclear testing zones, poisoning the environment in that area for decades if not centuries to come. In the 1950s to 1970s, pockets of Han residents were established, as general political campaigns washed across the region, bringing "sent-down youth" and others into the area.

But after 1979, hostilities mounted precipitously when developmental policies moved toward modernization and became highly prejudicial toward ethnic autonomy and noncapitalist or non-accumulative modes of economic and social life, such as subsistence oasis farming.

---

2   "Uyghur" is a twentieth-century invention of an identity. I use it here for familiarity and convenience. See Rian Thum, "Uyghurs in Modern China," Oxford Research Encyclopedia, accessed April 2018, oxfordre.com. Also see David Brophy, "Good and Bad Muslims in Xinjiang," Made in China Journal, July 11, 2019, madeinchinajournal.com.

Even while the openings of the 1980s allowed for a cultural flourishing in Xinjiang—huge numbers of religious, historical, and political texts were published in the Uyghur language at that time—extractive industries, led by oil drilling, and military farms (*bingtuan*/兵团), established to provision the now-modernizing PLA and to serve as models of new forms of agribusiness, facilitated state-subsidized Han in-migration, exacerbating the already-tense local social and political environment. Han "civilizers" looked down upon Uyghurs as a backward and inferior people, a chauvinism facilitated by the fact that Uyghurs are a Turkic people—thus are racially marked as different from the Han—and many keep to Islamic culinary and cultural codes. Out-migration of Uyghurs, meanwhile, has been hampered by Han employers' reluctance to hire such "others" in their factories, manufactures, or construction sites. Since the 1980s, the percentage of Uyghurs in the population of Xinjiang has fallen, while segregated residential patterns have pushed them into smaller ghettoized pockets. Lands previously used for pasturage are now being enclosed and rendered economic components of the new "One Belt, One Road" initiative. Economic life is oriented ever more toward Han-dominated cities and capital investments in Northern Xinjiang rather than the dispersed population and economy of the South.

After the attacks on the United States on September 11, 2001, the PRC connected their own growing state security rhetoric to the high pitch of global anti-terrorism, now alleging that rising Uyghur unrest had to be part of a fundamentalist network emanating from abroad that was intent on undermining China's territorial integrity, peace, harmony, and safety. As the US "War on Terror" has continued to fuel instability on China's borders, with war in Afghanistan and military bases established in the newly independent former Soviet nations surrounding China, real or imagined Chinese security concerns have led to exponential growth in the crackdown on Uyghurs. Most recently, this has entailed the targeted imprisonment of such major public thinkers as the economist Ilham Tohti, as well as over 300 leading Uyghur cultural and intellectual figures, as part of an attempt to lobotomize the brain trust of Uyghur life, and the wholesale imprisoning of a general population of suspected malcontents. A few incidents of ethnic violence perpetrated by Uyghurs against Han outside of Xinjiang solidified the state's conviction that Uyghurs as a people are being radicalized by fundamentalist Islamists from outside China and thus that all Uyghurs are potential terrorists. Anecdotal reports indicate that many Han appear to believe this to be true and seem positively disposed to Xi Jinping's "people's war on terrorism" targeting Uyghurs, and to the newly revealed network of mass incarceration and so-called "reeducation" of more than a million Uyghurs now ongoing in Xinjiang. As German researcher Adrian Zenz, who helped expose the extent of the carceral camps, has recently noted, mass internment "merely represents the logical culmination of Beijing's wider strategy to reassert control over the spiritual-moral realm of society,"[3] a strategy that has dominated the Xi Jinping domestic regime of extensive censorship, hyper-nationalism, Han Chinese culturalism, and Chinese capitalist expansion across continents. That Uyghurs—and Tibetans—are perceived as obstacles to the "great revival" of the Chinese nation (as a state and a people) has called forth the perceived need for a policy of ethnic "fusion" (*jiaorong*/交融) to replace the previous minority policy of ethnic difference.[4]

Uyghurs stand squarely in the geographical and ideological path of the One Belt, One Road (OBOR) policy, also known as the Belt and Road Initiative (BRI), an expansive bid for Chinese national infrastructural and economic control over resources spanning the globe. Formally proposed in 2013 by Xi Jinping, this initiative intentionally recalls an older Silk Road pastoral while pushing that mythic ancient trade ideal into the twenty-first century. Yet, as literary scholar Tamara Chin has explored, the Silk Road, far from being an ancient artifact, is a modern idea, a term first coined by a German geographer in 1877 as part of European imperialist expansion across the Euro-Asian continent. During the Cold War, China re-signified

---

3   Adrian Zenz, "Re-education Returns to China," *Foreign Affairs*, June 20, 2018, foreignaffairs.com.

4   Unknown author, "Minor Events and Grand Dreams: Ethnic Outsiders in China's Postcolonial World Order," *positions*, forthcoming.

the Silk Road (*sichou zhi lu* / 丝绸之路) as "the ancient prefiguration of its non-aligned diplomacy with the decolonized world." At that time, Mao Zedong and Zhou Enlai proposed the Silk Road as part of "a larger Afro-Asian framework in which historians and writers spatially could re-organize China's connected past."[5] In this process, Chin shows, China's Afro-Asian Silk Road differed from the imperialist Euro-Asian version of the nineteenth and early twentieth centuries. Xi Jinping's twenty-first century version fuses the discursive types to arrive at a supposedly nonthreatening consolidation, one that, in Chin's words, allows China to claim that "before globalization [China] already had a proto-globalized Silk Road world. OBOR's new order thus represents itself not as a challenge (to, say, U.S. hegemony), but as a renewal of an older order."[6] In this state-sanctioned idiom, Han Chinese scholar Hu Angang insists that OBOR presents a specifically "Eastern" combination of "consent and tribute" through which China can reach the position of superpower differently from the coercive version pursued by the United States or the former Soviet Union.[7]

One Belt, One Road runs through Xinjiang; it runs through Uyghur autonomy; it runs through Uyghur grievances about Han high-handedness, Han repression, and Han enrichment at Uyghur expense; and it runs through religious and cultural opposition to both assimilation and marginalization. With minority policy being transformed into a policy of "fusion"; with networks of camps intended to wipe out cultural, linguistic, intellectual, and religious identity; with gendered policies to force young Uyghur women into marriage with Han men, thus to subdue the population and dilute Uyghur racial and

---

5   Tamara Chin, "The Afro-Asian 'Silk Road' and the Rhetoric of Connected History," talk delivered at Columbia University, New York, April 11, 2018. The cited passages are from the publicity materials for the talk. Also see Tamara Chin, "The Invention of the Silk Road, 1877," *Critical Inquiry* 40:1, 2013, 194–219.

6   Mercy A. Kuo, "One Belt, One Road: A Convergence of Civilizations? Insights from Tamara Chin," *Diplomat*, May 24, 2017.

7   Hu Angang. *Zhongguo 2020: Yige xinxing chaoji daguo* [China in 2020: A new type of superpower], Zhejiang: Zhejiang Renmin Chubanshe, 2012.

cultural characteristics;[8] with possibilities of autonomous Uyghur leadership erased; with the full scale of technology being brought to bear on surveillance and suppression;[9] with OBOR establishing infrastructural alliances with global corporations from the United States and elsewhere, whose profits are more important than are ethics; and with global wars on terror constantly mutating, expanding, and converging, how the "Uyghur question" might persist and change remains open. What is clear is that, far from "consent and tribute," ethnic-cultural cleansing is being deployed as the current Chinese national strategy to garner kowtowing obedience among Uyghurs and others deemed threatening to current political, economic, social, cultural, and racial priorities.

---

8   Eva Xiao, "China Pushes Inter-ethnic Marriage in Xinjiang Assimilation Drive," *Hong Kong Free Press*, May 18, 2019, hongkongfp.com.

9   Darren Byler, "Ghost World," *Logic* 6, logicmag.io.

Conclusion: 2019

[The cinema of] the end of the first decade of the twenty-first century indicates that it is much easier to imagine the end of humanity than the end of capitalism.

—Dai Jinhua[1]

In July 2018, some workers at the Chinese-owned Jasic Technology factory near Shenzhen attempted to form an independent, nonparty union. They picketed their workplace and pressured local leaders in protest of the low pay, long hours, and horrible conditions in which they labored. A group of university students from Beijing, awakened to Marxism's class analysis and Maoism's focus on proletarian consciousness, learned of the Jasic case, wrote a letter of solidarity, then traveled south to stand with the workers in an attempt to force the Chinese state and the CCP to live up to their self-proclaimed communist ideals. By mid August, many workers and students had been detained and disappeared; sometime later, one by one they were selectively trotted out to perform public confessions to a TV audience. The Jasic episode has resonated internationally—Marxist and non-Marxist scholars around the world rallied to the cause with letters of solidarity and boycotts of conferences—in part, perhaps, because of the student involvement in the action. According to the online *China Labour Bulletin*, Jasic is just one of many worksites being challenged today: "China's economic slowdown, exacerbated by the Sino-US trade war, seems to have been most acutely felt in the coastal provinces, which are once again the focus of worker protests in the manufacturing sector."[2]

Worker protests never disappeared in the post-1989 era, yet only a few have become iconic interruptions to China's relentless pursuit of

---

1   Dai Jinhua, "Dimensions of the Future," 96
2   *China Labour Bulletin*, newsletter, January 7, 2019, clb.org.hk.

economic growth at any social cost. Foxconn, the Taiwan-owned "electronics workshop of the world" that manufactures iPhones and other Apple devices, has been a consistent target of worker activism, even if the popularity of the products it manufactures remains untouched by its and Apple's vile practices. Foxconn made international headlines repeatedly a few years ago when several of its workers serially committed suicide by throwing themselves from buildings at various worksites over poor treatment, corporate neglect of chronic medical problems stemming from chemicals used in the production process, bad pay, overwork, and state indifference.[3] As Xu Lizhi, one of the worker suicides of 2014, despairingly wrote in his posthumously celebrated poetry:

车间，流水线，机台，上岗证，加班，薪水 . . . (*chejian, liushuixian, jitai, shangganzheng, jiaban, xinshui . . .*)
Workshop, assembly line, machine, work card, overtime, wages . . .
我被它们治得服服贴贴 (*wo bei tamen zhide fufu tietie*)
They've trained me to become docile
我不会呐喊，不会反抗 (*wo buhui nahan, buhui fankang*)
Don't know how to shout or rebel
不会控诉，不会埋怨 (*buhui kangsu, buhui maiyuan*)
How to complain or denounce
只默默地承受着疲惫 (*zhi momode chengshouzhe pibei*)
Only how to silently suffer exhaustion[4]

Foxconn's slogan, "China rooted, global footprint," just about sums up not only its own, but China's more general capitalist aspirations: roots in China are premised on the political capacity of the state to field a docile workforce, or rather, to render its workforce quiescent; the global footprint is achieved by partnering with some of the

---

3 Jenny Chan, Pun Ngai, and Mark Selden, "Apple, Foxconn, and China's New Working Class," in R. Appelbaum and N. Lichtenstein, eds., *Achieving Workers' Rights in the Global Economy*, Ithaca, NY: Cornell University Press, 2016, 173–89.

4 "The Poetry and Brief Life of a Foxconn Worker: Xu Lizhi (1990–2014)," libcom. org/blog/xulizhi-foxconn-suicide-poetry.

largest manufacturers in the world to seize and maintain market hegemony over microelectronic processing and sourcing, among others. Command over global resources and local labor pools is central to both Foxconn's and China's cornering of their target markets. These imperatives have in part informed China's recent capitalist-extractive expansions into Africa, Latin America, and nearby Asian countries. While of course not unique to China—such racialized, gendered, and rapacious practices characterize the capitalist-imperialist world forged by Euro-America from the eighteenth century onward—the current Chinese iteration is nevertheless worth thinking through, not only because it is the sad legacy of China's abandonment of socialism but because it is symptomatic of counter-revolutionary trends taking hold all over our world today.

Meanwhile, peasant protests have not abated in number or intensity, even though it is quite rare that those dispersed village-based actions make headlines. The 2011 Wukan Village protest—during which peasants were so fed up with their corrupt leaders that they kicked them out of the village and then held off a police siege for a number of weeks—became known and iconic, in part because the village is located so close to Hong Kong. Once the TV cameras and journalists were gone, and the solidarity groups disbanded, the leaders of the protest were rounded up, silenced, and jailed or disappeared. The village mounted another protest in 2016, again over illegal land seizures by a real estate company intent on turning the village into a debt-financed city; the protest was ruthlessly suppressed, and the seventy-two-year-old leader was arrested and forced into a TV confession improbably admitting to his *own* corruption, while remaining villagers were evicted from their homes. The Wukan grievances are hardly unique. Villages in surrounding areas, and even at some distance from Wukan, have attempted to emulate earlier Wukan tactics in similar struggles against their local leaders' collusion with companies intent on seizing communal land for private real estate development. The snowball effect of these protests put Southern China's provincial governments on strict notice to keep their latently restive populations in line. Peasant protests and petitioning—over land seizures, poisoning of life environments by industrial runoff, village-level corruption, medical malpractice, and so much more—now are dealt with harshly, and even preemptively, before they can gather any momentum or social media presence. The trend toward community dispersal through depeasantization and emptying out the villages gathers steam, even while in the context of that forced collapse of agriculture as a family-based, village-located productive pursuit, what counts as economic activity in the remaining rural areas has changed utterly. It is now primarily structured through out-migration waged work performed by men, with residual farming activities now feminized as "merely" reproductive labor of an unremunerated and economically irrelevant and unrecognized sort.[5]

Four decades of unremitting development have left a growing ecological disaster as a living and dying reality of the current situation. Increasing numbers of rural and urban dwellers suffer from pollution-induced illnesses, whether cancer, HIV/AIDS, respiratory problems, dermatological diseases, or infant malformations, among others. This necropolitics—deliberate political neglect and conscious economic choice to let some live and some die—obviously is not unique to China, but because of China's scale, the trend does loom large. From dead rivers to heavily polluted urban air; from deforestation and desertification to depleted aquifers and industrially fouled agricultural zones; from overfished oceans to distressed coral reefs: China's warp-speed development with minimal environmental oversight has taken a massive toll on the natural world. And again, China's despoliation of nature is not appreciably different from the thorough poisoning by Euro-America-Japan, not only of their own regions but also of large swaths of the world in pursuit of imperialist domination and capitalist growth. And yet again, the rapidity of the creation in China of environmental crisis—and the export to other regions of the model of development that made the crisis so acute so

---

5   Tamara Jacka, "Inside Work: The Hidden Exploitation of Rural Women in Modern China," *Made in China*, special issue, "To the Soil," October 2018, madeinchinajournal.com.

quickly—is breathtaking (literally, sometimes). Combined with the vast destruction of human and natural habitats perpetrated by the endless wars pursued by the United States and its proxies, acute and chronic environmental crises are creating global-level "sacrifice zones," where life is either marginally or no longer livable.[6]

China also depends on some of the most intensively pursued dirty industries, such as coal extraction, which remains a staple source of household and industrial energy. Regulatory regimes, such as they are, rely upon provincial and local government implementation, and yet those very bodies also are answerable to Beijing for keeping economic growth at a torrid pace. The coal industry supports an ever more desperate stratum of rural male labor, which is all but enslaved to undersupervised mine owners with terrible safety records, while urban middle classes are rising up in disgust and despair over the air and water that they and their children are expected to breathe and consume. As China's dense air pollution does not remain in China—particulates regularly spread to Taiwan, Korea, Japan, Vietnam, and Russia, and sometimes even extend to Hawaii and the coast of California—the pressures on Beijing are growing. At the same time, the massive diversion of water from the Himalayas and the damming of the Three Gorges on the Yangzi River to address China's water shortages are causing zero-sum tensions between South and North, and with neighboring countries that use those same resources to sustain and develop their own livelihoods and economies. China now is the world's number two polluter behind the United States. Yet climate change, whose scientific basis and reality is denied by the current US government, has stimulated China's embrace of technology as a fix, in lieu of an attempt to change people's behaviors; in fact, China is host to some of the largest and fastest-growing green technologies, with research and markets heavily subsidized by the state. The paradox of China's

---

6   Robert Stolz, "Radiation's World: Japan's Fukushima Disaster and the Repetition Compulsion of National Sacrifice Zones," paper delivered at the American Association of Geographers, New Orleans, April 2018.

leadership in simultaneously solving and creating these problems is here on full view.

"China's rise," or "the rise of China," was originally coined and popularized in the late 1990s in American journalism by academic China watchers and policy pundits as a term of panic to describe China's contemporary challenge to modern Euro-America's historically hegemonic hold on global resources, wealth, and power. It carries the vague and yet unmistakable echo of that late-nineteenth- and early twentieth-century racial panic about "yellow hordes" overtaking Euro-American white purity, as well as directly echoing the cognate Cold War racial-political panic about the vast, putatively lobotomized, "blue ant" population of China overrunning the putatively peaceful freedom-loving democratic West.[7] "China's rise" thus names a panic-inducing challenge to white global supremacy and Euro-American-controlled capitalism, one depicted as devious and distorted—unfair, even—because it is presided over by a ruthless Communist authoritarianism that has thwarted all predictions of its inevitable political demise. However, "China's rise" (*zhongguo jueqi* / 中国崛起) is not as popular a phrase in China as the now-ubiquitous Chinese term for the contemporary moment: the "years of ascendancy and prosperity" (*sheng shi* / 盛世). This latter term is an entirely unironic echo of that used by the Kangxi Emperor in the eighteenth century to reflect on the achieved greatness of Qing territorial expansion—into Xinjiang, no less—and dynastic flourishing, which itself recalls much earlier versions of prosperity touted in the Han or Tang dynasties. "Ascendancy and prosperity" is thus a designation that presents a cultural internality to China's history, imagined as benign and peaceful, that can be posed as alternative to the "China's rise" designation, with its reference to global antagonism and direct challenge to the hitherto-existing Euro-American-dominated world order.

---

7   "Blue ant" refers to the ubiquity of the blue "Mao suit" (or Sun Yatsen suit) worn by many Chinese after 1949. It was used as an all-purpose racialized fear-mongering epithet in the 1950s McCarthy era of Chinese as unthinking collectivized followers of a leader.

Yet, the ongoing popular uprisings in Hong Kong over the tightening of PRC control in that territory powerfully demonstrate that not all who might be subject to China's "ascendancy and prosperity" are interested in succumbing to its version of the world. The "one-country two-systems" through which Hong Kong is governed—with promised local autonomy for fifty years after the 1997 hand-over of the British colony to the PRC—is fraying badly. While corporations and businesses count on social stability to accumulate profit and do not concern themselves with morality or ethics, increasingly huge numbers of ordinary Hong Kong citizens—who, until the 2014 Umbrella Movement, usually have been quiescent with regards to politics—are taking matters into their own hands. And Taiwan is watching, warily operating in an international and regional order more beholden to PRC economic and political constraints every day. As those in Hong Kong and Taiwan are aware, room for maneuver may be narrowing dramatically: the highly uneven ascendance and prosperity (for some) will be imposed if it is not "freely" embraced (by all).

Conceptual language has consequences for presenting the past. Facts and narratives are potent weapons in the ideological and material creation of how pasts are rendered present, and how that present shapes a desired or projected future. Today, the language of internal class conflict and revolutionary necessity has dropped from usage, both at the level of everyday understanding and at the level of scholarly discourse. Some decades ago, we were told to "say farewell to revolution,"[8] not only as an aspiration for the future but as a paradigm through which to understand China's modern past. This was and remains part of a broader global scholarly repudiation of twentieth-century histories of revolution (and of revolutionary histories) that locally challenged and globally contested the normative nature of the emerging and maturing process of capitalist globalization and

---

8   *Gaobie geming* (告別革命) was an influential book written by Li Zehou and Liu Zaifu, published in 1999.

neoliberal hegemony. It is also part of a broad academic rejection of the problem of modernity—a particular local experience of global time combined with a radical rethinking of the past—as a world-historical logic.

It may be that the worlds of revolution are at an end. Even as class polarization on a local, regional, and global level becomes ever more acute; as the share of global wealth is funneled ever upward into fewer and fewer hands; as the ferocious violence that punctuated the twentieth century now becomes a naturalized part of the everyday life of billions; and as ecological disaster bears down upon us all (albeit unevenly, threatening the poor and the weak more than the strong and the wealthy), different organizational answers to the threats that beset our individual and collective social life are needed. Theorist Dai Jinhua has argued that the cultural ascendance in the past decades of apocalyptic and postapocalyptic movies and narratives indicates that "in our time when the breakthroughs of modern science and technology come face to face with structural crises, what troubles humanity as a whole is not yet the survival of the species, but the increasingly accelerated fragmentation and disintegration of community."[9] I would argue that this forced disintegration is part of the creation of the sacrifice zones, and that, as Dai elaborates, lead to the social negation of whole populations: "For material producers across the world . . . a fantastical scene emerges: the increasingly automated production line, as well as the research, manufacture, and application of laboring robots, does not entail emancipation, but abandonment."[10] A savage world of disposable populations is coming into view.[11]

If nineteenth- and twentieth-century revolutions were premised upon the inexhaustibility of natural resources and upon the peasant/proletariat as the leading classes of universalized humanity, it seems clear that these premises can no longer serve exclusively or at all as the bases of a radical politics today. By the same token, in recalling

---

9   Dai Jinhua, "Dimensions of the Future," 99.

10   Ibid., 101.

11   Neferti Tadiar, "Lifetimes of Disposability within Global Neoliberalism," *Social Text* 115, Vol 31:2 (Summer 2013): 19-48.

revolutions as history, in remembering how and why revolutionary movements were thinkable and actively created in the nineteenth and twentieth centuries, in narrating China's recent history as a history of revolutions in the modern world, we force ourselves to recollect how worlds other than the given ones could be made thinkable and rendered possible. In this sense, China's twentieth-century revolutions left powerful local and global traces. So, even as the current Chinese state under Xi Jinping works hard to tame the future by appropriating the revolutionary past, by enshrining China's passage from the May Fourth Movement through Mao's era as if it had been fought to secure the victory of national capitalism over the critical spirit of its times,[12] we can recall this history otherwise: with China's and other modern world revolutions as the insistent modes through which normative presents consistently and repeatedly were challenged.

In narrating the rejection of the inevitability of capitalist globalization, this volume, written in 2019 in part as a centenary of the revolutionary "nine years" of the twentieth century beginning with May 4, 1919, reminds us that modern revolutions aimed to establish a permanent principle through which radical transformations in individual quotidian life would help animate collective sociopolitical transformations at a national and global scale. Revolutions were intimately intertwined with the century-long struggle in China and globally over the relationship between modernization and democracy, between the massification of production and culture and the massification of politics. Deeply embedded in the historical problem presented to and in China by the arrival, in the nineteenth century, of the most undemocratic form of global modernization—that form known as capitalist imperialism—was precisely the radical potential to reject the inevitability of surrender. From then on, China was intractably part of political and social movements worldwide that contested capitalist normality, including the twentieth-century challenge posed by socialism as anti-capitalist modernity and mass democracy. While the violence of

---

12   Paraphrasing Bensaid, *Marx for Our Times*, 67.

the problems helped produce and call forth the violence of the solutions, the various potentials articulated in these explorations took "the world" as a malleable revolutionary opportunity rather than as a settled normative principle.

Here, we might reconfigure the idea of the end of revolution as the end of the particular world-historical logic of the nineteenth and twentieth centuries. In that light, an urgent philosophical and collective attempt is required to grasp anew the relationship between development and democracy in our present and for our future. Without such an effort, China may well be condemned, along with all of us, to ever more dystopian versions of the future. Such dystopias can only spell ecological disaster along with the end to any promise of democratic control over the conditions of life itself.

Acknowledgments

This book was written at the suggestion of editors at Verso. I otherwise had no intention of writing such a narrative. I am grateful for the push, and I have enjoyed the task, which has occupied the better part of five months. I particularly thank Jessie Kindig for her editorial acumen, and Sam Smith for his copyediting diligence. Sophia Massie enthusiastically undertook the indexing and proofing.

Angela Zito helped with the title (although it ended up being something entirely different from what we thought). Judith Karl helped with readability. Gratitude is due to the London posse—Harriet, Bec, Isabella, Susan and Mike, Sanjay and Raj, among others—for making my writing retreat there so much fun; and to Mike and Anne Ellis, for their place near Hampstead Heath, where I remained undisturbed for as long as I could. The final parts of the book were finished in Taipei, where the Center for Chinese Studies offered support and I-Yi Hsieh, among others, made sure I was well fed and entertained. The Institute for New Economic Thinking generously has funded leave and research time for the last several years. While this is not the book I promised them—that one is still forthcoming—I wish to acknowledge their forbearance and assistance.

I am deeply saddened that my mother did not live to see this book. She always supported me in such an unconditional way; I miss her immensely.

I wrote this book with my past and future students in mind, and I dedicate it to teachers in general, and to three of my teachers in particular from whom I have learned so very much: Arif Dirlik, Marilyn B. Young, and Harry Harootunian. Incomparable intellects all. I wish Arif and Marilyn were still here.

Bibliography

Anderson, Benedict, *Imagined Communities: Reflections on the Origins and Spread of Nationalism*, London and New York: Verso, 1983.

Andreas, Joel, *Rise of the Red Engineers: The Cultural Revolution and China's New Class*, Palo Alto, CA: Stanford University Press, 2009.

Asen, Daniel, *Death in Beijing: Murder and Forensic Science in Republican China*, Cambridge, UK: Cambridge University Press, 2016.

Auden, W. H., and Christopher Isherwood, *Journey to a War*, London: Faber & Faber, 1973 [1939].

Averill, Stephen C., *Revolution in the Highlands: China's Jinggangshan Base Area*, New York: Rowman & Littlefield, 2006.

Battacharya, Tithi, ed., *Social Reproduction Theory: Remapping Class, Recentering Oppression*, London: Pluto Press, 2017.

Bei Dao, "The Answer," *The August Sleepwalker*, tr. Bonnie S. McDougall, New York: New Directions, 1990.

Bell, Lynda S., "From Comprador to County Magnate," in Joseph Esherick and Mary Rankin, eds., *China's Local Elites and Patterns of Dominance*, Berkeley, CA: University of California Press, 1990.

Benjamin, Jesse, and Robin D. G. Kelley, "Introduction: An African Perspective on the Russian Revolution," in Walter Rodney, *The Russian Revolution: A View from the Third World*, ed. Robin D. G. Kelley and Jesse Benjamin, London and New York: Verso, 2017.

Bensaid, Daniel, *Marx for Our Times*, tr. Gregory Elliott, London: Verso, 2010.

Benton, Gregor, *Mountain Fires: The Red Army's Three-Year War in South China, 1934–1938*, Berkeley, CA: University of California Press, 1992.

Brophy, David, "Good and Bad Muslims in Xinjiang," *Made in China Journal*, July 11, 2019, madeinchinajournal.com.

Bu, Liping, "Anti-Malaria Campaigns and the Socialist Reconstruction of China, 1950–80," *East Asian History* 39, 2014, eastasianhistory.org.

Byler, Darren, "Ghost World," *Logic* 6, logicmag.io.

Cai Xiang, *Revolution and Its Narratives: China's Socialist Literary and Cultural Imaginaries, 1949–1966*, tr. and ed. Rebecca E. Karl and Xueping Zhong, Durham, NC: Duke University Press, 2016.

Central Committee of the Communist Party of China, "May 16 Circular," available at *Marxists Internet Archive*, marxists.org.

Chan, Jenny, Pun Ngai, and Mark Selden, "Apple, Foxconn, and China's New Working Class," in R. Appelbaum and N. Lichtenstein, eds., *Achieving Workers' Rights in the Global Economy*, Ithaca, NY: Cornell University Press, 2016, 173–89.

Chen Duxiu, "On Literary Revolution," tr. T. Wong, in Kirk Denton, ed., *Modern Chinese Literary Thought: Writings on Literature, 1893–1945*, Palo Alto, CA: Stanford University Press, 1996.

Chen, Janet, *Guilty of Indigence: The Urban Poor in China, 1900–1953*, Princeton, NJ: Princeton University Press, 2012.

Chen Jian, "The Tibetan Rebellion of 1959 and China's Changing Relations with India and the Soviet Union," *Journal of Cold War Studies* 8:3, 2006, 54–101.

Chesneaux, Jean, *The Chinese Labor Movement, 1919–1927*, tr. H. M. Wright, Palo Alto, CA: Stanford University Press, 1968.

Chin, Tamara, "The Afro-Asian 'Silk Road' and the Rhetoric of Connected History," talk delivered at Columbia University, New York, April 11, 2018.

——, "The Invention of the Silk Road, 1877," *Critical Inquiry* 40:1, 2013, 194–219.

China Labour Bulletin, newsletter, January 7, 2019, clb.org.hk.

Chow Tse-tsung, *The May Fourth Movement*, Cambridge, MA: Harvard University Press, 1960.

Clifford, Nicholas, *Spoilt Children of Empire: Westerners in Shanghai and the Chinese Revolution of the 1920s*, Middlebury, VT: Middlebury College Press, 1992.

Clinton, Maggie, *Revolutionary Nativism: Fascism and Culture in China, 1925–1937*, Durham, NC: Duke University Press, 2017.

Cook, Alexander, *The Cultural Revolution on Trial: Mao and the Gang of Four*, Cambridge, UK: Cambridge University Press, 2016.

——, *Mao's Little Red Book: A Global History*, Cambridge, UK: Cambridge University Press, 2014.

Cook, James A., "Reimagining China: Xiamen, Overseas Chinese, and a Transnational Modernity," in Madeline Yue Dong and Joshua Goldstein, eds., *Everyday Modernity in China*, Seattle, WA: University of Washington Press, 2007.

Dai Jinhua, "Culture," tr. Rebecca E. Karl, in Christian Sorace, Nicholas Loubere, and Ivan Franceschini, eds., *Afterlives of Chinese Communism: Political Concepts from Mao to Xi*, London and New York: Verso, 2019.

——, "The Dimensions of the Future," tr. Zhou Shuchen, *Chinese Literature Today* 7:2, 2019, 100.

——, "Introduction," tr. Jie Li, in Lisa Rofel, ed., *After the Post-Cold War*, Durham, NC: Duke University Press, 2018.

Davidson, Neil, *How Revolutionary Were the Bourgeois Revolutions?* Chicago, IL: Haymarket, 2012.

"Decision of the Central Committee of the Chinese Communist Party concerning the Great Proletarian Cultural Revolution," *Peking Review* 9:33, August 12, 1966.

Deng Xiaoping, "The 'Two Whatevers' Do Not Accord with Marxism," May 24, 1977, available at dengxiaopingworks.wordpress.com.

Dikköter, Frank, *Mao's Great Famine: The History of China's Most Devastating Catastrophe, 1958–62*, London: Walker & Company, 2010.

Ding Ling, "Shanghai, Spring 1930," tr. Shu-ying Ts'ao and Donald Holoch, in Tani E. Barlow, ed., *I Myself Am a Woman: Selected Writings of Ding Ling*, Boston, MA: Beacon Press, 1986.

Dirlik, Arif, *Anarchism in the Chinese Revolution*, Berkeley, CA: University of California Press. 1991.

——, *Revolution and History: Origins of Marxist Historiography in China, 1919–1937*, Berkeley, CA: University of California Press, 1978.

———, *The Origins of Chinese Communism*, New York: Oxford University Press, 1989.

Dong, Madeline Yue, *Republican Beijing: The City and Its Histories*, Berkeley, CA: University of California Press, 2003.

Eastman, Lloyd, "Who Lost China? Chiang Kai-shek Testifies," *China Quarterly* 88, December 1981, 658–68.

Eisenman, Joshua, "Comrades-in-Arms: The Chinese Communist Party's Relations with African Political Organisations in the Mao Era, 1949–76," *Cold War History*, March 2018.

Engels, Friedrich, "On the Polish Question," in *Collected Works*, vol. 6, London: Lawrence Y. Wishart, 1976.

Esherick, Joseph, *The Origins of the Boxer Uprising*, Berkeley, CA: University of California Press, 1987.

Eyferth, Jacob, ed., *How China Works: Perspectives on the Twentieth-Century Industrial Workplace*, New York: Routledge, 2006.

Feng, Keli, "Seeing Red: China's Communist Revolution Captured on Camera," *Sixth Tone*, April 7, 2018, sixthtone.com.

Fields, Andrew, "Aftermath of the May 30th Incident of 1925," *Shanghai Sojourns: A Shanghai Flaneur's Website*, January 22, 2019, shanghaisojourns.net.

Fitzgerald, John, *Awakening China: Politics, Culture, and Class in the Nationalist Revolution*, Palo Alto, CA: Stanford University Press, 1996.

Galbiati, Fernando, *Peng Pai and the Hai-Lu-Feng Soviet*, Palo Alto, CA: Stanford University Press, 1985.

Gates, Hill, *China's Motor*, Ithaca, NY: Cornell University Press, 1996.

"The Genesis of the Tibetan Women's Struggle for Independence," Tibetan Women's Association official website, tibetanwomen.org.

Gramsci, Antonio, "Red October" (October 13, 1917), *Prison Notebooks*, vol. 1, New York: Columbia University Press, 2011.

Grunfeld, A. Tom, *The Making of Modern Tibet*, New York: Routledge, 1996.

Han Dongping, *The Unknown Cultural Revolution: Life and Change in a Chinese Village*, New York: Monthly Review, 2009.

Harrison, Henrietta, *Inventing the Nation: China*, London: Arnold Publishers, 2001.

——, *The Making of the Republican Citizen: Political Ceremonies and Symbols in China, 1911–1929*, Oxford, UK: Oxford University Press, 2000.

Hershatter, Gail, *Dangerous Pleasures: Prostitution and Modernity in Twentieth-Century Shanghai*, Berkeley, CA: University of California Press, 1997.

——, *The Gender of Memory: Rural Women and China's Collective Past*, Berkeley, CA: University of California Press, 2014.

——, *Women and China's Revolutions*, New York: Rowman & Littlefield, 2019.

Hoffman, Marcelo, *Militant Acts: The Role of Investigations in Radical Political Struggles*, Albany, NY: SUNY Press, 2019.

Hong-Fincher, Leta, *Leftover Women: The Resurgence of Gender Inequality in China*, London: Zed, 2016.

Honig, Emily, *Sisters and Strangers in the Shanghai Cotton Mills, 1919–1949*, Palo Alto, CA: Stanford University Press, 1986.

Hu Angang, *Zhongguo 2020: Yige xinxing chaoji daguo* [China in 2020: A new type of superpower], Zhejiang: Zhejiang Renmin Chubanshe, 2012.

Huan Jin, "Authenticating the Renewed Heavenly Vision: The Taiping Heavenly Chronicle (Taiping tianri)," *Frontiers of History in China* 13:2, 2018, 173–92.

Hu Shih, *The Chinese Renaissance: The Haskell Lectures*, Chicago, IL: University of Chicago Press, 1934.

——, "Some Modest Proposals for the Reform of Literature," tr. Kirk A. Denton, in K. Denton, ed., *Modern Chinese Literary Thought: Writings on Literature, 1893–1945*, Palo Alto, CA: Stanford University Press, 1996.

Isaacs, Harold, *The Tragedy of the Chinese Revolution*, Palo Alto, CA: Stanford University Press, 1951 [1938].

Israel, John, *Lianda: A Chinese University in War and Revolution*, Palo Alto, CA: Stanford University Press, 1998.

Jacka, Tamara, "Inside Work: The Hidden Exploitation of Rural Women in Modern China," *Made in China*, special issue, "To the Soil," October 2018, madeinchinajournal.com.

Jiang Hongsheng, "The Paris Commune in Shanghai: The Masses, the State, and Dynamics of 'Continuous Revolution,'" PhD diss., Duke University, 2010.

Jiang Qing, "On the Revolution of Peking Opera," wengewang.org.

Jiang Zemin, Selected Works of Jiang Zemin, Beijing: Foreign Languages Press, 2013.

Ji Fengyuan, "Language and Politics during the Chinese Cultural Revolution: A Study in Linguistic Engineering," PhD diss., University of Canterbury, 1998.

Johnson, Matthew D., "Cinema and Propaganda during the Great Leap Forward," in J. A. Cook et al., eds., Visualizing Modern China, New York: Rowman & Littlefield, 2014.

Judd, Ellen, "Revolutionary Drama and Song in the Jiangxi Soviet," Modern China 9:1, 1983, 127–60.

Kanagaratnam, Tina, "Roar, China! Langston Hughes in Shanghai," Historic Shanghai, historic-shanghai.com.

Karamouzis, Delia, The Shanghai Campaign of 1949, website, arcgis. com/apps/Cascade/index.html?appid=eb9435f82a484efcbf11fba 5d9ea1acd.

Karl, Rebecca E., "China," in Andrew Pendakis, Jeff Diamanti, and Imre Szeman, eds., Bloomsbury Companion to Marx, London: Bloomsbury Press, 2018.

———, "Compradors: The Mediating Middle of Capitalism in Twentieth-Century China and the World," in Joyce Liu and V. Murthy, eds., East Asian Marxisms and Their Trajectories, New York: Routledge, 2017, 119–36.

———, "Little Big Man," New Left Review 97, 2016, newleftreview.org.

———, Mao Zedong and China in the Twentieth-Century World: A Concise History, Durham, NC: Duke University Press, 2010.

———, Staging the World: Chinese Nationalism at the Turn of the Twentieth Century, Durham, NC: Duke University Press, 2002.

Kelley, Robin D. G. and Betsy Esch, "Black like Mao: Red China and Black Revolution," Souls 1:4, 1999, 6–41.

Ko, Dorothy, Cinderella's Sisters: A Revisionist History of Footbinding, Berkeley, CA: University of California Press, 2005.

Kristeva, Julia. "Beauvoir in China," tr. Susan Nicholls, kristeva.fr.

Kuo, Mercy A., "One Belt, One Road: A Convergence of Civilizations? Insights from Tamara Chin," *Diplomat*, May 24, 2017.

Lanza, Fabio, *Behind the Gate: Inventing Students in Beijing*, New York: Columbia University Press, 2010.

Lary, Diana, "Drowned Earth: The Strategic Breaching of the Yellow River Dyke, 1938," *War in History* 8:2, April 2001, 191–207.

——, *The Chinese People at War*, Cambridge, UK: Cambridge University Press, 2010.

Lee, C. K., *Gender and the South China Miracle*, Berkeley, CA: University of California Press, 1998.

——, *Against the Law: Labor Protests in China's Rustbelt and Sunbelt*, Berkeley, CA: University of California Press, 2007.

Lee, Leo Ou-fan, *Shanghai Modern: The Flowering of a New Urban Culture in China, 1930–1945*, Cambridge, MA: Harvard University Press, 1999.

Liang Qichao, "Lun Zhongguo zhi jiangqiang" (On the Future Strength of China), *Shiwu bao* 31, June 1897.

Lin Chun, "Rethinking Land Reform: Comparative Lessons from China and India," in Mahmood Mamdani, ed., *The Land Question: Socialism, Capitalism and the Market*, MISR Book Series, vol. 5, Kampala: Makerere Institute of Social Research, 2015, eprints.lse.ac.uk/59697.

Liu, Lydia, R. E. Karl, and D. Ko, trs. and eds., *The Birth of Chinese Feminism: Essential Texts in Transnational Theory*, New York: Columbia University Press, 2013.

Lu Xun, "In Memory of Miss Liu Hezhen" (April 1926), available at *Marxists Internet Archive*, marxists.org.

——, *Jottings under Lamplight*, tr. Bonnie McDougall, ed. Eileen Cheng and Kirk Denton, Cambridge, MA: Harvard University Press, 2017.

—— *The True Story of Ah Q*, in *A Call to Arms*, tr. Julia Lovell, New York: Penguin, 2010.

McElderry, Adriana, "Woman Revolutionary: Xiang Jingyu," *China Quarterly*, March 1986.

McGuire, Elizabeth, *Red at Heart: How Chinese Communists Fell in Love with the Russian Revolution*, New York: Oxford University Press, 2018.

Ma, Debin, "Money and Monetary System in China in the 19th–20th Century: An Overview," *LSE Working Papers*, January 2012.

Mao Zedong, "Always Keep to the Style of Plain Living and Hard Struggle," *Selected Works of Mao Tse-tung*, vol. 5, Beijing: Foreign Languages Press, 1977.

——, "American Imperialism Is Closely Surrounded by the Peoples of the World," available at *Marxists Internet Archive*, marxists. org.

——, "Analysis of Classes in Chinese Society," in Stuart Schram, ed., *Mao's Road to Power*, vol. 2, New York: Routledge, 1992.

——, "Bombard the Headquarters—My First Big-Character Poster," available at *Marxists Internet Archive*, marxists.org.

——, "The Chinese People Have Stood Up!" available at *Marxists Internet Archive*, marxists.org.

——, "Commentary on the Suicide of Miss Zhao", in Stuart Schram, ed., *Mao's Road to Power*, vol. 1, New York: Routledge, 1992.

——, "Criticize P'eng Chen [Peng Zhen]," available at *Marxists Internet Archive*, marxists.org.

——, "A Letter to the Red Guards of Tsinghua University Middle School," available at *Marxists Internet Archive*, marxists.org.

——, "The National Revolution and the Peasant Movement," in Schram, ed., *Mao's Road to Power*, vol. 2.

——, "On Protracted War," available at *Marxists Internet Archive*, marxists.org.

——, "Problems of War and Strategy," *Selected Works of Mao Tse-tung*, vol. 2, Beijing: Foreign Languages Press, 1954.

——, "Proclamation of the Central People's Government of the PRC," *People's Daily*, October 2, 1949.

——, "Request for Opinions on the Tactics for Dealing with Rich Peasants," available at *Marxists Internet Archive*, marxists.org.

——, "Speech Marking the 60th Birthday of Stalin," available at *Marxists Internet Archive*, marxists.org.

———, "A Study of Physical Education," *Xin Qingnian* [New Youth], in Schram, ed., *Mao's Road to Power*, vol. 1.

———, "Talks at the Yan'an Forum on Art and Literature," available at *Marxists Internet Archive*, marxists.org.

Marx, Karl, "Revolution in China and in Europe," *New York Daily Tribune*, June 14, 1853.

"The 'May 7' Cadre School," *Peking Review* 19, May 12, 1972, 5–7.

Meisner, Maurice, *Li Ta-chao and the Origins of Chinese Marxism*, Cambridge, MA: Harvard University Press, 1967.

———, *Mao's China and After: A History of the People's Republic*, 3rd ed., New York: Free Press, 1999.

Meyer-Fong, Tobie, *What Remains: Coming to Terms with Civil War in Nineteenth-Century China*, Palo Alto, CA: Stanford University Press, 2013.

Michael, Franz, *The Taiping Rebellion: History and Documents*, Seattle, WA: University of Washington Press, 1971.

Mitter, Rana, *China's War with Japan, 1937–1945: The Struggle for Survival*, London: Allen Lane, 2013.

Monson, Jamie, *Africa's Freedom Railway: How a Chinese Development Project Changed Lives and Livelihoods in Tanzania*, Bloomington, IN: Indiana University Press, 2009.

Moore, Aaron, "China's War with Japan, 1937–1945: The Struggle for Survival," *Reviews in History*, history.ac.uk.

Mullaney, Thomas, *The Chinese Typewriter: A History*, Cambridge, MA: MIT Press, 2017.

Ngok, Kinglun, "The Changes of Chinese Labor Policy and Labor Legislation in the Context of Market Transition," *International Labor and Working Class History* 73:1, Spring 2008, 45–64.

"On the Revolutionary 'Three-in-One' Combination," Beijing: Foreign Languages Press, 1968.

Perry, Elizabeth, *Rebels and Revolutionaries in North China, 1845–1945*, Palo Alto, CA: Stanford University Press, 1980.

Petersson, Fredrik, " 'We Are Neither Visionaries nor Utopian Dreamers' ": Willi Münzenberg, the League against Imperialism, and the Comintern, 1925–1933," PhD diss., Åbo Akademi University, Turku, Finland, 2013.

Platt, Stephen, *Autumn in the Heavenly Kingdom*, New York: Vintage, 2012.

"The Poetry and Brief Life of a Foxconn Worker: Xu Lizhi (1990–2014)," libcom.org/blog/xulizhi-foxconn-suicide-poetry.

Pun Ngai, *Made in China: Women Factory Workers in a Global Workplace*, Durham, NC: Duke University Press, 2005.

Qin Hui, *Zouchu dizhi: Cong Wanqing dao Minguo de lishi huiwang* [Out of the imperial polity: Historical reflections on the late Qing and the republic], Beijing: Qunyan, 2016.

Qu Qiubai, "Dazhong wenyide wenti" [Questions of mass literature], *Wenxue* [Literature], 1932.

——, "Puluo dazhong wenyide xianshi wenti" [The practical questions of proletarian mass literature], *Wenxue* [Literature], 1932.

Ramzy, Austin,"China Targets Prominent Uighur Intellectuals to Erase an Ethnic Identity," *New York Times*, January 5, 2019.

"Red Guards Destroy the Old and Establish the New," *Peking Review* 36, September 1966.

Reed, Christopher, *Guttenberg in China: Chinese Print Capitalism, 1876–1937*, Vancouver: UBC Press, 2004.

"Resolution on Certain Questions in the History of our Party since the Founding of the People's Republic of China," available at *Marxists Internet Archive*, marxists.org.

Riddell, John, ed., *Workers of the World and Oppressed Peoples, Unite! Proceedings and Documents of the Second Congress, 1920*, 2 vols., New York: Pathfinder, 1991.

Riskin, Carl, "Seven Questions about the Chinese Famine of 1959–61," *China Economic Review* 9:2, 1998.

Schmalzer, Sigrid, *Red Revolution, Green Revolution: Scientific Farming in Socialist China*, Chicago, IL: University of Chicago Press, 2016.

Schwarcz, Vera, *The Chinese Enlightenment: Intellectuals and the Legacy of the May Fourth Movement of 1919*, Berkeley, CA: University of California Press, 1986.

Shiroyama, Tomoko, *China during the Great Depression: Market, State, and the World Economy, 1929–1937*, Cambridge, MA: Harvard University Asia Center, 2008.

Smith, S. A., *Like Cattle and Horses: Nationalism and Labor in Shanghai, 1895–1927*, Durham, NC: Duke University Press, 2002.

Stolz, Robert, "Radiation's World: Japan's Fukushima Disaster and the Repetition Compulsion of National Sacrifice Zones," paper delivered at the American Association of Geographers, New Orleans, April 2018.

"Study the Documents Well and Grasp the Key Link," *People's Daily*, February 7, 1977.

Tadiar, Neferti. "Lifetimes of Disposability within Global Neoliberalism," Social Text 115, Vol 31:2 (Summer 2013): 19-48.

Terrill, Ross, *The White-Boned Demon: A Biography of Madame Mao Zedong*, New York: Morrow, 1984.

Thum, Rian, "Uyghurs in Modern China," *Oxford Research Encyclopedia*, oxfordre.com.

Tsering Shakya, *The Dragon in the Land of Snows*, New York: Penguin, 2000.

Tsui, Brian, *China's Conservative Revolution: The Quest for a New Order, 1927–1949*, Cambridge, UK: Cambridge University Press, 2018.

Unknown, "Minor Events and Grand Dreams: Ethnic Outsiders in China's Postcolonial World Order," *positions*, forthcoming.

Wakeman, Frederick, *Policing Shanghai, 1927–1937*, Berkeley, CA: University of California Press, 1995.

Walker, Kathy Le Mons, *Chinese Modernity and the Peasant Path: Semicolonialism in the Northern Yangzi Delta*, Palo Alto, CA: Stanford University Press, 1999.

Wang Chaohua, "China's First Revolution," *New Left Review* 106, Summer 2017, 125–40.

Wang Gungwu, "Juxtaposing Past and Present in China Today," *China Quarterly* 61, 1975, 1–24.

Wang Hui, "The 1989 Social Movement and the Historical Roots of Neoliberalism in China," tr. Rebecca E. Karl, *positions* 12:1, Spring 2004, 7–69.

———, *China's Twentieth Century*, tr. and ed. Saul Thomas, London and New York: Verso, 2016.

Wang Yang, "Urban Subjectivity in Representations of Peasant Women in the Early PRC," paper delivered at CHANGE conference, Brussels Free University, February 15, 2019.

Weber, Isabella, *Reassessing China's Reform Debate (1978–1988): Price Regulation and Market Creation*, forthcoming.

Weigelin-Schwiedrzik, S., "The Campaign to Criticize Lin Biao and Confucius (批林批孔) and the Problem of 'Restoration' in Chinese Marxist Historiography," in Viren Murthy and Axel Schneider, eds., *The Challenge of Linear Time*, Amsterdam: Brill, 2014.

Westad, Odd Arne, *Decisive Encounters: The Chinese Civil War, 1946–1950*, Palo Alto, CA: Stanford University Press, 2003.

Wong, Lorraine Chi-man, "The Chinese Latinization Movement: Language, History and Politics: 1917–1958," PhD diss., New York University, 2014.

Wu Qi and Yun Zhu, "Living in the End Times? An Interview with Dai Jinhua," *Chinese Literature Today* 7:2, 2018, 82–91.

Wu Yiching, *The Cultural Revolution at the Margins*, Cambridge, MA: Harvard University Press, 2014.

"Wusi shiqi lao tongzhi zuotanhui jilu," [Record of round-table discussion by old Comrades of the May Fourth period], in *Jinian wusi yundong liushi zhouniman xueshu taolunhui lunwen xuan* [Collected essays in celebration of the sixtieth anniversary of the May Fourth Movement], vol. 1, Beijing: Chinese Academy of Social Sciences, 1980.

Xiao, Eva. "China Pushes Inter-ethnic Marriage in Xinjiang Assimilation Drive," Hong Kong Free Press, May 18, 2019, hongkongfp.com.

Yan Fan [燕帆], 大串连：一场史无前例的政治旅游 [*Da chuanlian: Yichang shiwuqianlie de zhengzhi lüyou*/The great linking-up: A historically unprecedented political travel experience], Beijing: Jing guan jiaoyu chubanshe, 1993.

Yang Jisheng, *Tombstone: The Great Chinese Famine, 1958–1962*, New York: Farrar, Strauss, & Giroux, 2013.

Yao Dadui, "The Power of Persuasion in Propaganda," *Frontiers of History in China* 13:2, 2018, 193–210.

Yao Wenyuan, "On the New Historical Play 'Hai Rui Dismissed from Office,'" available at *Marxists Internet Archive*, marxists.org.

Yeh, Michelle, "The 'Cult of Poetry' in Contemporary China," *Journal of Asian Studies* 55:1, January 1996.

Zanasi, Margherita, *Saving the Nation: Economic Modernity in Republican China*, Chicago, IL: University of Chicago Press, 2006.

Zarrow, Peter, *China in War and Revolution, 1895–1949*, New York: Routledge, 2005.

Zenz, Adrian, "Re-education Returns to China," *Foreign Affairs*, June 20, 2018, foreignaffairs.com.

Zhang Daye, *The World of a Tiny Insect: A Memoir of the Taiping Rebellion and Its Aftermath*, tr. Xiaofei Tian, Seattle, WA: University of Washington Press, 2013.

Zhong, Yurou, "Script Crisis and Literary Modernity in China, 1916–1958," PhD diss., Columbia University, 2014.

Index